Palgrave Studies in Victims and Victimology

Series Editors
Matthew Hall
University of Lincoln
Lincoln, UK

Pamela Davies
Department of Social Sciences
Northumbria University
Newcastle upon Tyne, UK

In recent decades, a growing emphasis on meeting the needs and rights of victims of crime in criminal justice policy and practice has fuelled the development of research, theory, policy and practice outcomes stretching across the globe. This growth of interest in the victim of crime has seen victimology move from being a distinct subset of criminology in academia to a specialist area of study and research in its own right.

Palgrave Studies in Victims and Victimology showcases the work of contemporary scholars of victimological research and publishes some of the highest-quality research in the field. The series reflects the range and depth of research and scholarship in this burgeoning area, combining contributions from both established scholars who have helped to shape the field and more recent entrants. It also reflects both the global nature of many of the issues surrounding justice for victims of crime and social harm and the international span of scholarship researching and writing about them.

More information about this series at
http://www.palgrave.com/gp/series/14571

Julia Maria Muraszkiewicz

Protecting Victims of Human Trafficking From Liability

The European Approach

Julia Maria Muraszkiewicz
Trilateral Research & Consulting
London, UK

Palgrave Studies in Victims and Victimology
ISBN 978-3-030-02658-5   ISBN 978-3-030-02659-2   (eBook)
https://doi.org/10.1007/978-3-030-02659-2

Library of Congress Control Number: 2018959730

This Palgrave Macmillan imprint is published by the registered company Springer Nature Switzerland AG
The registered company address is: Gewerbestrasse 11, 6330 Cham, Switzerland

This is the first fruits of our efforts; let us persevere and our triumph will be complete. Never, never will we desist till we have wiped away this scandal from the Christian name, released ourselves from the load of guilt, under which we at present labour, and extinguished every trace of this bloody traffic, of which our posterity, looking back to the history of these enlightened times, will scarce believe that it has been suffered to exist so long a disgrace and dishonour to this country.
—William Wilberforce before the House of Commons, 18 April 1791

As punishments are only inflicted for the abuse of that free will, which God has given a man, it is just that a man should be excused for those act, which are done through unavoidable force and compulsion.
—Blackstone in his Commentaries on the Laws of England (1941)

Contents

Abbreviations

CJEU	The Court of Justice of the European Union
CoE	Council of Europe
CPS	Crown Prosecution Service
ECHR	European Convention for the Protection of Human Rights and Fundamental Freedoms
ECtHR	European Court of Human Rights
EU	European Union
EU Charter	Charter of Fundamental Rights of the European Union
GRETA	Group of Experts on Action Against Trafficking in Human Beings
ICCPR	International Covenant on Civil and Political Rights
ILO	International Labour Organisation
IOM	International Organisation for Migration
MSA	Modern Slavery Act 2015
NGO	Non Governmental Organisation
OHCHR	The Office of the United Nations High Commissioner for Human Rights
OJ	Official Journal
OSCE	Organisation for Security and Cooperation in Europe
TEU	Treaty on the European Union
TFEU	Treaty on the Functioning of the European Union

THB	Trafficking in Human Beings
UK	United Kingdom
UN	United Nations
UNDHR	The Universal Declaration of Human Rights
UNHCR	United Nations High Commissioner for Refugees
UNICEF	United Nations Children's Emergency Fund
UNODC	United Nations Office on Drugs and Crime

1

Introduction

Crime and punishment do not always go together. Sometimes, we must excuse those who break the law.

When victims of human trafficking escape their trafficking situation, they can be at serious risk of criminal or civil proceeding for violations they committed in connection with their human trafficking circumstances. Thus, one of the areas in which victims' rights need to be protected regards holding them not liable for those wrongdoings. European regional law has sought to do just that. However, perceiving a person who engaged in a criminal act as a victim is still counter-intuitive to the criminal justice system and there is "difficulty for a law enforcement officer to simultaneously view a trafficked person as both a criminal committing an offence and a victim compelled by a human-trafficking situation to commit that offence" (Cross 2013: 401). Nonetheless, these persons deserve protection for they were acting under control and broke law because of the unique circumstances they found themselves in. Their culpability was either significantly reduced or destroyed. That is to say, there was a lack of the foundation for criminal responsibility. Holding trafficked persons liable can lead to institutional victimisation and is far from the

© The Author(s) 2019
J. M. Muraszkiewicz, *Protecting Victims of Human Trafficking From Liability*, Palgrave
Studies in Victims and Victimology, https://doi.org/10.1007/978-3-030-02659-2_1

victim centred approach that is championed in anti-human trafficking discourse.

This book is a reaction to the regrettable truth that many of the victims who break the law are looked at in terms of their breaches and their irregular migration status. Meanwhile, the serious crime which has been committed against them gets lost. For these persons, the amplified rhetoric that victims deserve support and human trafficking is a heinous crime seems to have drifted away. Instead, their fate is one of arrests, prosecutions, trials and punishment. It is one of secondary victimisation. The book is also born out of the belief that a proper application of protective measures requires understanding the law. However, there are significant uncertainties about the scope of the principle of non-punishment and non-prosecution of trafficked persons who have been compelled to commit crimes, or as this book calls it the principle of non-liability. It is not just the principle that poses difficulties, i.e. the idea of excusing someone for breaching the law. Societies' perception of who is a victim of human trafficking also thwarts the application of the non-liability principle. Indeed, an accurate political and social construction of victimhood is central to the successful protection of trafficked persons, but it is missing. This book shows that it remains difficult to, in theory and practice, protect victims of human trafficking from being held liable for crimes they were compelled to commit in the course or as a consequence of being trafficked. European laws, from the Council of Europe and the European Union, and in turn their transposition, remain vague and potentially inadequate to achieve the aim of safeguarding the human rights of victims and avoiding further victimisation.

This book also explains how the non-liability principle is justified through the ethos of criminal and human rights law and critically analyses the existing law and its transposition. This is done in order to test the efficiency of the non-liability principles as contained in European legal frameworks. Towards the end, this book concludes with a concrete recommendation on how European law, or any other law (be it domestic or regional), can enhance protection for trafficked persons against unjust liability. In turn, in doing so the book provides relevant stakeholders, e.g. policy makers, civil society and law enforcement authorities, with a better understanding of the non-liability principle. Moreover, national policy makers and future regional policy makers can use the proposed alternative provision if they are serious about protecting the rights of the victims.

How Trafficked Persons Commit Crimes

The purposes for which victims of human trafficking are exploited include forced criminality. In France, for example, child victims have been compelled to commit theft (French Commission Nationale Consultative des Droits de l'Homme 2016). Other crimes that victims are forced to commit include, albeit are not limited to, drug trafficking and cultivation, benefit fraud, pickpocketing, robbery and burglary. The Recital to the 2011 EU Human Trafficking Directive at para. 14 explicates that the exploitation of criminal activities should be understood as "the exploitation of a person to commit, inter alia pick-pocketing, shoplifting, drug trafficking and other similar activities which are subject to penalties and imply a financial gain…" According to UK statistics, in 2011 thirty victims were identified as exploited for the purposes of cannabis cultivation, whilst by 2012 this number increased to sixty-nine (SOCA 2013: 17). A UK police operation, Operation Golf, found over one thousand children from a single Romanian Village who were trafficked "to Western Europe for forced labour and sexual exploitation. The exploitation of the children in the UK was largely connected to 'street crime' offences such as pickpocketing, bag snatching, shoplifting and ATM and distraction thefts, as well as through forced begging" (Anti-slavery 2014: 21).

In addition, trafficked persons may commit crimes that are not part of the exploitation element but are related to their migration status. Stoyanova writes that "this is very likely since countries of destination have introduced a panoply of criminal offences related to breaches of immigration laws" (2015: 224). Masika (2007: 14) concludes: "trafficked women and children often have an illegal immigration status in destination countries. Since legal frameworks relating to trafficking and prostitution vary, victims of trafficking are commonly deported, without adequate support, or imprisoned. Law enforcement may trap the victim of trafficking rather the trafficker." We can also consider the work of Campbell (2016), a British Anthropology and Sociology scholar, who raises attention of the numerous immigration offences used to criminalise irregular migrants. Moving away from immigration offences, Stoyanova (2015: 224) highlights that "involvement in prostitution, soliciting for the purpose of prostitution, or other prosecution-related activities could be qualified as criminal offences in some national jurisdiction." Indeed, in Croatia persons engaging in prostitution breach the national law. Furthermore, as highlighted by Schloenhardt and Markey-Towler (2016: 13) "victims of trafficking may commit criminal offences in an attempt to escape the trafficking situation, especially by using force or threats against traffickers and those associated with them."

Although forcing a person to commit crimes is a recognised form of exploitation, research and case law show that many victims are prosecuted (Anti-slavery 2014). Hales and Gelsthorpe (2012) from the Institute of Criminology at the University of Cambridge confirm this. Between May 2010 and November 2011, they studied migrant women in prison and immigration holding estates in the South-East of England and found that fifty-eight women (out of one hundred and thirteen studied) had strong indicators of being victims of human trafficking. They were predominantly charged with offences related to false identification possession or the production of cannabis. The civil society organisation Fair Work (2011) also shows with respect to the Netherlands that trafficked persons who were forced to commit criminal activities are incarcerated in prisons. It thus follows that authorities sometimes look at trafficked persons in terms of their immigration status or the crimes which they have committed, rather than the violations that they have endured. This could be a result of a number of reasons including: lack of identification of a person as a victim, lack of clarity as to relevant law that protects these persons or a need to meet government quotas and policies such as the war on drugs. Consequently, as stated by the organisation Anti-slavery (2014) "states are failing to implement the non-punishment and non-prosecution provisions enshrined in international legislation. By doing so, miscarriages of justice are being committed against victims whilst their traffickers go unpunished."

In turn, for the traffickers the punishment of victims is to a great advantage. It gives them further control over the victim; they can threaten victims with state punishment. Moreover, "it ensures that their victims are the ones to bear the criminal penalties while the real offenders can operate with impunity" (OSCE: 10).

Aims of the Book Through the Prism of Multiple Looking Glasses

The following legal provisions aim to protect trafficked persons against being held liable:

Article 26 of the *2005 Council of Europe Convention on Action Against Trafficking in Human Beings* states:

> Each Party shall, in accordance with the basic principles of its legal system, provide for the possibility of not imposing penalties on victims for their involvement in unlawful activities, to the extent that they have been compelled to do so.

Article 8 of Directive *2011/36 on preventing and combating trafficking in human beings and protecting its victims* states:

> Member States shall, in accordance with the basic principles of their legal systems, take the necessary measures to ensure that competent national authorities are entitled not to prosecute or impose penalties on victims of trafficking in human beings for their involvement in criminal activities which they have been compelled to commit as a direct consequence of being subjected to any of the acts referred to in Article 2.

The provision is supported by the Recital, which at para. 14 states that:

> Victims of trafficking in human beings should, in accordance with the basic principles of the legal systems of the relevant Member States, be protected from prosecution or punishment for criminal activities such as the use of false documents, or offences under legislation on prostitution or immigration, that they have been compelled to commit as a direct

consequence of being subject to trafficking. The aim of such protection is to safeguard the human rights of victims, to avoid further victimisation and to encourage them to act as witnesses in criminal proceedings against the perpetrators. This safeguard should not exclude prosecution or punishment for offences that a person has voluntarily committed or participated in.

Noting these provisions, the overarching aim of the book is to use a legal conceptual framework to answer the central research questions: *How are victims of human trafficking in Europe protected against unjust liability? Could the law be improved?* These questions evoke three overall aims: (i) determine what Article 26 of the *2005 Council of Europe Convention on Action Against Trafficking in Human Beings* and Article 8 of Directive *2011/36 on preventing and combating trafficking in human beings and protecting its victims* oblige states to do; (ii) ascertain whether the current obligations on non-liability fulfil the aim of delivering protection to trafficked persons; and (iii) if they do not, what could be the alternative provision.

To undertake the analysis, it is important to situate the principle of non-liability in broad scholarly domains, that of human rights, victimology and criminal law. The choice of criminal law is straightforward, much of the prosecuting and punishing is done in within the criminal justice space, and the responses of European and national legislators and policy makers have been that of criminal law or criminal focused policy. On one hand, this is a positive, firstly because having the law is important for trafficked persons as a group of victims, as the law informs the public conscious, it tells us a situation such as the one it seeks to address is a reality. It gives the experience of being compelled to commit a crime a voice and shapes public discourse. Secondly, it allows trafficked persons who committed crimes to see themselves as worthy of protection at regional and national level. However on the other hand, criminal law should not be and is not where the story ends, and we must bring in human rights. Kaiafa-Gbandi (2011: 7) rightly writes that: "[d]isassociating criminal law from the protection of fundamental rights or even loosening such association – albeit for the sake of addressing transnational crime by means of enhancing judicial cooperation – is liable to emasculate elemental values inherent in democratic societies, which subject the exercise of State authority to the rule of law. Even within international entities, then, no legitimate approach to criminal law can ignore its dual nature as a means of protecting fundamental interests as well as a yardstick of civil liberties".

Fortunately, the regional frameworks do not ignore human rights. The *2005 Council of Europe Convention on Action Against Trafficking in Human Beings* in the preamble states that trafficking in human beings constitutes a violation of human rights and an offence to the dignity and the integrity of the human being and that respect for victims' rights, protection of victims and action to combat trafficking in human beings must be the paramount objectives. The ethos of human rights is also echoed in the sentence that all actions or initiatives against trafficking in human beings must be non-discriminatory, take gender equality into account as well as a child-rights approach. In similar vein, *Directive 2011/36 on preventing and combating trafficking in human beings and protecting its victims* adopts a victim-focused approach that places the victim's welfare as one of the key pillars. The Recital at paragraph Seven states that rigorous prevention, prosecution and protection of victims' rights are major objectives of this Directive. This is in line with the EU Strategy on Human Trafficking (2012–2016), which highlights victim protection. The strategy includes, as it's first of five key priorities, identifying, protecting and assisting victims of trafficking.[1]

Bearing these aims in mind, it is unsurprising that the human rights legal framework is one of the prisms to inform the critical analysis in this book. Human rights play an important role in ensuring that each person's dignity and equality are met. With respect to the non-liability principle, they are particularly significant and appropriate because traditionally human rights protect individuals from government action that would threaten or harm their rights; the very thing that holding someone unjustly liable does. As such, a human rights approach is central to this work.

A human rights approach was initially established in the field of international development cooperation. It places the individual at the centre of efforts. With respect to human trafficking, the United Nations Human Rights Office of the High Commissioner (OHCHR 2014: 7) states that "[a] human rights-based approach is a conceptual framework for dealing with a phenomenon such as trafficking that is normatively based on international human rights standards and that is operationally directed to promoting and protecting human rights. Such an approach requires analysis of the ways in which human rights violations arise throughout the trafficking cycle, as well as of States' obligations under international human rights law." A human rights approach is therefore very much about protection. Rijken and Koster (2008: 9) emphasise the importance of victim protection and state that: "the position of the victims, the violations of their human rights and their vulnerable position are the starting points for taking countermeasures against THB [Trafficking in Human Beings]…A human rights based approach thus takes the protection of the human rights of victims of trafficking as the guideline for adopting measures, policy, and legislation in the field of combating THB."

Applying the human rights approach to a provision on non-liability for victims of human trafficking allows us to substantively ascertain that States have a responsibility under international law to act with due diligence to protect trafficked persons from unjust prosecution, trials or punishment. Further, it stipulates a methodological structure that offers assistance on how to design, implement and monitor the provision. In other words, it helps us determine what the law should be. In brief, the law ought to be characterised by fundamental rights derived from human rights law.

Using human rights is also important as it can act as a preventing force against law enforcement and political priorities taking over from a victim focus. Most criminal justice practitioners recognise the need to safeguard victim rights as an essential element of ensuring that victims are able to play an effective role in the investigation and prosecution of their exploiters. In other words, they are helped because they then can be used as witnesses. This approach, however, misses the point that safeguarding victim's rights is about protecting the dignity and equality of the victims. To avoid the danger of wrongly trying to frame victim protection within a criminal justice space, this book takes securing of human rights as the only valid reason for why we have principles such as non-liability. In other words, the concern is not the efficiency of the justice system per se, but instead that each person, including the victim, is treated with respect and worth. That is why in subsequent chapters there is caution in justifying the principle of non-liability with regard to seeing it as a way of achieving higher numbers of prosecutions of traffickers. For this author, anti-trafficking efforts are not to be measured successful by the number of convictions of traffickers but by the quality and quantity of protection offered to victims. Human beings, including victims of human trafficking, are not a means to an end, but an end in themselves.

Thus, human rights will provide standards to revise current law and to develop forward-looking human trafficking legislation that truly protect persons in need of protection. Admittedly, not all scholars see human rights as the "go-to" field when discussing human trafficking; fair labour practices, migration, criminal law and social justice all play a role. However, it is contended that the human rights agenda has much to offer, in particular with regard to the non-liability provision, which focuses on state responsibility towards the individual. Human rights are not only a framework through which to assess the existing legislation and thus determine if trafficked persons are truly protected. It is also acknowledged that holding trafficked persons liable is a human rights violation in itself. A violation often closely linked to discrimination and to deep-seated misconceptions of who is a victim worthy of protection. This is where victimology comes into play.

Victimology is one of the youngest disciplines within the domain of justice studies. She separated herself from the other more traditional disciplines—law, criminology, etc.—as one that primarily concerns itself with the victims of crime. In criminal law, there are two parties: an offender and a victim. The crime itself is a result of the direct or indirect interaction between the offender and the victim. Victimology defends the importance of victims against the offenders and even against the state. A full exploration of victimology is beyond the scope of this book however, on the whole victimology concerns itself with who are the victims, what social structures or other contexts led to the harm of an individual or a group of individuals. Moreover, it looks at the types of victims, and it researches the relationship between the offender and the victim, the will and role of the victim in the crime as well as the treatment of victims by the criminal justice system. We owe victimology a lot, including the acknowledgement that the effectiveness of our justice systems requires the hearing of victim voices. In addition, authors such as Mawby and Walklate (1994) evolved discourse and highlighted that the experiences of certain groups such as women or minorities need to be understood within broader structural contexts. The same is very much true of the group of victims who are subjected to human trafficking. The impact that victimology has had on practice and our legal documents, has meant that hearing victims' voices transcended into rights for victims, e.g., in terms of criminal procedure. With time, these manifested into enforceable human rights, including (as argued in this book) the right to non-liability for victims of trafficking who were compelled to commit a crime.

A lot of the questions that victimology asks are relevant to this book and will be asked throughout. Thus, the reader will find victimology as a leitmotif in many of the chapters. In particular, the book explores that the position of victim is not awarded solely because of the trafficking experience, but by the perceptions and held stereotypes of those that play a role in ensuring the right non-liability manifests itself. "Evidence suggests that unless victims fit into stereotypical roles of 'victimhood' as defined by law enforcement officials, they may not be identified as trafficking victims and may be labelled as criminals and further victimized" (Malloch and Rigby 2016: 5). Chapter 7 shows that there is a hierarchy of victims, and some will be more successful of enforcing their rights as contained in European legislations. Notions of innocence and blamelessness are set to distinguish the victim from the trafficker, yet matters are not often so two-dimensional. This theory forms the template for when we explore what thwarts the application of the law.

Terminology

The following terminology is used in this book:

Non-liability: The wording of the principle in question varies across different legal instruments and discourses. There is language such as "non-criminalisation," "non-prosecution," "non-punishment," "non-application of penalties" and "exemption," to name some of the more common examples. However, this book finds a key problem with the terminology, for it does not appear to be intended for use outside of criminal law, and it is not conceived for cases of administrative/civil law. Case in point, the words "non-criminalisation" or "non-prosecution" are exclusively linked to criminal law. With regard to the latter, it specifically refers to the possibility that prosecutors may refrain from pressing charges against victims of trafficking, and no mention is made of cases outside of the prosecutions' domain. Mere reference to criminal law leaves trafficked persons unaware of the consequences of wrongful acts committed external of it; and yet, as will be shown trafficked victims can engage in non-criminal offences. To reflect this reality, when speaking about the principle generally, this book will rely on the phrase "non-liability." This is borrowed from Article 10 of UNODC's Model Law,[2] which states that trafficked persons should not be held "criminally or administratively liable for offences." There is breadth and accuracy in the term "non-liability."

Victims: The subjects at the heart of the principle of "non-liability" are persons who are victims of human trafficking. Broadly speaking, in literature the term victim: "has come to describe any person who has experienced injury, loss, or hardship due to the illegal action of another individual, group, or organization" (Ferguson and Turvey: 2). However, this word can still give rise to debates, especially as those who have experienced a non-fatal crime may prefer the term "survivor" (Letschert and Staiger 2010: 16). This book will nevertheless use the term victim, as that is the language contained in relevant legislation, it will also use interchangeably: "victim of human trafficking," "victim of trafficking," "trafficked person" and "human trafficking victim."

Prosecution and Punishment: In accordance with general principles of interpretation, penalties are likely to include: cautions, fines and imprisonment. The meaning of prosecution most likely relates to the conventional court-based prosecution, where the State seeks penalties after guilt has been proven.

Notes

1. The strategy was published by the European Commission in 2012; it aims to "provide a coherent framework for existing and planned initiatives, to set priorities (and) to fill gaps." In brief, the strategy details

the EU's counter-trafficking policy and legislation, which also includes actions regarding external work of EU with third countries. The EU Anti-Trafficking Coordinator, appointed in 2011 by the Commission, has a mission to oversee the implementation of this strategy. At the time of writing, this post is held by Dr. Myria Vassiliadou.

2. The UNODC Model Law against Trafficking in Persons was developed by the United Nations Office on Drugs and Crime (UNODC) in response to the request of the General Assembly to the Secretary-General to promote and assist the efforts of member states to become party to and implement the United Nations Convention against Transnational Organized Crime and the Protocols thereto…The Model Law will both facilitate and help systematize provision of legislative assistance by UNODC as well as facilitate review and amendment of existing legislation and adoption of new legislation by States themselves. It is designed to be adaptable to the needs of each State, whatever its legal tradition and social, economic, cultural and geographical conditions.

References

Anti-slavery. (2014). *Trafficking for Forced Criminal Activities and Begging in Europe. RACE in Europe Project* [Online]. http://www.antislavery.org/includes/documents/cm_docs/2014/t/trafficking_for_forced_criminal_activities_and_begging_in_europe.pdf.

Campbell, J. R. (2016). Asylum v. Sovereignty in the 21st Century: How Nation-State's Breach International Law to Block Access to Asylum. *International Journal Migration and Border Studies, 2*(1), 24–39.

Cross, A. L. (2013). Slipping Through the Cracks: The Dual Victimization of Human-Trafficking Survivors. *McGeorge Law Review, 44*, 395–422.

European Commission. (2012). *The EU Strategy Towards the Eradication of Trafficking in Human Beings (2012–2016)* [Online]. https://ec.europa.eu/anti-trafficking/eu-policy/new-european-strategy-2012-2016_en.

Fair Work. (2011). *Signaling Victims of Labor Exploitation and Criminal Exploitation in Alien Detention* [Online]. http://www.fairwork.nu/assets/structured-files/Publicaties/Rapporten/RapportageVDarbeids-encrimineleuitbuitingDEF3007201.pdf.

Ferguson, C., & Turvey, B. (date unknown). *Victimology: A Brief History with an Introduction to Forensic Victimology* [Online]. http://booksite.elsevier.

com/samplechapters/9780123740892/Sample_Chapters/02-Chapter_1. pdf.

French Commission Nationale Consultative des Droits de l'Homme. (2016). *La lutte contre la traite et l'exploitation des êtres humains* [Online]. http:// www.cncdh.fr/sites/default/files/cncdh_traite_des_etres_humains_vdef.pdf.

Hales, L., & Gelsthorpe, L. (2012). *Institute of Criminology*. Cambridge: University of Cambridge.

Kaiafa-Gbandi, M. (2011). The Importance of Core Principles of Substantive Criminal Law for a European Criminal Policy Respecting Fundamental Rights and the Rule of Law. *European Criminal Law Review, 1*(1), 7–34.

Letschert, R., & Staiger, I. (2010). Introduction and Definitions. In R. Letschert, A. Pemberton, & I. Staiger (Eds.), *Assisting Victims of Terrorism*. Dordrecht: Springer.

Malloch, M., & Rigby, P. (2016). Contexts and Complexities. In M. Malloch & P. Rigby (Eds.), *Human Trafficking: The Complexities of Exploitation*. Edinburgh: Edinburgh University Press.

Masika, R. (2007). *Gender, Trafficking and Slavery*. Oxford: Oxfam.

Mawby, R., & Walklate, S. (1994). *Critical Victimology*. London: Sage.

Rijken, C., & Koster, D. (2008). A Human Rights Based Approach to Trafficking in Human Beings in Theory and Practice. *SSRN Electronic Journal* [Online]. http://dx.doi.org/10.2139/ssrn.1135108.

Schloenhardt, A., & Markey-Towler, R. (2016). Non-criminalisation of Victims of Trafficking in Persons—Principles, Promises and Perspectives. *Groningen Journal of International Law, 4*(1), 10–38.

SOCA. (2013). UKHTC: *A Baseline Assessment on the Nature and Scale of Human Trafficking in 2012* [Online]. http://www.soca.gov.uk/ news/462-human-trafficking-assessment-published.

Stoyanova, V. (2015). *Human Trafficking and Slavery Reconsidered: Conceptual Limits and States' Positive Obligations*. Lund: Lund University.

United Nations Human Rights Office of the High Commissioner. (2010). *Recommended Principles and Guidelines on Human Rights and Human Trafficking*. Geneva: OHCHR [Online]. www.ohchr.org/Documents/ Publications/Commentary_Human_Trafficking_en.pdf.

United Nations Human Rights Office of the High Commissioner. (2014). *Human Rights and Human Trafficking*. New York and Geneva: United Nation [Online]. http://www.ohchr.org/Documents/Publications/FS36_en.pdf.

United Nations Office on Drugs and Crime (UNODC). (2009). *Model Law Against Trafficking in Persons*. V.09–81990 (E).

2

Human Trafficking

Introduction

GRETA (the Council of Europe's Group of Experts on Action against Trafficking in Human Beings) states that where trafficking "is not officially established or remains vague, persons who are victims of THB [trafficking in human beings] are convicted of criminal offences, for example purse snatching, pickpocketing or drug smuggling" (2014: para. 189). This statement clearly exemplifies the importance of understanding the meaning of what human trafficking is. Yet as will be shown, terminological uncertainty creates many difficulties in successfully applying measures that protect victims of human trafficking. This chapter explores the definition of human trafficking.

Whilst international legal consensus on the characterisation of the crime has been reached, the definition of human trafficking continues to be a moot point. The various international and regional definitions are similar if not identical; however, individual states, literature and civil society bodies still remain divided on a number of topics that make up the definition of human trafficking. As summarised by Rijken (2013: 10), "much remains unclear in relation to the actual definition."

© The Author(s) 2019
J. M. Muraszkiewicz, *Protecting Victims of Human Trafficking From Liability*, Palgrave
Studies in Victims and Victimology, https://doi.org/10.1007/978-3-030-02659-2_2

The story of human trafficking can be summarised as having three key developments. Firstly, the white slave movement, secondly the progression to traffic in women and children, and finally, the adoption of the universal definition in 2000. Alternatively, one can follow Allain's (2017: 1) categorisation: "[T]he evolution in the legal regime governing human trafficking can be separated neatly into three eras: The Pre-League of Nations, the League of Nations, and the United Nations." It should be noted that it is beyond the scope of this book to describe the historic development of the human trafficking definition and the book begins with the year 1998.

What Is Human Trafficking: The Legal Definitions

In an attempt to develop a binding structure on transnational crimes, in 1998 the UN tasked an ad hoc committee with building a new international legal framework. This eventually gave rise to Resolution 55/25 of 15 November 2000 and the adoption of the Convention against Transnational Organised Crime which sought to tackle organised crime through outlying how states can cooperate on issues such as joint investigations or mutual legal assistance with regard to transnational organised crime. The Convention has three additional protocols, including the Protocol to Prevent, Suppress and Punish Trafficking in Persons, Especially Women and Children. Obokata (2015: 174) highlights that "one of the important contributions which the Trafficking Protocol has made so far is the adoption of a definition of human trafficking." Article 3 of the 2000 UN Protocol on Human Trafficking states that trafficking in persons shall mean:

a. The recruitment, transportation, transfer, harbouring or receipt of persons, by means of the threat or use of force or other forms of coercion, of abduction, of fraud, of deception, of the abuse of power, or a position of vulnerability, or the giving or receiving of payments or benefits to achieve the consent of a person having control over another person, for the purpose of exploitation. Exploitation shall include, at a minimum, the exploitation of the prostitution of others

or other forms of sexual exploitation, forced labour or services, slavery or practices similar to slavery, servitude or the removal of organs.
b. The consent of a victim of trafficking in persons to the intended exploitation set forth in subparagraph (a) of this article shall be irrelevant where any of the means set forth in subparagraph (a) have been used.
c. The recruitment, transportation, transfer, harbouring or receipt of a child for the purpose of exploitation shall be considered "trafficking in persons" even if this does not involve any of the means set forth in subparagraph (a) of this article.

The Protocol entered into force on 25 December 2003, and 117 states and regional economic integration organisations have signed it. The definition includes three elements. An action (recruitment, transportation, transfer, harbouring or receipt), a means (threat or use of force or other forms of coercion, of abduction, of fraud, of deception, of the abuse of power, or a position of vulnerability, or the giving or receiving of payments or benefits to achieve the consent of a person having control over another person) and a purpose (at a minimum, the exploitation of the prostitution of others or other forms of sexual exploitation, forced labour or services, slavery or practices similar to slavery, servitude or the removal of organs). According to Piotrowicz (2007: 277) "[T]hese elements indicate that [trafficking in human beings] includes a number of actors, each of whom may play a role in 'creating' a victim of trafficking, from the acquaintance in the victim's village who knows someone who can organise a job or visa, to the individual who facilitates illegal crossing of the frontier, to the person who supplies rooms to accommodate victims in transit and the bar owner who eventually 'buys' the victim."

A key point to note for the purposes of discussing victims who were compelled to commit crimes is that consent of the victim is irrelevant. This is stated in Art. 3(b) and so even if a trafficked person consented to breaking the law, e.g. committing an immigration offence or engaging in drug manufacturing, such consent is irrelevant in the eyes of the law. As such, a victim who consents to break the law ought to still be classified as a victim and thus be entitled to protection and support granted in international and national legislation.

The first European definition came with the *2005 Council of Europe Convention on Action Against Trafficking in Human Beings*. The Convention evolved the UN legislation and provided stricter measures on protecting and promoting the rights of trafficked persons. In terms of definition, Article 4 states:

a. "Trafficking in human beings" shall mean the recruitment, transportation, transfer, harbouring or receipt of persons, by means of the threat or use of force or other forms of coercion, of abduction, of fraud, of deception, of the abuse of power or of a position of vulnerability or of the giving or receiving of payments or benefits to achieve the consent of a person having control over another person, for the purpose of exploitation. Exploitation shall include, at a minimum, the exploitation of the prostitution of others or other forms of sexual exploitation, forced labour or services, slavery or practices similar to slavery, servitude or the removal of organs;
b. The consent of a victim of "trafficking in human beings" to the intended exploitation set forth in subparagraph (a) of this article shall be irrelevant where any of the means set forth in subparagraph (a) have been used;
c. The recruitment, transportation, transfer, harbouring or receipt of a child for the purpose of exploitation shall be considered "trafficking in human beings" even if this does not involve any of the means set forth in subparagraph (a) of this article;
d. "Child" shall mean any person under eighteen years of age;
e. "Victim" shall mean any natural person who is subject to trafficking in human beings as defined in this article.

A key aspect of the Convention is that it established the first monitoring body. The Group of Experts on Action against Trafficking in Human Beings (GRETA) completes country evaluation rounds. GRETA visits each member state and assesses it on its compliance with the 2005 European Convention against Trafficking. Subsequently, detailed country reports are published. Unlike some UN monitoring bodies, GRETA is unable to receive individual complaints. However, in its country visits the organisation speaks to a wide range of stakeholders including non-governmental organisations (NGOs).

What has the EU been doing in the space of human trafficking? In 2002, the EU adopted the Council Framework Decision on the Fight against Trafficking in Human Beings. In that instrument, the definition does not replicate word for word the UN definition, albeit it is largely based on it. The entry of the Lisbon Treaty in 2009, and in particular the Treaty on the Functioning of the European Union (TFEU), afforded a chance to further develop the existing human trafficking law. Art. 79(1) and (2)(d) of the TFEU provide that in the development of a common EU immigration policy the EU will prevent and combat trafficking in human beings. Additionally, human trafficking is listed in Article 83(1) TFEU as a crime that falls within the EU competence for harmonisation. *Directive 2011/36 on preventing and combating trafficking in human beings and protecting its victims* was adopted by the European Parliament on 5 April 2011 and entered into force on 15 April 2011. Article 2 of the Directive concerns the definition of human trafficking:

1. The recruitment, transportation, transfer, harbouring or reception of persons, including the exchange or transfer of control over those persons, by means of the threat or use of force or other forms of coercion, of abduction, of fraud, of deception, of the abuse of power or of a position of vulnerability or of the giving or receiving of payments or benefits to achieve the consent of a person having control over another person, for the purpose of exploitation.
2. A position of vulnerability means a situation in which the person concerned has no real or acceptable alternative but to submit to the abuse involved.
3. Exploitation shall include, as a minimum, the exploitation of the prostitution of others or other forms of sexual exploitation, forced labour or services, including begging, slavery or practices similar to slavery, servitude, or the exploitation of criminal activities, or the removal of organs.
4. The consent of a victim of trafficking in human beings to exploitation, whether intended or actual, shall be irrelevant where any of the means set forth in paragraph 1 has been used.
5. When the conduct referred to in paragraph 1 involves a child, it shall be a punishable offence of trafficking in human beings even if none of the means set forth in paragraph 1 has been used.

6. For the purpose of this Directive, "child" shall mean any person below 18 years of age.

The EU definition differs to that contained in the *2000 UN Protocol on Human Trafficking* and the *2005 Council of Europe Convention on Action Against Trafficking in Human Beings*. Firstly, it includes a further "action": exchange or transfer of control. Secondly, the Directive includes a new "purpose": begging and exploitation of criminal activities. The Recital also includes illegal adoption or forced marriage as examples of exploitation. Paragraph 11 states: "The definition also covers trafficking in human beings for the purpose of the removal of organs, which constitutes a serious violation of human dignity and physical integrity, as well as, for instance, other behaviours such as illegal adoption or forced marriage in so far as they fulfil the constitutive elements of trafficking in human beings."

The European Court of Human Rights has also steered the discourse on human trafficking and state responsibilities, including towards victims. The court has ruled that human trafficking falls within the remit of Article 4.

Breaking Down the Definition

For trafficked persons who have been compelled to commit a crime as a result of their trafficking situation, the definition is of primary importance. Without falling within the remit of the definition they will not be granted protection and will be labelled as perpetrators. Yet, the definition is riddled with ambiguities and limitations. The least problematic is the first element, the action. However, the subsequent means and purpose are riddled with concerns. Below they are examined, however first some observatory remarks as to the definition as a whole.

Framing of the Definition

It is possible to argue that the definition of human trafficking is, in its wording, gender unbiased. The international legal community first approached human trafficking through a discourse on the white slave movement, which referred to forcibly or under fraud recruiting white women and children into prostitution. Contrary to the predeceasing focus, existing definitions include a more gender-neutral language, referring to persons rather than women, and do not solely focus on sexual exploitation. The definitions' breadth, as is shown below, seeks to capture the experiences of all genders. Whilst this book accepts that male power is systematic and reflected in our laws, it would appear that the definition of human trafficking was created not just from the point of view of the man. Although riddled with emotive issues surrounding sex work (e.g. when does it become trafficking?), the definition does appear to include the feminist and victimologist voices. Indeed, even the controversies around sex work contained in the definition are feminist, for feminism is not a single theory. Instead, it is a discipline that expands into different perceptions, agendas and different definitions of key concepts. Mutually, however, these viewpoints wish to ensure all gender interests are addressed properly. The gender-neutral stance can be attributed to the significant, unprecedented and influential contribution from NGO actors, many of whom included female voices and those attune to notions of victimology, who assisted in providing more information regarding the phenomenon of human trafficking, something that may be considered as a lacuna in the knowledge of the drafters (Gallagher 2010: 1003). Such involvement contributed to the development of a broad international definition of trafficking in persons, one that recognises that a victim can be a 70-year-old woman forced to work as a domestic slave, a transgender person compelled to shoplift or a male forced to cultivate cannabis.

Our optimism is however quickly curtailed. Whilst the definition on the surface does not make assumptions about who can and who cannot be a trafficker or a trafficked person, the law itself is not the end of the story. Due to hidden factors at play, including gender biases, there are many "victimological others," persons who are not seen as victims (Walklate 2005) and who are excluded from receiving the required protection. Perception is prejudiced by poor media illustrations, a patriarchal political and justice system, the political climate (e.g. hostile environment for migrants) all of which lead to the creation of an ideal victim as the only person entitled to assistance (see chapter 7).

Moreover, issue can be taken with how human trafficking is framed, and thus defined, in the first place. Rather than seeing it solely as a crime, it could equally be conceptualised as an issue of power, capitalism, greed. To put differently, it is possible that the problem with human trafficking is that it tends to be predominantly framed as an issue of criminal justice. Here, a weak, young, blameless victim—who is often seen as female—has her rights invaded by an individual offender or an organised criminal group. This simplified framing of a multifarious and global issue has practical implications for national and international definitions and thereby approaches to human trafficking. States focus on arrests, prosecutions and collecting numbers of how many victims they helped. Potentially, this misidentified construction of human trafficking as a heinous product of a relationship between individuals—victim and offender—has diverted our focus from broader and more appropriate notions. Namely, how existing socio-economic structures impact, and possibly support, human trafficking. If that is the case, then perhaps the definition is not as gender-neutral as first shown. Ignoring the existing capitalist structures that propel human trafficking could be seen as male centred, for the economy is still very much a patriarchal space. Perchance, a truly gender-neutral definition would portray human trafficking more as a social and economic problem rather than just as an expression of violence. Moreover, re-framing human trafficking as not just a criminal law issues would shift attention from the aftermath and instead would more likely take prevention seriously. Applying the criminal law lens is potentially not effective because it accepts that trafficking will happen. However, an emphasis on prevention, through a more socio–economic–political approach, would declare that people are truly not for sale.

Currently, there is not enough recognition of human trafficking as a socially constructed phenomenon. Rather, we look at it as a product of objective criminal behaviour. The consequence of this is on policy. More cynical questions can be posed: are there stakeholders who benefit from normalising elements of labour exploitation and if so do they have an impact on policy? There is not enough space in this book to unpack whether human trafficking ought to be framed through a definition different to criminal law, yet it is worthy to ponder it and further research is due on how this may affect victims' access to rights.

It is now time to break down the definition of human trafficking.

Action Element of the Definition

There are six action elements in *Directive 2011/36 on preventing and combating trafficking in human beings and protecting its victims*:

1. Recruitment
2. Transportation
3. Transfer
4. Harbouring
5. Receipt of persons
6. Exchange or transfer of control.

The 2005 Council of Europe Convention on Action against Trafficking in Human Beings does not have the sixth element. The actions themselves may be neutral but they take on a different meaning when undertaken through the various means and with the intent to exploit. A study on organ trafficking rightly highlights that the actions in the definition precede exploitation, and a person can already be guilty of human trafficking once a victim was subjected to one of the actions and by one of the means, provided the intention to exploit was there (Council of Europe and United Nations 2009). In other words, the definition asks states to criminalise the action for the purpose of exploitation. The actions themselves are relatively straightforward. They encompass a broad range of activities that can occur nationally or transnationally. Additionally, the actions do not have to be carried out by the same person, but each of the acts will constitute a criminal conduct.

Turning to the six actions we begin with recruitment. Recruitment is the act of enlisting new people to be exploited. According to the Council of Europe and UN study (2009: 78), recruitment "is to be understood in a broad sense, meaning any activity leading from the commitment or engagement of another individual to his or her exploitation." As was highlighted by the Spapens et al. (2014: 15): "The trafficker needs to 'find' the persons he wants to exploit. Usually this involves gaining the trust of the later victim and drawing an attractive picture of the type of work on offer, the working conditions and the salary, which will later turn out to be (partly) false." Recruitment may be interpreted extensively and is limited only by the creativity of the traffickers; agencies, chat rooms and bars can all be used to lure potential victims. The term covers the search for potential victims and the enlistment of victims by whatever means.

Transportation is also a broad term, and it can occur nationally or across borders, and there is no limit as to the type of transportation. It can include carriage by car, foot, flights, etc., and regard long or short distances. As such if a person is moved from one house to another by a means (e.g. deceit or force) for the purpose of exploitation, this is enough to constitute human trafficking.

The transfer element refers to the handing over of an individual from one person/group to another. There is also an element of transfer of control over the victim which may be key in situations where family members transfer a child from one family unit to another, e.g. for the purpose of domestic servitude. The same is recognised in the EU Directive by the inclusion of the phrase "the exchange of transfer of control over those persons."

Harbouring regards accommodating/housing a victim. In the case of trafficking in human beings for the purpose of the removal of organs, harbouring also contains accommodating intended donors in the medical clinic or other locations where the organ removal is to take place (Council of Europe and United Nations 2009: 78). The receipt of persons is an extensive term and regards receiving victims at the place where they will be exploited or meeting victims at various places along their journey.

Means Element of the Definition

The problem of ambiguity begins with the means elements. It is the means that are of particular relevance to the non-liability principle as they go to the heart of the distortion of free will of the person, which as will be shown in this chapter is part of the justification for why trafficked persons ought to be excused. The means used concern the action and not the exploitation. In accordance with the definitions, there are seven means:

1. Threat or use of force
2. Coercion
3. Abduction
4. Fraud
5. Deception
6. Abuse of power or vulnerability
7. Giving or receiving payments or benefits.

The means list is closed. Thus, in a situation where a trafficker uses a different means to achieve his/her purpose, this may cause problems for a victim. Sitarz (2010: 340) uses the example of a situation when a person blackmails or seduces a victim. Blackmail is not on the list. However, by including an array of different means, the legislators have given a wide scope for determining that a particular method is within the realms of this definition. Taking blackmail as an example, even using strict interpretation, it is easily imaginable that it would fall under the category "abuse of power or of a position of vulnerability." The "means" specified could be taken as umbrella terms for related phenomena. This is not to suggest that there is free reign to add whatever means. However, the list can be extended to additional specifies, provided they in some way fit within a constructive reading of the means listed and follow the documents' spirit and purpose.

More problematic, however, is the ambiguous meaning of the various means contained. Perhaps, the vaguest term is "abuse of power or of a position of vulnerability." Article 2(2) of the Directive 2011/36 on preventing and combating trafficking in human beings and protecting its victims states: "A position of vulnerability means a situation in which the person concerned has no real or acceptable alternative but to submit to the abuse involved." What does such a situation involve? The Explanatory Report to the 2005 Council of Europe Convention on Action against Trafficking in Human Beings (para. 83) explains that: "By abuse of a position of vulnerability is meant abuse of any situation in which the person involved has no real and acceptable alternative to submitting to the abuse. The vulnerability may be of any kind, whether physical, psychological, emotional, family-related, social or economic. The situation might, for example, involve insecurity or illegality of the victim's administrative status, economic dependence or fragile health. In short, the situation can be any state of hardship in which a human being is impelled to accept being exploited. Persons abusing such a situation flagrantly infringe human rights and violate human dignity and integrity, which no one can validly renounce."

Despite the explanation, there are still uncertainties. Most problematic is the assessment of vulnerability, as it includes having no real or acceptable alternative, and this is a subjective criterion. Equally problematic is the word "abuse"; what does it actually include? In 2009, the Dutch Supreme Court considered a case of a defendant who had not taken any steps to recruit the workers in question; they had themselves begged for a job. However, it was found that their irregular migration status was enough to put them in a position of vulnerability. In this case, the Supreme Court found that "the conscious use of a position of vulnerability itself constitutes the abuse" (Esser and Dettmeijer-Vermeulen 2016).

Through highlighting that "vulnerability may be of any kind," the definition becomes very elastic and it is possible to contend that an expansive interpretation means that more victims will be entitled to protection. Moreover, there appears to be no consistency on the definition of abuse of a position of vulnerability amongst states, thus further showing the lack of clarity.

The formulation of the term "position of vulnerability" includes an underlying theme of compulsion or involuntariness. In relation to the debate on the principle of non-liability, these considerations are relevant since the principle relies on the victim being compelled to do an act. The circumstances in which trafficked person is compelled to commit crimes are varied and can be very case specific. However, their vulnerability certainly appears to play a central role. This, as is shown in subsequent chapters, can be problematic because vulnerability is not always obvious. A strong looking male from Ukraine may not appear vulnerable to the English society, yet many trafficked persons are made vulnerable by their migration status. Traffickers abuse this vulnerability and threaten their victims with various authorities (police, immigration). We thus need to recognise that abuse of power or of a position of vulnerability is not always visible.

Turning to the other means, coercion and force and threat of force are the more direct means by which individuals become victims of human trafficking. However, there is no indication whether coercion or force is restricted to physical acts or can include psychological means as well. As stated by Stoyanova (2013: 66–67), "it is also unclear whether economic coercion is included." Gallagher (2010: 31) highlights that deception and fraud are examples of the less direct means and "will generally relate to the nature of the promised work or service, and/or the conditions under which an individual is to undertake that work or perform that service." On close examination, there is ambiguity as to the difference between fraud and deception. It is possible to try and advocate that by including both terms the definition applies to jurisdictions that use one or the other terms. As such, any overlap between the various means is to the benefit of states. Clarity is, however, further compromised by a lack of precision as to the required threshold of deception or fraud.

As to the last means—"the giving or receiving of payments or benefits to achieve the consent of a person having control of another person"—this too is opaque. For instance, the term control is not defined; is it only legal control (parents and children), contractual control (employer and employee), physical control or all of these? This provision adds to the overall ambiguity surrounding the meaning of the means element.

Exploitation Element of the Definition

One of the most problematic elements of the definition is the meaning of exploitation. The exploitation of the prostitution of others or other forms of sexual exploitation is perhaps the most challenging, especially as key concepts are not defined in international law (Fergus 2005: 5).

As argued by Sullivan (2003: 81) with respect to the 2000 UN Protocol on Human Trafficking, "it is a compromise definition of trafficking but one which takes no clear position on the relation between prostitution and trafficking." The lack of definition of the exploitation of the prostitution of others or other forms of sexual exploitation in any of the relevant instruments, including the human trafficking documents, is deliberate so as to not prejudice how states deal with prostitution and sexual exploitation in domestic law. However, by not defining the terms, the international instruments have left a vacuum, now filled by a polarised moral debate. The discussion on human trafficking and prostitution predominantly focuses on whether prostitution can ever be chosen, whether it is a form of work or whether it is a product of a patriarchal society. The diverging positions on prostitution complicate the common knowledge on what is human trafficking. In fact, some stakeholders, such as the ILO, advocate for the term "sexual exploitation" to be taken out of the definition. The ILO (1999) notes: "We suggest deleting the reference to sexual exploitation, which is a rather undefined term and subject to different interpretations."

Other than the above brief remarks, this book will not engage in the contested debate as to whether sex work is exploitation or what exactly constitutes forced labour, slavery, servitude, removal of organs, etc. There is after all a plethora of work on these topics. Instead, a scrutiny of exploitation itself is undertaken.

Where the concept of human exploitation arises in international legal instruments, it is not defined. Neither the *2000 UN Palermo Protocol* nor the *2005 Council of Europe Convention on Action Against Trafficking in Human Beings* or *Directive 2011/36 on preventing and combating trafficking in human beings and protecting its victims* define exploitation. This in turn creates problems for those working in the anti-human trafficking field; one needs to have some knowledge when a situation is qualified as exploitation to be able to prevent it, punish it and protect those affected. *A lack of definition has led to a divergence in state practice on criminalising exploitation. As pointed out by Rijken (2015: 432) "in some countries a mere violation of labour rights is considered exploitation, whereas in other countries only cases of severe violation qualify as such, albeit without further defining such severity."*

To a certain degree, international human trafficking law has sought to clarify the meaning of exploitation by listing examples. Although these examples are not defined, elaborations can be obtained from reputable international conventions and other sources of international law, for instance with respect to what servitude is. However, there are also other practices—old and emerging—that do not have long-standing instruments that explain their meaning, e.g. exploitation for forced begging. Moreover, the examples listed in the *2005 Council of Europe Convention on Action Against Trafficking in Human Beings* and *Directive 2011/36 on preventing and combating trafficking in human beings and protecting its victims* and other sources of human trafficking law are perhaps the most severe forms of exploitation, e.g. slavery. How are we to understand whether a practice of, for example, forcing someone to engage in fraudulent car accidents can be classified as exploitation? Can that person then be excused for committing fraud?

Undeniably, defining exploitation is problematic and currently is resolved at a national level. Macedonian law, for example, includes forced fertilisation as a form of exploitation, whilst in Moldova exploitation includes using a woman as a surrogate mother or for reproductive purposes. It is, however, important for the purpose of applying the principle of non-liability to try defining exploitation. For one, part of that exploitation may be a criminal activity.

One could suggest inflicting harm as an obvious place to draw a line for unacceptable behaviour. This gives exploitation a John Mill flavour, where actions (exploitative) are prohibited in order to prevent harm to others. Harm is understood in the context of Derek Parfit's (1984) theory: an action harms a person if it makes it the case that the person is worse off than he/she would have been had the action not occurred. For instance, human trafficking of children for the purpose of using them as child soldiers wrongfully exploits the children because it violates their autonomy and harms them on both psychological and physiological levels. The advantage of using harm as a benchmark to define exploitation is that it is resistible to, although not completely immune from, time and culture. There are, however, issues that remain. Some may, for example, renounce the above definition of harm. Others may ask: are all levels of harm wrong? Let us consider the example of men who work in car washes for 10 Euro a day, a wage below minimum standard. This is an agreed form of exploitation but these men, who otherwise may not have had a job, are technically not worse off, unless, of course, there are other elements present such as physical or psychological abuse. Thus, we are still left with the question of what is exploitation? Robert Goodin (1987) claims that exploitation involves making an unusual or uncommon use. This definition is, however, problematic; indeed, the practice of making workers work below minimum wage, for long period and without access to overtime pay, may not be so uncommon amongst, for example, seasonal workers or au pairs.

Wood (1995: 150) frames exploitation through the concept of vulnerability, arguing that: "proper respect for others is violated when we treat their vulnerabilities as opportunities to advance our own interest or projects." Although trafficked persons are often perceived as vulnerable, the concept alone cannot be enough to demarcate exploitation. Let us consider a football game, a player from team A is sent off. Team A is now vulnerable because it has fewer players. Team B scores a goal and wins the game. We would not, however, say that team B "exploits" the opponent's vulnerability. In essence, there is nothing exploitative about team B's actions. Equally, a school bully, who chooses to steal lunch from students with height impairment, although indecent and wrong, is not exploiting them. Rijken (2015: 435) confronts the use of only the element vulnerability because it is not a static element, "but depends on time, the person and the specific situation."

Allain in his book *Slavery in International Law* writes about exploitation within the terms of an unfair advantage; in this approach, it is not the act which is important, but the means by which the person is made to do the activity. Allain's work draws on other scholars who contextualise exploitation as an unfair or opportunistic advantage. Wertheimer (1996), one of the most prominent political philosophers to scrutinise exploitation defined it as: "A exploits B when A takes unfair advantage over B." Understanding exploitation as an unfair advantage still leaves some questions unanswered. Primarily, we need to understand at what point the unfair advantage turns into exploitation. On the free market, there are numerous examples of stronger parties taking, what may seem as, an unfair advantage over weaker ones. Think here of the power exercised by monopolies. As summarised by the UNODC (2015: 22), "the inequalities of power that enable the unfair advantage are themselves considered to be acceptable within that time and place – as is the disproportionate benefit accrued through the taking of unequal / unfair advantage."

Labour law is of some help in determining what is unfair; in the above example, earning 10 Euro a day is unfair because labour law says it is so. However, using labour standards as a determination for exploitation is problematic on copious levels. Firstly, we are hindered by the divergences of political systems. To paraphrase Rijken: having detailed labour laws and standards will be perceived by some as a form of labour protection, whilst others will view labour indicators as paternalism. "In a free market approach, freedom for the individual to enter into an agreement is valued and restrictions on entering into a labour agreement and negotiating labour issues are less likely to be adopted, even if they are imposed to protect the (migrant) workers. In a more social democratic regime, protection of (migrant) workers is considered more important than economic gain and, as a result, migrant workers can only enter into an agreement that guarantees fundamental rights" (Rijken 2015: 437–438). Secondly, answering the question of exploitation with reference to labour law and workers' rights creates a lack of certainty as to practices that are beyond this sphere. There are other practices that could be deemed exploitative that have nothing to do with work. Of course, the methodology of using labour law as a benchmark could be transcended, and we could try to rely on human rights, family law, contract or criminal law as a gauge. This is in line with a proposition of Allain et al. (2013): "…a person will be exploited where they have been taken unfair advantage of by another person acting unlawfully – be it by reference to criminal, human rights or employment law –…" Thus, an action carried that is contrary to national and/or human rights law—e.g. illegal adoption—can constitute as human trafficking.

However, such an approach ought to be contested on two bases. Firstly, such an understanding could significantly and disproportionately broaden the scope of what situations are categorised as human trafficking. Secondly, such an approach assumes that the law will be available and clear. This is not necessarily the case, in particular in rogue states. In addition, consider, for example, Valdman's (2009) example of the Antidote case: "Person B is bitten by a rare poisonous snake while hiking in a remote forest. His death is imminent. Fortunately, another hiker, A, happens by and offers to sell B the antidote…Though it retails for $10, A insists that he will accept no less than $20,000. Since B would rather lose his money than his life, he accepts A's offer." In this case, A does not act against the law, yet we can argue that he has exploited B.

The work of J. L. Hill, a US professor of law and philosophy, can offer a solution to the question of how exploitation should be comprehended. For Hill (1994: 636), "[e]xploitation is a psychological, rather than a social or an economic, concept. For an offer to be exploitative, it must serve to create or to take advantage of some recognised psychological vulnerability which, in turn, disturbs the offeree's ability to reason effectively. In the absence of some adverse effect upon the capacity to reason, no offer can reasonably be deemed 'exploitative'." In summary, a situation is exploitative when A takes advantage of B's vulnerability, so that B is unable to make a reasonable decision. In other words, vulnerability and exploitation are interconnected; however, it is the inability to form a reasoned decision that is key. Hill (1994: 686) defined vulnerability as a "disposition of personality or circumstance of life that serve to hamper the rational-emotive process."

It becomes clear that the conceptualisation of someone as a trafficked person requires an acknowledgement of their vulnerability; as already stated at time, this is a difficult task. Importantly, it ought to be remembered that vulnerability alone does not turn someone into a victim of trafficking. The difference between a vulnerable person and the trafficking victim is that the trafficking victim is influenced not only by his/her vulnerabilities, but also by the actions of the trafficker. Likewise, traffickers can also have vulnerabilities, indeed that is perhaps why they turn to crime in the first place. However, for the purpose of granting the principle of non-liability when conceptualising the victim, we acknowledge that their vulnerability is exploited for the gain of another.

Exploitation Is Not a Crime in the Context of Directive 2011/36 on Preventing and Combating Trafficking in Human Beings and Protecting Its Victims

Under the *2005 Council of Europe Convention on Action Against Trafficking in Human Beings* or the *Directive 2011/36 on preventing and combating trafficking in human beings and protecting its victims*, exploitation alone is not a crime. Instead, for a crime of human trafficking to occur, the exploitation has to be related to the acts and means. This is a missed opportunity as the most disagreeable element of the human trafficking process is the exploitative part.

Conversely, Gallagher argues that by including the terms harbouring and receipt, which do not require movement and include the final place where the exploitation occurs, the definition makes the crime of human trafficking of both process and end result. Gallagher (2010: 30) explains this by writing: "The references to harbouring and receipt operate to bring not just the process (recruitment, transportation, transfer) but also the end situation of trafficking within the definition. In other words, whereas buying or otherwise taking possession of an individual through any of the stipulated means for purposes of exploiting would fall within the definition of trafficking, maintaining an individual in a situation of exploitation through any of the stipulated means would, according to the plain meaning of the text, also amount to trafficking. The breadth of the action element has the effect of bringing, within potential reach of the definition, not just recruiters, brokers, and transporters but also owners and managers, supervisors, and controllers of any place of exploitation such as a brothel, farm, boat, factory, medical facility, or household." Gallagher argues that the purpose element alone can be human trafficking because the character of the exploitation will always imply at least harbouring or receipt of persons. However, the convergence of the expression "for the purpose of exploitation" with the other elements of the definition makes for a perplexed landscape. Amongst scholars, there is some divergence of Gallagher's perception. Krieg (2009: 779) analyses the definition and remotely touches on the issues by using phrases such as "trafficking chain"; thus, illustrating that exploitation alone does not constitute human trafficking. Rijken explains that "the fact that the existence of an aim to exploit is sufficient to qualify as a case of [trafficking in human beings] without the need of the actual exploitation taking place, contributes to the effect that focus is more on forced recruitment". Elsewhere she writes: "What is problematic in the definition is that it criminalises 'forced recruitment' for the aim of exploitation and not the exploitation in and of itself... the criminalisation of exploitative practices does not necessarily follow from the definition in Article 2 of the directive even though the most objectionable aspect of trafficking is the actual exploitation" (Rijken and Bosma 2014: 18). Similarly, Stoyanova (2013: 94) contends: "...if Gallagher's expanded version of the definition of human trafficking is followed, then all the exploitative practices included in the purpose element, including slavery, servitude and forced labour, have to be relabelled as human trafficking, based on her interpretation of harbouring and receipt. The result would be a complete convergence between the concepts of trafficking, and of slavery, servitude and forced labour, which would defeat the purpose for which these different concepts were introduced in international law."

This book agrees that the definition of human trafficking does not focus on actual exploitation. *This stems from the wording of the definition but is also an approach rooted in history.* The 1926 Slavery Convention recognises two issues: (i) slavery and (ii) the slave trade. It may be helpful to look at the wording of the Convention:

Article 1

For the purpose of the present Convention, the following definitions are agreed upon:

1. Slavery is the status or condition of a person over whom any or all of the powers attaching to the right of ownership are exercised.
2. The slave trade includes all acts involved in the capture, acquisition or disposal of a person with intent to reduce him to slavery; all acts involved in the acquisition of a slave with a view to selling or exchanging him; all acts of disposal by sale or exchange of a slave acquired with a view to being sold or exchanged; and in general, every act of trade or transport in slaves.

Accordingly, Article 1 of the 1926 Convention is very similar to the human trafficking discussion, where the process resembles the slave trade and the exploitation resembles slavery. It thus becomes apparent that there is a deep history of distinguishing between process and the actual exploitation. The same is also evident in the *1949 Convention for the Suppression of the Traffic in Persons and of the Exploitation of the Prostitution of Others*.[1] This book contends that there is a missed opportunity to include the criminalisation of exploitation and more importantly to protect exploited persons who have not been trafficked. There is a risk that the protective measures that are available to victims of human trafficking will not be applicable to victims of forced labour or slavery, where the same were not proceeded by the trafficking process. This is particularly important for the provision of non-liability. Article 8 of the *Directive 2011/36 on preventing and combating trafficking in human beings and protecting its victims* and Article 26 of the *2005 Council of Europe Convention on Action Against Trafficking in Human Beings* apply only to human trafficking victims; a victim of forced labour alone may not be entitled to protection. Logic commands that we should aim to "extend the victim protection to victims of these practices as well. Concluding differently will undermine the human rights based approach in combating human trafficking" (Rijken and Bosma 2014: 18). This, however, may require enacting new laws, for a broader reading of the human trafficking definition may be against the principle of legality.

A Few Words on the Context of Human Trafficking

This section provides a brief contextual analysis of human trafficking, particularly in Europe. The European Commission (2005) has described human trafficking as: "a serious crime against persons." It is a complex occurrence rooted in political, socio-economic and cultural factors. As summarised by Rijken and Koster (2008: 5), "[b]oth the situation in the country or region of origin and the situation in the country or region of destination play a role in the occurrence of THB [Trafficking

in Human Beings]." At the European regional level, the European
Union Strategy towards the Eradication of Trafficking in Human Beings
(2012–2016) attributed causes of human trafficking to, for example:

• Poverty
• Lack of democracy
• Gender inequality and violence against women
• Conflict and post-conflict situations
• Lack of social integration
• Lack of employment opportunities
• Lack of (access to) education
• Discrimination.

Traffickers make use of these elements, targeting their recruitment
to places such as homeless shelters, online forums, jobcentres, war
zones, refugee camps and impoverished geographical areas. There, the
traffickers prey on a person's determination to move and/or change
something in their life and recruit their victims by offering work,
experiences and/or education. Upon arrival, the person is controlled
and exploited. Alternatively, some trafficked persons are taken into
exploitation by force, such as through kidnapping or threats, or they are
sold by their families.

    Trafficking in persons can be seen as an economic process, made up
of supply and demand driving an illicit market. Destination countries
are pushing the demand for sex, organs, cheap labour and goods, and
countries of origin supply people who have a desire for a better life and
will accept poor working conditions for a monetary reward. In terms
of economics, humans are a "good" perhaps better than many others;
a weapon can only be sold once, but you can exploit a person's labour
numerous times.

    In addition, we ought to acknowledge the emergence of globalisation
as a factor contributing to human trafficking, which is the international
movement of knowledge, the sharing of cultures and the closer
economic–social integration of the countries of the world through the
increased flow of goods and services, labour and capital (Stiglitz 2006).
Globalisation has played a role in allowing human trafficking to thrive,

and so, human trafficking has been called one of the darkest sides of globalisation (Jones et al. 2007). Similarly, Derks (2000: 32) draws our attention to the fact that "economic desires fuelled by the global spread of images of wealth, modernity and beauty contribute to this abusive movement of people for work or services." In their study of Nigerian women who migrated to Europe, Skilbrei and Tveit (2008: 18) highlight the perception these women held of Europe—a continent of possibilities where money could be earned; "sending a family member to Europe was seen as an investment for the whole family, in addition to hopefully improving the life of the migrant herself."

The crime is strongly associated with migration. In the context of migration, we talk about victims coming from countries of origin, through transit countries (the carriage trail) and arriving at the country of destination. The country of destination receives the victim; it is usually where the person is exploited, although they can also be exploited on route. The destination country is also where the initial assistance will have to be provided to the trafficked person. The new migration reality is witnessing a large number of people seeking opportunities to enter Europe. In turn, this has significantly increased the risk of abuse and exploitation of migrants. As border controls become more restrictive, migrants are compelled to turn to smugglers to assist them to enter the EU irregularly and use more and more dangerous routes. This can put them at the risk of exploitation. A Human Trafficking and Exploitation Prevalence Indication Survey conducted by the IOM (2016) on the Central Mediterranean Route in Sicily demonstrates a worrying trend: 76% of interviewed migrants have experienced at least one of the trafficking and other exploitative practices indicators. Thus, we note that strict migration policies in areas of destination, such as in Europe, can be a contributing factor to a person's vulnerabilities and have an increasing impact on the scale of human trafficking.

However, human trafficking can also be domestic, i.e. the crime occurs in only one country. A recent Dutch report quoted in DutchNews (2016) notes that there has been an increase in Dutch national victims exploited in the Dutch sex trafficking industry. Domestic trafficking is also illustrated by the case of a group of men in Rochdale, UK, who were, amongst other things, found guilty of human trafficking. Indeed, the Eurostat report (2014) states that domestic human trafficking is prevalent. The same report (2014: 34) also highlights that in Europe: "of the registered victims confirmed as EU citizens, the top 5 countries of citizenship are Bulgaria, Romania, the Netherlands, Hungary and Poland."

The exact number of people trafficked is unknown, and in reality, currently, it is impossible to calculate. Indeed, we should treat statistics with doubt due to poor or unavailable data. Kelly (2002: 7) also highlights that our knowledge of the magnitude of trafficking is limited by our "infant" research methods; we still rely on overviews, commentaries and limited data from service providers, rather than mature sociological studies. Although this is somewhat changing, there is an increasing use of sophisticated statistical methods such as the multiple system estimation. This book will not try to account for the numbers as the sources can be unreliable; it is undeniable that this is a serious offense at an international, regional and domestic level. It takes place for the purpose of exploitation of vulnerable people. Arrays of rights are breached, including but not limited to "person's personal and physical dignity, the right to personal freedom and security, and the principle of non-discrimination" (Rijken and Koster 2008: 8) in addition to the right to freedom of movement, and of course the right not to be held in slavery, servitude or be required to perform forced or compulsory labour.

Conclusion

The stated key aim of this chapter was to understand the term human trafficking. Until 2000, there was no agreed definition, and prior to that, trafficking was thought of as a problem referring to sexual exploitation of women and girls. This changed with the *2000 UN Protocol on Human Trafficking*, which was followed by the *2005 Council of Europe Convention on Action Against Trafficking in Human Beings* and *Directive 2011/36 on preventing and combating trafficking in human beings and protecting its victims*. The EU definition is very similar to the UN and Council of Europe demarcation. The difference lies in the addition of a further "action": exchange or transfer of control. In addition, the European Directive also includes a new "purpose": begging and exploitation of criminal activities.

Contextually, we must understand that the drafting process of the first definition (contained in the *2000 UN Protocol on Human Trafficking*) was the result of bargaining between states. Hence, compared to some crimes defined in national criminal codes, the definition is more ambiguous. Until this day, there remain complexities with regard to the definition, and in turn difficulties in efficiently identifying who is a victim. Yet, a failure by the state to identify a victim and provide appropriate assistance risks violation of human rights, Council and EU law. That is why it is so important to understand what trafficking in persons is. As summarised by Bosma and Rijken (2016: 329): "As long as it is unclear who has become victim and who is responsible for their identification, those persons cannot be protected…."

The answer to the question of what human trafficking is, on the surface, is as follows. Human trafficking encompasses three core elements: an action, a means and the purpose. The actions are broad, which means a range of persons will fall within the definition: recruiters, transporters, controllers of exploitation and the exploiters, to name but some examples. The means only apply to adults. The purpose is exploitation, which is an open list, including the prostitution of others or other forms of sexual exploitation, forced labour or services, slavery or practices similar to slavery, servitude or the removal of organs. None of the instruments define exploitation, thus "leaving the entire notion of human trafficking, which is premised on it, somewhat legally and theoretically shallow" (Jovanovic 2017: 45). As shown above, this book relies on work of J. L. Hill who frames exploitation as a psychological concept: A exploits B when A takes advantage of B's vulnerability, so that B is unable to make a reasonable decision. This lies at the heart of the justification for a principle of non-liability.

The definition covers an array of victims, women, men and children, and based on the definition, we can identify human trafficking in a variety of situations. It is trafficking in the cases of Nigerian women who are recruited and subjected to voodoo practices to force compliance through psychological pressures and who are then transported to

Europe where they are sexually exploited or forced into various types of labour. Individuals who "contact parents who are living in poverty in countries such as Romania and Bulgaria, either to buy or hire their sons and daughters with the purpose of exploiting them for purposes of theft or begging, or to exploit them sexually in prostitution' are also committing human trafficking" (Spapens et al. 2014: 45). Equally, women who are promised well-paid jobs in Ireland, Great Britain and Cyprus, but later are forced to marry third country nationals, are subjected to human trafficking.

At the same time, there remains an unanswered ambivalence about what constitutes human trafficking due to terminological contradictions and disagreements. The definition we can argue has numerous open-ended terms. The question of what the meaning of exploitation is or what is the difference between fraud and deception highlights the existing difficulties. Equally, the threshold for the means is uncertain. In sum, the definition is not always user friendly: it lacks precision, for defendants, victims and the state.

Note

1. Article 1 states: The Parties to the present Convention agree to punish any person who, to gratify the passions of another:
   (1) Procures, entices or leads away, for purposes of prostitution, another person, even with the consent of that person;
   (2) Exploits the prostitution of another person, even with the consent of that person.

References

Allain, J. (2017). White Slave Traffic in International Law. *Journal of Trafficking and Human Exploitation, 1*(1), 1–40.

Allain, J., Crane, A., LeBaron, G., & Behbahani, L. (2013). *Forced Labour's Business Models and Supply Chains*. Joseph Rowntree Foundation [Online]. https://www.jrf.org.uk/report/forced-labour%E2%80%99s-business-models-and-supply-chains.

Bosma, A., & Rijken, C. (2016). Key Challenges in the Combat of Human Trafficking: Evaluating the EU Strategy and EU Trafficking Directive. *New Journal of European Criminal Law, 7*(3), 315–330.

Council of Europe. (2005). *Explanatory Report on the Convention on Action Against Trafficking in Human Beings,* ETS 197, 16 May 2005.

Council of Europe's Group of Experts on Action Against Trafficking in Human Beings. (2014). *Report Concerning the Implementation of the Council of Europe Convention on Action Against Trafficking in Human Beings by Italy. First Evaluation Round.* Council of Europe [Online]. http://www.coe.int/t/dghl/monitoring/trafficking/Docs/Reports/ GRETA_2014_18_FGR_ITA_w_cmnts_en.pdf.

Council of Europe and United Nations. (2009). *Trafficking in Organs, Tissues and Cells and Trafficking in Human Beings for the Purpose of the Removal of Organs* [Online]. https://www.coe.int/t/dghl/monitoring/trafficking/Docs/ News/OrganTrafficking_study.pdf.

Derks, A. (2000). *From White Slaves to Trafficking Survivors: Notes on the Trafficking Debate.* The Center for Migration and Development: Working Paper Series [Online]. http://www.nswp.org/sites/nswp.org/files/CMD-0002M.pdf.

DutchNews. (2016). *More Dutch are Victims of Human Trafficking for Sex Industry: Report.* DutchNews [Online]. http://www.dutchnews.nl/news/ archives/2016/08/more-dutch-are-victims-of-human-trafficking-for-sex-in- dustry-report/.

Esser, L. B., & Dettmeijer-Vermeulen, C. E. (2016). The Prominent Role of National Judges in Interpreting the International Definition of Human Trafficking. *Anti-trafficking Review, 6,* 91–105.

European Commission. (2005). Fighting Trafficking in Human Beings—An Integrated Approach and Proposals for an Action Plan. Communication to the European Parliament and the Council, COM (2005) 514.

European Commission. (2012–2016). *The EU Strategy Towards the Eradication of Trafficking in Human Beings* [Online]. https://ec.europa.eu/ anti-trafficking/eu-policy/new-european-strategy-2012-2016_en.

Eurostat. (2014). *Trafficking in Human Beings, Statistical Working Papers* [Online]. http://ec.europa.eu/dgs/home-affairs/what-is-new/news/news/docs/20141017_ working_paper_on_statistics_on_trafficking_in_human_beings_en.pdf.

Fergus, L. (2005). Trafficking in Women for Sexual Exploitation. *Briefing: Australian Centre for the Study of Sexual Assault, 5* [Online]. http://www3. aifs.gov.au/acssa/pubs/briefing/acssa_briefing5.pdf.

Gallagher, A. (2010). *The International Law of Human Trafficking.* New York: Cambridge University Press.

Goodin, R. (1987). Exploiting a Situation and Exploiting a Person. In A. Reeve (Ed.), *Modern Theories of Exploitation* (pp. 171–178). London: Sage.

Hill, J. L. (1994). Exploitation. *Cornell Law Review, 79,* 631–699.

HR 27 oktober 2009,ECLI:NL:HR:2009:BI7097.

International Labour Organisation. (1999). *Note on the Additional Legal Instrument Against Trafficking in Women And Children,* A/Ac.254/Crp.14 [Online]. http://www.ilo.org/public/libdoc/igo/1999/479829.pdf.

International Organization of Migration. (2016). *Analysis: Flow Monitoring Surveys. The Human Trafficking and Other Exploitative Practices Prevalence Indication Survey* [Online]. http://migration.iom.int/docs/Analysis%20-%20 Flow%20Monitoring%20and%20Human%20Trafficking%20Surveys%20 in%20the%20Mediterranean%20and%20Beyond%20-%2011%20 August%202016.pdf.

Jones, L., Engstrom, D. W., Hilliard, T., & Diaz, M. (2007). Globalization and Human Trafficking. *Journal of Sociology & Social Welfare, 34*(2), 107–122.

Jovanovic, M. (2017). The Principle of Non-punishment of Victims of Trafficking in Human Beings: A Quest for Rationale and Practical Guidance. *Journal of Trafficking and Human Exploitation, 1*(1), 41–76.

Kelly, E. (2002). *Journeys of Jeopardy: A Review of Research on Trafficking in Women and Children in Europe.* IOM Migration Research Series, no. 11. Geneva: International Organization for Migration.

Krieg, S. (2009). Trafficking in Human Beings: The EU Approach Between Border Control, Law Enforcement and Human Rights. *European Law Journal, 15*(6), 775–790.

Obokata, T. (2015). Human Trafficking. In N. Boister & R. J. Currie (Eds.), *Routledge Handbook of Transnational Criminal Law.* London and New York: Routledge.

Parfit, D. (1984). *Reasons and Persons.* Oxford: Clarendon Press.

Piotrowicz, R. (2007). Trafficking of Human Beings and Their Human Rights in the Migration Context. In R. Cholewinski, R. Perruchoud, & E. MacDoland (Eds.), *International Migration Law: Developing Paradigms and Key Challenges.* The Hague: Asser Press.

Protocol to Prevent, Suppress and Punish Trafficking in Persons, Especially Women and Children, supplementing the United Nations Convention against Transnational Organized Crime, GA Res. 55/25, Annex II, UN GAOR, 55th Sess., Supp. No. 49, at 53, UN Doc. A/45/49 (Vol. I) (2001), Nov. 15, 2000, entered into force December 25, 2003.

Rijken, C. (2013). Trafficking in Human Beings for Labour Exploitation: Cooperation in an Integrated Approach. *European Journal of Crime, Criminal Law and Criminal Justice, 21*(1), 9–35.

Rijken, C. (2015). Legal Approaches to Combating the Exploitation of Third-Country National Seasonal Workers. *The International Journal of Compatartive Labour Law and Industrial Relations, 31*(4), 431–452.

Rijken, C., & Bosma, A. (2014). *Deliverable D1.1: A Review of the Implementation of the EU Strategy on Human Trafficking by EU Members.* TRACE Project [Online]. http://trace-project.eu/wp-content/uploads/2016/01/TRACE_D1.1_Final.pdf.

Rijken, C., & Koster, D. (2008). A Human Rights Based Approach to Trafficking in Human Beings in Theory and Practice. *SSRN Electronic Journal* [Online]. http://dx.doi.org/10.2139/ssrn.1135108.

Sitarz, O. (2010). Wątpliwości I Kontrowersje Wokół Definicji Handlu Ludźmi. *Archiwum Kryminologii, XXXII,* 328–344.

Skilbrei, M., & Tveit, M. (2008). Defining Trafficking Through Empirical Work: Blurred Boundaries and Their Consequences. *Gender, Technology and Development, 12*(1), 9–30.

Spapens, T., Tamas, A., Lulle, A., Durieux, H., Polatside, V., Dragota, C., et al. (2014). *TRACE, D1.3: A Report Concerning the Macro and Micro Analyses of Human Trafficking.* TRACE Project [Online]. http://trace-project.eu/wp-content/uploads/2014/11/TRACE_D1.3_Final.pdf.

Stiglitz, J. (2006). *Making Globalization Work.* London: Allen Lane.

Stoyanova, V. (2013). The Crisis of a Definition: Human Trafficking in Bulgarian Law. *Amsterdam Law Forum, 5*(1), 64–79.

Sullivan, B. (2003). Trafficking in Women: Feminism and New International Law. *International Feminist Journal of Politics, 5*(1), 67–91.

United Nations Office on Drugs and Crime (UNODC). (2015). *Issue Paper: The Concept of 'Exploitation' in the Trafficking in Persons Protocol.* Vienna: United Nations [Online]. https://www.unodc.org/documents/human-trafficking/2015/UNODC_IP_Exploitation_2015.pdf.

Valdman, M. (2009). A Theory of Wrongful Exploitation. *Philosophers Imprint, 9*(6), 1–14.

Walklate, S. (2005). *Criminology: The Basics.* London: Routledge.

Wertheimer, A. (1996). *Exploitation.* Princeton, NJ: Princeton University Press.

Wood, A. (1995). Exploitation. *Social Philosophy and Policy, 12,* 136–158.

3

Rationale for the Non-liability Principle

Introduction

Before engaging in descriptions and debates on the European approach to protecting human trafficking victims from liability, it is important to understand why such persons, who were compelled to break the law, ought to be protected at all. The answers can be found in scholarly and civil society writings, legal principles and national justifications. For criminologists, the answers are rooted in criminal law principles, and responses can be provided by referring to notions of responsibility and non-responsibility. Elsewhere, e.g. for many civil societies, the answers are provided conclusively by emphasising human rights and the rights of victims. There are also rationalisations to be found in more practical spheres, ones that move away from theory. Namely in the reality that by affording protection to trafficked persons, states are encouraging victims to come forward, disclose their story and cooperate. Thereby, aiding states in their obligation to investigate and prosecute those responsible for human trafficking. This, however, is criticised in the last part of this chapter.

© The Author(s) 2019
J. M. Muraszkiewicz, *Protecting Victims of Human Trafficking From Liability*, Palgrave Studies in Victims and Victimology, https://doi.org/10.1007/978-3-030-02659-2_3

This chapter explains the three different rationales for the principle of non-liability, which in turn can help us determine what we can come to expect from the non-liability principle. However, before the justifications are presented, this chapter bestows onto the reader an explanation of who, legally speaking, is a victim of human trafficking and subsequently showcases stories of victims being held liable for a range of wrongdoings they were compelled to commit. This in turn aids the understanding and acceptance of the rationale for the non-liability principle. Important however is the recognition that by having a non-liability principle there is, in theory, a movement away from victim-blaming approaches. In other words, on the surface the notion of the non-liability principle accepts that an external force placed on someone is responsible for a crime, rather than the crime being a product of one's fault. The phraseology "in theory" and "on the surface" are chosen deliberately for as subsequent chapters show state understanding of the principle has been linked to the concept of duress, with is riddled with blaming the victim.

Who Is a Victim of Human Trafficking: The Legal Definition

"The word 'victim' has its roots in many ancient languages that covered a great distance from north-western Europe to the southern tip of Asia and yet had a similar linguistic pattern: *victima* in Latin" (Dussich, n.d.). *Victima* means an animal offered as sacrifice. The Polish word *ofiara* reflect this perfectly for it means two things, "victim" and "something sacrificed." Equally in German, the word *opfer* means those two things. There is thus a direct link "between someone who has suffered from crime or the actions of others and the idea of sacrifice" (Wit and Wa 2013: 2).

But who is a victim? Fattah suggests that the word victim is used in a variety of contexts to describe someone who suffers a negative outcome, a loss, harm or injury whether it is physical, material or psychological in nature (Fattah 1997: 147). Shoham et al. have suggested that victimisation happens to those who are forced "to cope with important potentially uprooting events that can be actuated against him or her by other humans. Omissions are deemed equivalent to active deeds provided there is a duty to be active" (Shoham et al. 2010: 13). Carlos Fernández de Casadevante Romani states that one becomes a victim "as a consequence of acts or omissions that are in violation of criminal laws operative within states including those laws proscribing abuse of power. Therefore, the qualification of a victim is subject to the previous legislative action of the state adopting the necessary measures to make such acts become criminal offences under national law" (Fernández de Casadevante Romani 2012: 90). In 2018 as we begin to accept, understand and address victimhood these scholarly descriptions feel almost instinctive, they are an easy pill for us to swallow. But what about the law, how does European law recognise a victim?

The answer can be found in the *EU Directive 2012/29/EU Establishing Minimum Standards on the Rights, Support and Protection of Victims of Crime* (here forth 2012 EU Directive on Victims of Crime). It has been described as an instrument with a "vast and comprehensive obligation to establish common minimum rights related to victims of crime on the international level" (Buczma 2013: 236). For Rasquete, Ferreira and Marques, the 2012 EU Directive on Victims of Crime is "potentially the greatest step forward seen so far towards better recognition for the status of victims" (2014: 121). The definition of a victim is contained in Article 2(1) (a) of the 2012 EU Directive on Victims of Crime:

(a) 'victim' means:

(i) a natural person who has suffered harm, including physical, mental or emotional harm or economic loss which was directly caused by a criminal offence;

(ii) family members of a person whose death was directly caused by a criminal offence and who have suffered harm as a result of that person's death;

On reading the definition we note that once an offence occurs, one becomes a victim. As it stands, the definition is broad. Firstly, it does not specify who has to inflict the harm, meaning it can be a state, a private body or a person. Secondly, the definition also establishes the notion of direct and indirect victims, where the latter are the family members of a person whose death has been caused by a criminal offence.[1] The 2012 EU Directive on Victims of Crime does however have some deficiencies: it does not stipulate who should be responsible for identifying the offence. As highlighted by Klip, if it is a court that is to take on this responsibility, this "may amount to a violation of the presumption of innocence if the finding that the person is a victim coincides with the finding that the victim is a victim of the accused" (Klip 2015: 186). In fact, the definition does not place a responsibility of distinguishing between victim and alleged victim: "There is a presumption in the Directive that the victim is a victim of the accused standing trial, or at least a victim of any crime" (Klip 2015: 186).

Nevertheless, despite some weaknesses this piece of legislation is important for helping us understand who is a victim of human trafficking. Based on the definition provided by the 2012 EU Directive on Victims of Crime, it can be asserted that an individual can be considered a victim of human trafficking if they suffered harm, including both physical and mental, or emotional or economic loss that was caused by the offence of human trafficking. That is it was someone who was subjected to an action, through the means and for the purpose of exploitation; the three core elements of human trafficking as pronounced by international definitions (see chapter 1). Interestingly, *Directive 2011/36 on preventing and combating trafficking in human beings and protecting its victims* itself does not contain a definition of a human trafficking victim. However, *the 2005 Council of Europe Convention on Action Against Trafficking in Human Beings* does, and it supports the assertion above. The 2005 Convention on Action Against Trafficking in Human Beings in Article 4(e) states the following: "'Victim' shall mean any natural person who is subject to trafficking in human beings as defined in this article."

As with other crimes, a trafficked person becomes a victim immediately on suffering the crime of human trafficking, their recognition is immediate and not conditional, i.e. it does not require a judge's sanction of for the person to cooperate with the police. This validation, or confirmation, of their status can have a positive impact on the victim's recovery process. We should also note that a human trafficking victim gains victim status by virtue of being subject to human trafficking, and it does not matter how they got into that situation or how they escaped it. This is important, particularly as some persons may commit crimes to escape the situation, yet these crimes do not nullify their trafficking status. As exemplified by Rijken (2017: 241): "a distinction can be made between who left the exploitative situation on their own initiative, and victims who were taken out of exploitative situation by others, most often the police. A trigger situation often makes a person decide to leave the situation and to stand up against the trafficker. Examples of such situations are extreme violence, pregnancy, and opportunity to escape. This is different from those victims who come out of the exploitative situation as a consequence of police intervention. They are still under the influence of the trafficker, try to protect the trafficker, and some of them want to go back so as to avoid getting into trouble with the trafficker. They do not want to report to the police, and decline support and assistance." Often when a victim is taken out of the trafficking situation by the police they may not be mentally ready to share their story, including proving their victimhood. This is important for the purpose of this book because those victims may also be unable to deliver evidence that would qualify them for the right not to be held liable for wrongdoings they were compelled to commit. Yet it needs to be recognised by stakeholders, that even as the victim may not share their story or may not fit our image of what a victim should look like (more on this later in the book) they are under the law still to be considered a victim. Thus, they are still entitled to protection.

As mentioned afore, a trafficked person becomes a victim immediately on suffering the crime of human trafficking. Here however lies the biggest hurdle which brings us back to the problem of the definition. The scope of who is a victim is as wide as the definition of human trafficking. And as shown in chapter 1, the definition covers a range of eventualities; from trafficking for the purpose of sexual exploitation to trafficking for the purpose of forced labour. Thus, we should always shy away from identifying one trafficking narrative; there is no typical human trafficking victim.

Although the definition is broad, and many will benefit from it, it is also ambiguous. Without really understanding the key terms that make it up it becomes difficult to award the victim status. Moreover, as already stated by Hoyle et al. (2011: 317) "we should be cautious in assuming that the Palermo Protocol's broad definition of trafficking has been translated into actual practices of identifying trafficking victims."

What does this all mean for the non-liability principle? As with other multifaceted definitions, a difficulty arises. To identify the trafficked person, and thus grant them their rights, requires understanding the definition. Not an easy task given the complexity of the description. Consequently, too often will persons who endured the crime, or the intent of the crime, will not be recognised and will not receive assistance. "It is more likely that they will be arrested, detained and charged with immigration offences, for soliciting prostitution or engaging in illegal work, making false statements; or else, they are fined for violations of administrative laws and regulations" (Piotrowicz and Sorrentino 2016: 670). The very notions that the non-liability seeks to protect trafficked persons from.

Examples of Trafficked Victims Held Liable

The narratives of cases of trafficked persons are reproduced in this sub-section to bring to life the misfortunes bestowed on persons who have already endured physical and psychological tragedies. In some of these cases, and others not listed here, the decision to hold the defendant liable was overturned, but this is not always the case. Moreover, even when (often on appeal) the case is overturned the victim has already endured further trauma.

1. "A young Nigerian woman was exploited in prostitution in Belgium; she was forced by her trafficker to use a false passport in order to receive a residence permit. Despite being recognized as a victim by a criminal court in Brussels, she was later prosecuted and convicted in her absence for the use of a false passport by another criminal court in Antwerp, which was not aware of the earlier decision. On appeal,

the victim and later the prosecutor, alleged that a justification existed, i.e., that the victim was not free to act and the trafficker coerced her into using a false passport; the judge ruled that she was not liable because she was constrained by force to commit the offence" (Centre for Equal Opportunities and Opposition to Racism 2008).

2. Three Polish women were deceived into sex work by a man who presented himself as a member of the Russian Mafia. The man took the women's money, humiliated and abused them. The women saw no means of escape and in desperation paid for the man to be killed. They were found guilty and convicted for 8–12 years of imprisonment. A possible mitigation related to their status as trafficked persons was not considered (Koba 2015: 78).

3. In 2014 a case was heard in the Irish High Court against the Governor of the Clover Hill Prison, the Attorney General and the Director of Public Prosecutions for a failure to identify a victim of trafficking and for his unlawful detention (Lin -v- Governor of Cloverhill Prison & Ors). The case concerned a Vietnamese national, Mr. Lin, who fell into debt and was violently threatened by money-lenders; eventually he was coerced into travelling to Europe to pay off the debt. In Ireland he worked in cannabis factories.

   "Mr Lin's lawyers highlighted that there were several indicators of trafficking present, namely that Mr Lin was found locked into a building, living in squalor, he spoke no English and was confused about his location. He had never received any money nor was he in possession of his travel documents…The Judge, Mr Justice Hogan found that Mr Lin was exploited and that his incarceration in the grow house amounted to conditions of servitude…However, he had not found that Mr Lin had been trafficked, arguing that 'key details in terms of identity, method of travel and dates of arrival had not been independently confirmed'" (Anti-slavery 2014: 44).

4. The case of R v L and Others (The Children's Commissioner for England and Equality and Human Rights Commission intervening) concerned Vietnamese children found working in cannabis farms in the UK. The minors were subsequently prosecuted under the Misuse of Drugs Act 1971 for the production of a controlled drug. One of the minor defendants had been prosecuted as an adult, despite being

a child. On hearing all the facts the Court of Appeal found that the criminal activities undertaken were integral to the status of a trafficked child and the children should not have been prosecuted. In consequence the Court overturned the convictions.

Amongst the defendants was also THN. He was found in a house in Bristol were there was large amounts of cannabis. He was arrested and on arrest told officers he was glad to see them. He explained that he had been brought to England in a freezer container, that he owed money in Vietnam and the deeds to his family home had been taken as collateral. On 18th October his solicitors wrote to the prosecution inviting them not to prosecute arguing that THN was a victim of trafficking. A request to stay the indictment was repeated in December. In January 2012 the case came to court, no abuse process application was pursued and the appellant pleaded guilty. He was sentenced to a Detention and Training Order for 12 months. On release from prison he was placed in the care of a local authority, however shortly after he went missing. It is believed that he had been re-trafficked.

What these cases, and others like them, reveal is that holding trafficked persons liable is not out of the ordinary, even in circumstances where relevant authorities know that a person was subjected to a number of practices that signal human trafficking. Thus, officially obtaining the status of victimhood, and the rights that come with it, is not as simple as satisfying the elements of the definition presented in above. It is possible at this stage to deduce that there are a number of factors that thwart a trafficked persons victim status and subsequently right not to be held liable.

Furthermore, the cases illustrate the range of offences that victims can commit; murder, immigration offences and production of drugs. In other words it is important to note, for this will be key in subsequent discussions, that trafficked persons do not only commit crimes that are part of their exploitation. Victims may break the law in trying to escape from trafficking or by breaching immigration regulations. Moreover, victims may commit serious crimes. The cases also show that victims may on appeal be successful in overturning their conviction, however at this point they would have already endured elements of secondary victimisation. Thus, having a well-worded and properly implemented provision on non-liability should work on a what this book calls "protection by design" approach. This regards being proactive rather than reactive in the endeavours to protect trafficked persons. That is having a principle that will prevent a trafficked person from going to court in the first place, and thus preventing any form of secondary victimisation and trauma (related to prosecution) from occurring. The protection is before the fact, not after e.g. during an appeal.

It is of course acknowledged that various states report that there are no cases of trafficked persons being held liable (Piotrowicz and Sorrentino 2016: 690). Yet, it is more likely that across Europe, numerous trafficked persons are being held liable either because they remain unidentified or because local authorities are unaware of existing international provisions.

We now turn to the justifications, rationales, for having a non-liability principle.

Criminal Law Theory

The non-liability principle is in some way, like victimology, a corrective to criminology (Spencer and Walklate 2016: xii). It does however also find roots in traditional criminal law thinking, and so it is logical to first turn to criminal theory combined with moral philosophy insofar as to explain why it is wrong to hold a compelled trafficked person liable.

Every criminal law system allows some forms of defence, whether an excuse or a justification, through which liability can be excluded. In other words, even when there is proof that there is an actus reus with the required mens rea, the defendant may have a recognised defence. Indeed, as stated by Lanham: "as a matter of analysis we can think of a crime as being made up of three ingredients, actus reus, mens rea and (a negative element) absence of a valid defence" (Lanham 1976: 276). Defences reflect the reality that in some instances a state cannot prosecute or punish a person for the offence for which they are accused. To reiterate Westen's construction of defences, they: "...refer to all claims to the effect that, given such evidence as is otherwise admissible and given such burdens of proof as otherwise apply, the state may not lawfully try and/or convict a defendant of an offense at issue" (Westen 2006: 293). Naturally, the array of available defences varies between countries and as highlighted by Gallant: "the law of crimes and substantive defences is a product of theories of criminal law and its underpinnings in the philosophy of individual responsibility" (Gallant 2003: 322). It follows that defences are related to a state's perspective on controlling crime and the relationship between the sovereign and the people.

To determine why responsibility is excluded one should look at the circumstances in which the act was committed. Denying a compelled trafficked victim a defence means holding them liable for actions over which, for either psychological or physical reasons, they had no control. This naturally feels unjust. Criminal law is not designed to be cruel, it aims to be logical. Logic and humanity commands that we ought not to hold people liable in situations where human instincts overcome the ability to abide by the rules of the land. It is a concession to human frailty. As summarised by Worley: "The phrase 'A concession to human frailty' can simply be described as a human being conceding or yielding in their moral weakness when faced with a threatening situation. If, when in this threatening situation, the human being commits a criminal act, it is possible that the courts may excuse the criminal conduct" (Worley 2009). Thus, liability should not be imposed because the act was excusable. Of course, the breach of law is wrong, however, given the circumstances of compulsion the act is pardonable. As stated by Dubber and Hörnle: "[p]raise is indeed not bestowed, but pardon is, when one does a wrongful act under pressure which, in the words of Aristotle in *The Nicomachean Ethics,* overstrains human nature and which no one could withstand" (Dubber and Hörnle 2014: 425).

Here it may be helpful to remind of the difference between an excuse and a justification. Dressler writes: "a justification claim...seeks to show that the act was not wrongful whereas an excuse tries to show that the actor is not morally culpable for his wrongful conduct" (2001: 202–203). Similarly, Hart (1968: 23) excuses committed crimes when the person lacks a capacity or fair opportunity to choose the actions.

Berman summarised the difference as: "a justified action is not criminal, whereas an excused defendant has committed a crime but is not punishable" (2003: 4). Finally, Gardner summarises that "only those who are responsible in the basic sense can offer excuses" (2007: 181). It follows that by giving trafficked persons an excuse, we are not saying that the act committed was lawful. Instead, we recognise that the trafficked person was not blameworthy of the unlawful act. Zornosa notes that: "[p]articularly relevant to the context of trafficking victims who commit crimes at the discretion of their traffickers is the 'excuse' defence, because such a defence is deemed appropriate based on the defendant's lack of responsibility" (2016: 187). Such a viewpoint is true, the defendant (who is a trafficked person) is not responsible, the mental and/or physical strain endured place them outside a domain that requires punishment.

Indeed, "in the criminal law of the current era, the classic exemplar of ascription of criminal responsibility is capacity, with its hallmarks of individual agency, choice and autonomy" (Loughnan 2016: 29). In other words, for one to be liable they must be responsible; persons, who act because of the actions of a third person, are not responsible because they did not exercise full agency. Such contextualisation is related to key liberal ideas of autonomy. As summarised by Fletcher: "the notion of voluntariness adds a valuable dimension to the theory of excuses" (Fletcher 2000: 800). Of course, at most times the trafficked person's act is not involuntary because of some physical impartment. For example, the trafficker pushes their hand to commit a crime. In such an instance "there is no act at all, no wrongdoing and therefore no need for an excuse. The notion of involuntariness at play is what we should call moral or normative involuntariness. Were it for the external pressure, the actor would not have performed the deed" (Fletcher 2000: 798). The trafficker selects the victim's vulnerability—anxiety related to irregular migration status, fear for the well-being of their family, or other weaknesses—in order to compel them into committing a crime and thus reduces their capacity to act lawfully. That is to say, the crime is committed with significantly limited or absent cognitive aptitudes. Giving the trafficked person an excuse in criminal law is thus a logical concession to psychology and takes stock of the criminal context.

Such an analysis rightly makes the law not a response to criminal deeds but focuses more on the inward thoughts of the defendant (Gardner 1993). It is important to highlight that the non-liability principle does not excuse victims who offended because of feelings of fury, revenge or injustice.

In similar, vein Piotrowicz and Sorrentino rationalise the principle of non-liability with regard to the culpability of the victim, which is: "significantly diminished or extinguished because of the personal circumstances, in particular their situation of being under the control of the traffickers" (Piotrowicz and Sorrentino 2016: 674). The UK Lord Chief Justice supports this: "The criminality, or putting it another way, the culpability, of any victim of trafficking may be significantly diminished, and in some cases effectively extinguished, not merely because of age (always a relevant factor in the case of a child defendant) but because no realistic alternative was available to the exploited victim but to comply with the dominant force of another individual, or group of individuals" (L, HVN, THN and T v. R: para. 13).

Here however it is worthy to pause and advance a warning. By saying victims are not responsible or culpable, we ought not to extinguish their agency. Too often victims of trafficking are infantilised and constructed as persons of no free will in need of saving. At the same time, we have to acknowledge that their trafficking experience as a whole and the crime they were compelled to commit was not the making of their true will. How to balance their agency with the truism that their will and culpability were manipulated? Hoyle and Sanders (2000: 21, 29) give thought to this in an interesting way and draw on comparisons with women who stay in violent relationships. They write: "rationally chosen in the context of their current lives…[they are] situationally coerced by their circumstances…Their choices are reluctant choices, a product of the coerced circumstances of their relationships." It is also important to remember that the degree to which their culpability is affected lies on a continuum; from limited self-rule to complete suppression. And although the law craves clarity, it is impossible to mark where on that continuum the right to non-liability prevails. In practice it will be within the justice system that those responsible, prosecutor, judge, jury etc. will need to undertake a multifaceted and detailed factual and psychological examination of the trafficking situation, the trafficker's actions and the victim's state of mind.

Moving away from rationalising the non-liability principle by reference to defence theories, it is also suggested that victims of human trafficking who are compelled to commit crimes do not fall within any of the primary purposes of punishment. Namely: retribution, incapacitation, rehabilitation and deterrence. This is another reason for applying the principle of non-liability, particularly the non-punishment aspect of it. A qualification first: this book does not engage in or repeat the, somewhat exhausted, discussions surrounding punishment. Discussions on moral philosophy, which so often quote great thinkers such as Kant, Binding, Liszt and Bentham, are beyond the scope of this book. Instead, we use the established principles and adopt the so-called mixed theory for justifying punishment, to show why punishing trafficked persons is contradictory.

Retribution expresses the people's condemnation of the crime committed, and it asserts societies values. If we focus on the latter, namely societies values, and even take into account the lessons learnt from the proceeding paragraphs, then the value has to be that we do not punish those who were not responsible for their actions. This book argues that the most fundamental values of any society are to recognise human autonomy and at times its lack. It is submitted that it would be too draconian, and outside of societies values, to prosecute or punish a trafficked person for events that were not of their own making. If retribution recognises "the criminal as a responsible human actor, someone who deserved punishment for his crime" (Fletcher 1998: 32), then this is not a time for retribution. We could even ask whether the punishment of a non-responsible criminal would weaken the respect for law? It is put forward that it would.

Moreover, if retribution is as Kant outlines, for the purpose of giving the wrongdoer what they deserve for their past crime, then here the rationale of just deserts does not hold. For the trafficked victim was never truly a wrongdoer and punishing him/her would not cancel out the wrong suffered by society. Instead the focus should be on the trafficker, an argument to also be used when thinking about incapacitation.

Incapacitation aims to protect the people from the offender by imprisoning him/her. The punishment of the offender is explained as a necessity to keep the safety and welfare of everyone else. Yet, in the case of human trafficking our focus should be on protecting people from the trafficker not the victim, who as a matter of fact does not have a propensity towards crime. Indeed, the victim's connection to the criminal world has disappeared with their escape from their trafficking situation. One way of protecting society from the trafficker(s) is in fact by enforcing the non-liability principle, for it may encourage victims to cooperate with the police. It is a truism that direct witnesses of a crime are often a crucial element of a successful prosecution. That is why trafficking investigations and prosecutions require that law enforcement officials establish a trusting relationship with the victim. Reasonably, one way to do this is by not punishing them for wrongs they were compelled to commit. In effect, the principle of non-liability can help secure criminal evidence against traffickers, who inflict real and intentional harm on society. However as shown later, this book is vigilant not to place too much weight on this line of thought.

Rehabilitation, once admired by utilitarians like Bentham, seeks to protect the people, by encouraging the criminal not to commit further crimes. In the case of trafficked persons, there is nothing to rehabilitate. The victim did not commit the crime because of some inherent wrong or confusion over what is right and what is wrong. Rehabilitating trafficked persons is not necessary for they are not criminally inclined and would produce negative results. As such, this justification for punishment fails in cases of trafficked persons.

Lastly we have deterrence; as argued by Kara deterrence falls into two categories: "special deterrence (dissuading a specific criminal from committing future crimes) and general deterrence (dissuading other individuals from offending by making an example of particular offenders)" (2011: 130). None of these would appear to logically apply to trafficked persons. As summarised by Dennis with regard to persons (not just victims of human trafficking) who commit crimes due to compulsion: "it can be argued that since such conduct cannot realistically be deterred, punishment can serve no consequentialist purpose. Courts have sometimes expressed this idea in terms that the defendant's will not to commit the crime was overborne" (Dennis 2009: 35). Certainly, one can agree that deterrence will not work, because in circumstances when threats are made, force is used or other compulsion means are utilised by the trafficker, these are stronger then the power of deterrence. As noted by Fletcher (2000: 813): "there is a good utilitarian explanation for defences based on involuntary conduct. The argument is that involuntary conduct cannot be deterred and therefore it is pointless and wasteful to punish involuntary actors. This theory, which we shall call the theory of pointless punishment, carries considerable weight in current Anglo-American legal thought."

All of these four justifications for punishment can be explained through reference to consequentialist notions (incapacitation, rehabilitation and deterrence) or deontological ones (retribution). Given the nature in which the trafficked victim commits the crime—their involuntariness—it is hard to argue that society requires protection or would deem punishment fair; punishment would be pointless and serve no purpose.

Human Rights Law and the Non-liability Principle

Victimology confronts criminology's poor, or even lack of, engagement with the victim and focuses on the victim as the integral subject. In this section, we follow such an ethos and looking deeper into the victim's need and rights. The above justifications for a provision on non-liability regarded criminal law yet the EU Directive, in validating the inclusion of Article 8, focuses more on human rights concepts. The Recital says: *The aim of such protection is to safeguard the human rights of victims.* Whilst lauding its considerable impact, it would be unwise to not question the Recital. Indeed, it is interesting to contemplate why we are, through protecting trafficked victims from non-liability, safeguarding human rights. It is of course not new to marry human rights with victimology; radical vicitmologists have concerned themselves with human rights since the 1970s. Robert Elias advocated for a "victimology of human rights" and wrote: "a victimology that encompasses human rights would not divert attention from crime victims and their rights, but rather would explore their inextricable relationship to more universal human rights concerns" (1985: 17). Moreover, by being able to show that a concept—such as non-liability—can be grounded in human rights provides the said concept with a more universal influence.

Human Rights Law and the Non-liability Principle: Dignity

Radical victimology acknowledges the state's ability to oppress and turn people into victims. In turn, human rights seek to protect against abuse of power (including by the use of criminal law), which affect the physical well-being and liberty of persons. They prevent the arbitrariness of the sovereign from seizing control of a citizen through appropriating their legal standing, labour or otherwise. Locke voiced these ideas as the state's duty not to act capriciously towards its people (Locke 1990: 213). Donnelly describes human rights from a different, albeit related, approach: "We have human rights not to the requisites for health but to those things 'needed' for a life of dignity, for a life *worthy* of a human being, a life that cannot be enjoyed without these rights" (Donnelly 1989: 17). This spurs from the United Nations' *1948 Declaration of Human Rights*, which, although says little about the source of rights does view human rights as a foundation of freedom, justice and peace; all of, which contribute to sustaining dignity and humanity.

The elements that we deem as human rights need to be protected by the very essence of their relation to humanity. Consequently, the compelled actions of trafficked persons, even those that include serious crimes, are a manifestation of one's frailty, and should not lead to the deprivation of the victim's dignity. Indeed, much dignity is eroded when trafficked persons are held liable. For Hoshi (2013), the need to include principles of non-liability arises because of the exacerbated traumatisation of a victim when they are treated as a criminal. Thus, a non-liability provision exists to prevent secondary victimisation. This is a fair justification, especially if we consider the trauma that prosecution or punishment can have on a victim. The EU Agency for Fundamental Rights, for example, highlights that: "detention is a major interference with the right to liberty of any individual [and] its impact on persons with specific health needs, survivors of torture and other groups at risk may be proportionally higher than for others" (Fundamental Rights Agency 2010). Additionally, Boister highlights that human rights are threatened when trafficked persons become subject to "detention as illegal aliens rather than treated as the victim of crime" (Boister 2012: 21–22). Whilst the OSCE Special Representative vigorously argues that punishing trafficked persons: "is a violation of their fundamental dignity. It constitutes a serious denial of reality and of justice. Such punishment blames victims for the crimes of their traffickers, for crimes that, but for their status as trafficked persons, they would not have perpetrated. The criminalisation of trafficked victims may be tantamount to persecution of victims by the State: not only does it fail to take into account the serious crimes committed against the victim by the traffickers, and which should be investigated, it fails to recognise trafficked persons as being victims and witnesses of those serious crimes and exacerbates their victimisations and trauma by imposing on such persons State-sanctioned, unjust punishment" (OSCE Office of the Special Representative and Co-ordinator for Combating Trafficking in Human Beings 2013: 10).

Human Rights Law and the Non-liability Principle: Human Rights Instruments

Adherence to the core of human rights—dignity—informs our understanding of why trafficked persons should not be held liable. Moreover, to link the principle of non-liability with human rights one can also rely on the source of human rights, namely the instruments. For primary knowledge, it is worth noting that the notion of a defence is not absent from human rights or international law documents. Article 31(d) of the *Rome Statue* (dealing with duress) excludes liability as to crimes within the jurisdiction of the International Criminal Court. Here the Rome Statue recognises that there is a possibility of a suppression of freedom and autonomy, thus relating to the *mens rea* of the culprit.

The *Directive 2011/36 on preventing and combating trafficking in human beings and protecting its victims*, the *2005 Council of Europe Convention on Action Against Trafficking in Human Beings* and the *Association of Southeast Asian Nations (ASEAN) Convention Against Trafficking in Persons, Especially Women and Children* all address the non-liability of victims. However, none of these documents are core human rights instruments, although they do take on human rights characteristics (respect, protect, fulfil) and aim to protect persons. Importantly, the legally binding ILO Protocol—*ILO Protocol of 2014 to the Forced Labour Convention, 1930 (No. P029)*—obliges States to ensure that competent authorities are entitled not to prosecute victims for unlawful activities that they have been compelled to commit. The document's relation to human rights and its UN origin gives weight to argue that there is an emergence of the principle of non-liability in human rights instruments.

There is also a rich body of soft human rights law that addresses the principle of non-liability. Amongst the most cited is Principle 7 of the UN Trafficking Principles and Guidelines, which states: "Trafficked Persons shall not be detained, charged or prosecuted for their illegal entry into or residence in countries of transit or destination, or for their involvement in unlawful activates to the extent that such involvement is a direct consequence of their situation as trafficked persons." In similar vein the UN Working Group on Trafficking in Persons, which advises the Conference of the Parties to the United Nations Convention against Transnational Organized Crime, has recommended in its first session that: "With regard to ensuring the non-punishment and non-prosecution of trafficked persons, States parties should: (a) Establish appropriate procedures for identifying victims of trafficking in persons and for giving such victim support; (b) Consider, in line with their domestic legislation, not punishing or prosecuting trafficked persons for unlawful acts committed by them as a direct consequence of their situation as trafficked persons or where they were compelled to commit such unlawful acts…" Equally in Europe, the *Brussels Declaration on Preventing and Combating Trafficking in Human Beings* adopted by the European Conference on Preventing and Combating Trafficking in Human Beings, 20 September 2002 (Brussels Declaration) states:

"Trafficked victims must be recognised as victims of serious crime. Therefore they should not be re-victimised, further stigmatised, criminalised, prosecuted or held in detention centres for offences that may have been committed by the victim as part of the trafficking process."

Aside from these mentioned documents, there are other soft law texts that stress the importance of not holding trafficked persons liable (see Table 4.1). These soft law instruments operate in harmony and point to a growing acceptance of the need to reject the idea of criminalising trafficked persons for offences they committed as a result of their status. Of course, soft law does not impose a legal obligation on states and its weight should be taken with a forewarning. Nevertheless, soft law instruments are helpful in recognising or confirming legal attitudes and can shed light on the substantive content of hard law. One should also bear in mind the activism of the Fundamental Rights Agency (FRA), which although "has no legislative or regulatory powers, no quasi-judicial competence and no authority to adopt legally binding decisions with effect upon third parties" (Dutheil De La Rochere 2011: 1776), has become very prominent in shaping EU fundamental rights domains. The Agency has stated that "EU legislation should include a formal policy of non-punishment of victims of child trafficking to ensure that they can develop a relationship of trust with state authorities, in order to escape their dependency on their traffickers" (European Union Agency for Fundamental Rights 2009).

Thus far it has been demonstrated that the principle of non-liability can be rooted in sources of human rights law. There is a growing human right obligation "to which states must give effect so as to ensure that their domestic law conforms to that duty, irrespective of the requirements or complexities of their own legal systems. Accordingly, all states should, where necessary, adopt measures and take steps to bring their laws into conformity with the principle" (Piotrowicz and Sorrentino 2016: 677).

Separately from the direct reference to non-liability of trafficking victims, there are other well-established human rights provisions, also rooted in legislation, that are related to the principle. Their philosophies reject situations of trafficked persons being held liable for crimes they were compelled to commit by virtue of their trafficking situation.

Let us consider *The 1985 Declaration of Basic Principles of Justice for Victims of Crime and Abuse of Power*, this instrument highlights the importance of recognising someone as a victim and treating them with compassion and respect for dignity. Further it gives victims the right to justice and a redress mechanism. These principles are in conflict with holding trafficked persons liable for crimes they were forced to commit. A state would not be said to fulfil its responsibilities arising from the 1985 Declaration if it was holding a human trafficking victim liable.

Other established rights also reject prosecution and punishment of compelled trafficked persons. For one the right to freedom of movement, a key human right. Indeed, the OHCHR (Office of the High Commissioner for Human Rights) (2010: 134) confirms that "for trafficked persons who are lawfully within the relevant country, their detention in any kind of public or private facility would generally violate their right to freedom of movement." The principle on non-liability can also be related to rights enshrined in the EU Charter of Fundamental Rights such as: human dignity (Art. 1), prohibition of torture and inhuman or degrading treatment or punishment (Art. 4), right to liberty and security (Art. 6), protection from being expelled or extradited to a State where there is a serious risk that he or she would be subjected to the death penalty, torture or other inhuman or degrading treatment or punishment (Art. 19), equality before the law (Art. 20), non-discrimination (Art. 21), right to an effective remedy and to a fair trial (Art. 47), presumption of innocence and right of defence (Art. 48).

Proper conception of what holding trafficked persons liable can result in, goes against the key doctrines such as those listed in the preceding paragraph. And thus, acknowledging these rights and their full meaning allows us to excuse trafficked persons for crimes they were compelled to commit.

Human Rights Law and the Non-liability Principle: Case Law

This subsection considers case law from the European Court of Human Rights (the Court or ECtHR) as providing further justification for why we ought to protect the victim from liability. Yet primarily three points of caution are mandatory. Firstly, states are rarely found to violate Article 4 (prohibition of slavery and forced labour), and so the scrutiny herein is limited to a handful cases. Secondly, the Court has faced criticism with regard to the few cases it did consider. Some scholars find that the Court did not properly contemplate and/or understand the relevant law (Allain 2010; Stoyanova 2012). Thirdly, the Court has to date not considered the provision on non-liability of trafficked persons.

In *Siliadin v. France (2005)*, the Court held that Article 4 of the European Convention on Human Rights gives rise to the positive obligation on member states to penalise and prosecute effectively any act aimed at maintaining a person in a situation of human trafficking. As summarised by Rijken and Koster: "The Court then held that a violation of Article 4 is a serious violation of the personal integrity. Since this is a fundamental value, only criminal law can guarantee the effective and necessary protection by the state against these violations. Because France did not have adequate criminal legislation that unambiguously made punishable the behaviour at issue and since the perpetrators of this behaviour had not been convicted, the Court judged that the state had violated its positive obligations under Article 4" (Rijken and Koster 2008: 22). In 2012 the Court, in *CN v France*, reiterated that point and confirmed it also in *C.N. v. The United Kingdom*, where the judges found "that the investigation into the applicant's complaints of domestic servitude was ineffective due to the absence of specific legislation criminalising such treatment." Accordingly, in all three cases there was a violation of Article 4 of the Convention because the state did not have adequate laws in place.

The Court again confirmed the direct relationship between human trafficking and human rights in the landmark case of *Rantsev v Cyprus and Russia (2010)*.[2] However, on this occasion it went further than before and highlighted additional obligations that states have; the court made it clear that it is not enough to just have legislation that criminalises aspects of human trafficking. In respect of both countries, the Court found a violation of human rights. As summarised: "the ECtHR considered the absence of a proper criminal investigation a procedural violation of Article 4, inasmuch as Cyprus had failed to train law enforcement officials to initiate an investigation in cases where there were sufficient indicators of possible trafficking. Likewise, Russia's procedural failure to comply with Article 4 stemmed from its failure to undertake criminal investigation into the recruitment aspect of cross-border trafficking" (Vijeyarasa and Bello y Villarino 2013: 47). As to directly referring to human rights the Court stated: "There can be no doubt that trafficking threatens the human dignity and fundamental freedoms of its victims and cannot be considered compatible with a democratic society and the values expounded in the Convention…the Court concludes that trafficking itself, within the meaning of Article 3(a) of the Palermo Protocol and Article 4(a) of the Anti-Trafficking Convention, falls within the scope of article 4 of the Convention" (para. 282).

The *Rantsev* case is an important contribution to outlying the positive obligations with respect to victim protection. One of the most significant contributions of the judgements states: "The Court considers that the spectrum of safeguards set out in national legislation must be adequate to **ensure the practical and effective protection of the rights of victims or potential victims of trafficking**. Accordingly, in addition to criminal law measures to punish traffickers, Article 4 requires member states to put in place adequate measures regulating businesses often used as a cover for human trafficking. Furthermore, a state's immigration rules must address relevant concerns relating to encouragement, facilitation or tolerance of trafficking" [para. 284, emphasis added]. This quote from the Court's judgement "is a reflection of a well-settled aspect of states' positive obligations under the ECHR, namely, states are under an obligation to ensure an adequate and effective regulatory environment so that individuals are protected" (Stoyanova 2016: 292). It is suggested in this book that the obligation to ensure effective protection extends to excusing trafficked persons: "[t]o penalize a trafficked persons where they have been compelled to break the law actually denies the right to protection from the state" (Piotrowicz and Sorrentino 2016: 681).

The Court then continued: "In order for a positive obligation to take operational measures to arise in the circumstances of a particular case, it must be demonstrated that the State authorities were aware, or ought to have been aware, of circumstances giving rise to a credible suspicion that an identified individual had been, or was at real and immediate risk of being, trafficked or exploited" (para. 286). The Court's holding in *Rantsev* indicates that a human rights obligation arises once there is an awareness of a person as exploited or if it can be demonstrated that the state ought to have been aware of the person's status as a victim. Stoyanova (2012: 192–193) points out that the operational duty is less demanding in human trafficking than in other human rights cases. In *Osman v. United kingdom*, the Court phrased the positive duty as "the authorities knew or ought to have known," in *Rantsev* the Court stated: "States must demonstrate that where they 'were aware, or ought to have been aware, of circumstances giving rise to a credible suspicion that an identified individual had been, or was at real and immediate risk of being trafficked or exploited', they must remove that individual from the situation of risk or find themselves in violation of Article 4" (para. 286).

The law however is imprecise as regards to identification and it is unclear what due diligence is required. In *Rantsev*, the court highlighted the need to "ensure adequate training to those working in relevant fields to enable them to identify potential trafficking victims" (para. 296). However, a year later in *V.F. v. France,* the Court appears to apply reduced demands on state authorities. In this case, the applicant was under investigation of irregular migration and she did not state that she was a victim of human trafficking. Subsequently, the Court held that France had not violated Article 4 because they could not reasonably have known that she was a victim of human trafficking: "It was therefore of the opinion that the evidence submitted by the applicant was not sufficient to demonstrate that the police authorities knew or ought to have known that the applicant was the victim of a human trafficking network when they decided to deport her" (European Court of Human Rights 2014: 15).

Whilst the law on the due diligence of the duty to identify trafficked persons remains opaque, it is evident that in case of an affirmative identification the state has to take appropriate protection measures. Taking this situation to its logical consequences extends the obligations to protecting victims from liability (Turner 2015: 303). This is based on the conception that prosecution or penalising a victim can cause physical, psychological as well as socio-economic harm and can leave the victim at the risk of re-trafficking. The OSCE fittingly argued: "This emphasis on the protection of victims' rights in reality indicates that the obligation extends to include ensuring that such persons are not punished for offences that were caused or directly linked to their having been trafficked: few acts could constitute a more flagrant violation of a victim's rights than for the State to prosecute or otherwise punish a person for acts they were compelled by their trafficker or trafficking to do" (OSCE Office of the Special Representative and Co-ordinator for Combating Trafficking in Human Beings 2013: 15).

Moreover, the Court in *Rantsev* held that: "...there will be a violation of Article 4 of the Convention where the authorities fail to take appropriate measures within the scope of their powers to remove the individual from that situation or risk" (para. 286). This ruling can also be extended so as to argue that a state has to protect victims from being re-trafficked, which is a situation of risk, and ultimately from holding them liable. A report by the UK Anti-Trafficking Monitoring Group (2013: 93) highlights that "if trafficked persons are dealt with as offenders there is also an increased risk of re-trafficking." This point is rooted in case of *S.B. Moldova v Secretary of State for the Home Department*, where the trafficked victim who was imprisoned for three months for immigration offences and then deported to Moldova was re-trafficked to the UK for a further two years. Criminalisation of trafficked persons and re-trafficking are linked, which leads to a human rights violation as the victim was not removed from a situation of risk.

The ECtHR's rulings on positive obligations with respect to protecting trafficked persons serve as further justification for embedding the principle of non-liability in human rights discourse. Where a state fails to protect a victim from prosecution we can consider a human rights breach.

Human Rights Law and the Non-liability Principle: Final Points

On all the grounds described in the previous subsections, it can be argued that the principle of non-liability is also rooted in the doctrine of human rights. The effect of this is that there is a need for states to protect trafficked persons with due diligence. As such we need to acknowledge that: "trafficked persons have been the victims of one of more serious criminal offences. States have obligations to assist such person, and not treat them as criminals" (OSCE Office of the Special Representative and Co-ordinator for Combating Trafficking in Human Beings 2013: 15). A breach of this obligation can happen directly or indirectly. Indirect violation occurs when a state does not identify the relevant person as a trafficked victim which consequently leads to an inadequate understanding of the circumstances in which the crime was committed, and possibly a prosecution and penalisation of the victim. A direct violation occurs in circumstances when a state is or should have been aware of the victim's status but fails to apply the non-liability principle. The consequence of a failure to identify or to act appropriately on the identification means that a victim may be denied protection measures and will be treated as an ordinary defendant.

By articulating that the principle of non-liability should be channelled through a human rights-based approach we also acknowledge that pressure can be exerted on states to comply with the standard and when the same is not fulfilled there can be consequences for the state. As is argued by Mantouvalou "through human rights law, state obligations can become central because this body of law was primarily developed to protect individuals from state action. Most human rights documents incorporate state obligations to respect and secure individual rights" (Mantouvalou 2015: 349).

However, it is not enough for the law to exist on paper. The positive obligation means that there needs to be awareness of the rights and obligations in national law. Regrettably, there continue to be police officers who do not know what human trafficking is, states that prosecute or punish victims and victims who are unidentified. The Anti-Trafficking Monitoring Group in the UK (2013) highlighted that: "Whilst the positive obligation to investigate trafficking has been established in law, there is still a discrepancy between the number of potential trafficked persons identified and the number of prosecutions of traffickers... The most worrying finding of the research was that a significant number of victims continue to be prosecuted for offences they have committed as a direct consequence of their trafficking." Consequently, states need to ensure they have competent systems in place for victim identification. This includes ensuring there is adequate training to all frontline professionals who are likely to come into contact with a potential victim: e.g. health workers, police, lawyers, social workers and civil society. Training of front-line staff has the potential to overcome the barriers of victim identification associated with the clandestine nature of the crime.

Need to Fight Human Trafficking

Another justification that is often put forward for a provision on non-prosecution or non-application of penalties is that it will encourage victims to come forward to authorities, disclose their story and cooperate. Thereby, aiding states in their obligation to investigate and prosecute those responsible for human trafficking. The UN Working Group on Trafficking in Persons highlighted that: "Criminalisation limits the trafficking victims' access to justice and protection and decreases the likelihood that they will report their victimization to the authorities. Given the victims' existing fears for the personal safety and of reprisals by the traffickers, the added fear of prosecution and punishment can only further prevent victims from seeking protection, assistance and justice." In similar vein, we find arguments from psychologists. Herman (1997) notes that victims who have experienced a trauma are likely to be better witnesses if they have the choice whether to participate in criminal proceedings. That choice will logically be informed by whether the criminal justice system treats them justly. Similarly, Rijken recognises that punishing or expelling trafficked persons compromises criminal evidence (Rijken 2013: 31). Thus, exempting trafficked persons can serve a practical purpose in the aim of fighting human trafficking.

However, we ought to be sceptical about giving this rationalisation too much weight, for it undermines the commitment that the victim should be at the centre of conceptualisation. Any justification of rights within the framework of prosecution certainly dilutes the much-needed victim focus. In fact, such a justification runs the danger of promoting the now outdated view that human trafficking approaches ought to primarily focus on criminal justice.

In 2006 Davidson wrote the now famous, article *Will the real sex slave please stand up*, in it she recognised a held assumption from that era "that by casting a net to catch immigration offenders and individuals involved in a specific set of criminal activities such as those associated with prostitution, drug running, and people smuggling/trafficking, the authorities will also catch victims" (Davidson 2006: 10). Is it possible that today a different, equally poor, assumption prevails? That by casting a net to rescue victims the authorities are in truth hoping to catch victims? In both situations, an obvious conflict of interest emerges.

The granting of protection to a victim should be framed outside of reference to efficient prosecutions. In other words, victim empowerment by the non-liability principle should not be measured by the success of prosecution of trafficking cases. Likewise, for further critique we can borrow some of the language used by Nils Christie's (1977) "theft" concept; where victim's voices are used to suit the needs of the prosecution. Their story and endured harm is stolen by the state, through law enforcement professionals. It is stolen for, supposedly, the purposes of producing a desired state of affairs, i.e. more prosecutions of trafficking cases and ergo more prevention of future cases through deterrence. However, this approach falls to similar criticism as consequentialist penal theories; namely there is a dependency on empirical proof and success. What happens if empirical study shows that the non-liability principle does not lead to greater cooperation of victims with the authorities, and thus successful prosecutions?

It is thus put forward in this book that any justification that treats victims as a means to an end will end up with a system that is found wanting.

Are We Impending the Rights of the Accused Traffickers?

One of the manners in which any non-liability clause could be contested is that the rights guaranteed are grounded on assertions, which do not have to be proven beyond reasonable doubt in court. As a result it could be questioned whether by exempting a victim from punishment, a trafficker can receive a fair trial? Or to put another way: is the alleged trafficker's innocence assumed even when his alleged victim is receiving protection and exoneration? Such questions are made against the backdrop of Article 47 of the Charter of Fundamental Rights of the European Union, which provides the right to an effective legal remedy and fair trial. Amongst other things, as summarised by De Hert (2016: 116) this includes "an independent and impartial tribunal, including the right to be defended and represented." In this book, it is held that granting trafficked persons victim status and thus protection does not have a negative effect on the trafficker's right to a fair trial.

Firstly, the scope of any non-liable clause regards victims that have been recognised as victims, albeit the standard of proof may be lower than in criminal courts. Secondly, it is suggested that granting victim rights is independent of the criminal responsibility of the defendant. This has been determined in the most recent ECtHR case concerning human trafficking. Here the Court highlighted that there is independence between crime investigation and victim identification. The Court stated in J. and Others v. Austria (para. 115): "[…]the Court does not consider that the elements of the offence of human trafficking had been fulfilled merely because the Austrian authorities treated the applicants as (potential) victims of human trafficking (see paras. 110–111 above). Such special treatment did not presuppose official confirmation that the offence had been established and was *independent of the authorities' duty to investigate*" [emphasis added].

Additionally, an alleged trafficker will have equality of arms in court and can challenge a State decision as to victim status. Thus, protecting victim does not preclude an alleged trafficker from being able to exercise any of his/her rights and arguments. It is recommended that in instances where a victim has received exonerations, to prevent disadvantage to the defendant a court must take into account the victim's status with scrupulous care and must ensure that all measures are taken for the trial to be fair.

Conclusion

Protecting trafficked persons against liability is an important provision. The principle of non-liability concerns itself with providing an excuse for trafficked persons when they have breached the law as a result of compulsion arising out of their trafficking situation. It is a means of protection against the violation of fundamental rights and against secondary victimisation of persons who were not able to exercise full control over their actions but were compelled to commit crimes. Using concepts of radical vicitmologists, the principle is a shield against the state and its ability to produce victimisations. As summarised by Piotrowicz and Sorrentino: "in reality, if the state punishes a trafficked person for offences related to their trafficking, it is punishing them for being trafficked" (Piotrowicz and Sorrentino 2016: 674).

This chapter has sought to capture arguments that rationalise the non-liability principle and demonstrate that it is founded on established and recognised philosophies emanating from criminal law and human rights. Rather than being in competition with each other, it is argued that the presented in this chapter rationales complement one another. What must be said is that the multi-faced foundation provides a strong platform from which we can call on states to protect human trafficking victims from liability. In particular, by affiliating the principle with human rights we note there is a specific duty for states to put in place structural conditions where the right is secured. However, as the next chapters show, how this is done is very much at the discretion of the state.

Notes

1. The term family members includes the "spouse, the person who is living with the victim in a committed intimate relationship, in a joint household and on a stable and continuous basis, the relatives in direct line, the siblings and the dependants of the victim." Directive 2012/29/EU of the European Parliament and of the Council of October 2012 establishing minimum standards on the rights, support and protection of victims of crime, and replacing Council Framework Decision 2001/220/JHA, 14 November 2012, L 315/57, Art. 2(b).

2. The case concerned Ms. Rantsev who was brought to Cyprus on an artiste visa, applied for by the owners of a cabaret where she was supposed to work as a dancer. She started work on 16 March but after three days she escaped. On 28 March she was seen at a club in Limassol, and her previous employer, Mr. Athanasiou was informed. With the

assistance of another, Mr. Athanasiou took Ms. Rantseva to a police station where she was put into custody. Mr. Athanasiou's aim was that she would be detained and extradited, so that he could employ someone else. However, because her immigration status was not irregular the police noted that they could not do anything and contacted the employer to pick her up. Mr. Athanasiou collected Ms. Rantseva and took charge of all her documents. Subsequently he took her to an apartment of his employee and placed her in a room, allegedly against her will. At 6.30 a.m. Ms. Rantseva was found dead on the street below, there was a bed sheet tied to the balcony of the 5th floor apartment. For the purposes of understanding where the human rights breach comes from, it is important to note that the police did not question Ms. Rantseva or make an enquiry into the background of her case. They were not alerted that her employers held her documents or that she had run away from the cabaret. Ms. Rantseva's father complained under Articles 2, 3, 4, 5 and 8 of the ECHR, claiming that there had been a failure by Russia and Cyprus to protect his daughter from the risk of trafficking and that there had been a failure to adequately investigate her death.

References

Allain, J. (2010). Rantsev v Cyprus and Russia: The European Court of Human Rights and Trafficking as Slavery. *Human Rights Law Review, 10*(3), 546–557.

Anti-slavery. (2014). *Trafficking for Forced Criminal Activities and Begging in Europe Exploratory Study and Good Practice Examples* [Online]. http://www.antislavery.org/wp-content/uploads/2017/01/trafficking_for_forced_criminal_activities_and_begging_in_europe.pdf.

Anti-Trafficking Monitoring Group (ATMG). (2013). In the Dock. [Online] http://www.antislavery.org/includes/documents/cm_docs/2013/i/inthedock_final_small_file.pdf.

Berman, M. N. (2003). Justification and Excuse, Law and Morality. *Duke Law Journal, 53*(1), 1–77.

Boister, N. (2012). *An Introduction to Transnational Criminal Law.* Oxford: Oxford University Press.

Buczma, S. R. (2013). An Overview of the Law Concerning Protection of Victims of Crime in the View of the Adoption of the Directive 2012/29/EU Establishing Minimum Standards on the Rights, Support and

Protection of Victims of Crime in the European Union. *ERA Forum, 14*(2), 235–250.

Centre for Equal Opportunities and Opposition to Racism, Providing information on cases from the Criminal Court of Antwerp (Belgium), 26 April 2006 and 2 April 2008 quoted in OSCE Office of the Special Representative and Co-ordinator for Combating Trafficking in Human Beings. (2013). Policy and legislative recommendations towards the effective implementation of the non-punishment provision with regard to victims of trafficking. Vienna: OSCE. [Online] http://www.osce.org/secretariat/101002?download=true.

Christie, N. (1977). Conflicts as Property. *British Journal of Criminology, 17*(1), 1–15.

Davidson, J. O. (2006). Will the Real Sex Slave Please Stand Up? *Feminist Review, 83*, 4–22.

De Hert, P. (2016). EU Criminal Law and Fundamental Rights. In V. Mitsilegas, M. Bergstrom, & T. Konstadinides (Eds.), *Research Handbook on EU Criminal Law*. Chelteham: Edward Elgar.

Dennis, I. H. (2009). On Necessity as a Defence to Crime: Possibilities, Problems and the Limits of Justification and Excuse. *Criminal Law and Philosophy, 3*(1), 29–49.

Donnelly, J. (1989). *Universal Human Rights in Theory and Practice*. Ithaca: Cornell University Press.

Dressler, J. (2001). *Understanding Criminal Law*. New York: Lexis Publishing.

Dubber, M. D., & Hörnle, T. (2014). *Criminal Law: A Comparative Approach*. Oxford: Oxford University Press.

Dussich, J. P. J. (n.d.). *Victimology—Past, Present and Future* [Online]. http://www.unafei.or.jp/english/pdf/RS_No70/No70_12VE_Dussich.pdf.

Dutheil De La Rochere, J. (2011). Challenges for the Protection of Fundamental Rights in the EU at the Time of the Entry into Force of the Lisbon Treaty. *Fordham International Law Journal, 33*(6), 1776–1799.

Elias, R. (1985). Transcending Our Social Reality of Victimisation: Towards a New Victimology of Human Rights. *Victimology, 10*, 6–25.

European Court of Human Rights. (2014). *Guide on Article 4 of the European Convention on Human Rights Prohibition of Slavery and Forced Labour* [Online]. http://www.echr.coe.int/Documents/Guide_Art_4_ENG.pdf.

European Union Agency for Fundamental Rights. (2009). Report on strengthening the role of the EU in the fight against child trafficking [Online] http://fra.europa.eu/sites/default/files/fra_uploads/504-Child-trafficking-media-memo_en.pdf.

Fattah, E. A. (1997). *Criminology: Past, Present and Future*. London, UK: Palgrave Macmillan.

Fernández de Casadevante Romani, C. (2012). *International Law of Victims*. Heidelberg: Springer.

Fletcher, G. P. (1998). *Basic Concepts of Criminal Law*. Oxford: Oxford University Press.

Fletcher, G. P. (2000). *Rethinking Criminal Law*. Oxford: Oxford University Press.

Fundamental Rights Agency. (2010). *Detention of Third Country Nationals in Return Procedures, European Union Agency for Fundamental Rights*. Vienna [Online]. http://fra.europa.eu/en/publication/2010/detention-third-country-nationals-return-procedures.

Gallant, K. S. (2003). Politics, Theory and Institutions: Three Reasons Why International Criminal Defence Is Hard, and What Might Be Done About One of Them. *Criminal Law Forum, 14*(3), 317–334.

Gardner, J. (2007). *Offences and Defences*. Oxford: Oxford University Press.

Gardner, M. R. (1993). The Mens Rea Enigma: Observations on the Role of Motive in the Criminal Law Past and Present. *Utah Law Review, 1993*, 635–750.

Hart, H. L. A. (1968). *Punishment and Responsibility: Essays in the Philosophy of Law*. Oxford: Clarendon Press.

Herman, J. (1997). *Trauma and Recovery*. New York: HarperCollins.

Hoshi, B. (2013). The Trafficking Defence: A Proposed Model for the Non-criminalisation of Trafficked Persons in International Law. *Groningen Journal of International Law, 1*(2), 54–72.

Hoyle, C., & Sanders, A. (2000). Police Response to Domestic Violence: From Victim Choice to Victim Empowerment? *The British Journal of Criminology, 40*(1), 14–36.

Hoyle, C., Bosworth, M., & Dempsey, M. (2011). Labelling the Victims of Sex Trafficking: Exploring the Borderland Between Rhetoric and Reality. *Social & Legal Studies, 20*(3), 313–329.

Kara, S. (2011). Designing More Effective Laws Against Human Trafficking Designing More Effective Laws Against Human Trafficking. *Northwestern Journal of International Human Rights, 9*(2), 123.

Klip, A. (2015). On Victim's Rights and Its Impact on the Rights of the Accused. *European Journal of Crime, Criminal Law and Criminal Justice, 23*(3), 177–189.

Koba, L. (2015). Niekaralnosc ofiar handle ludźmi w Polsce – Punkt Widzenia Fundacji Przeciwko Handlowi Ludzmi I Niewolnictwu La Strada. In Z.

Lasocik, Z. (Ed.), *Niekaralnosc ofiar handle ludźmi – nowe perspektywy, Ośrodek Badań Handlu Ludzmi* (pp. 73–80). Warsaw: Warsaw University.

Lanham, D. (1976). Larsonneur Revisited. *Criminal Law Review*, May, 276–281.

Locke, J. (1990). *Questions Concerning the Law of Nature*. Ithaca: Cornell University Press.

Loughnan, A. (2016). Asking (Different) Responsibility Questions: Responsibility and Non-responsibility in Criminal Law. *Bergen Journal of Criminal Law and Criminal Justice, 4*(1), 25.

Mantouvalou, V. (2015). "Am I Free Now?" Overseas Domestic Workers in Slavery. *Journal of Law and Society, 42*(3), 329–357.

OHCHR. (2010). Recommended Principles And Guidelines On Human Rights And Human Trafficking. Geneva: OHCHR [Online] http://www.ohchr.org/Documents/Publications/Traffickingen.pdf.

OSCE Office of the Special Representative and Co-ordinator for Combating Trafficking in Human Beings. (2013). *Policy and Legislative Recommendations Towards the Effective Implementation of the Non-punishment Provision with Regard to Victims of Trafficking*. Vienna [Online]. http://www.osce.org/secretariat/101002?download=true.

Piotrowicz, R. W., & Sorrentino, L. (2016). Human Trafficking and the Emergence of the Non-punishment Principle. *Human Rights Law Review, 16*(4), 669–699.

Rasquete, C., Ferreira, A., & Moyano Marques, F. (2014). Why Do We Need Concrete Measures for Victims at EU Level? A View from the Coalface. *ERA Forum, 15*(1), 119–129.

Rijken, C. (2013). Trafficking in Human Beings for Labour Exploitation: Cooperation in an Integrated Approach. *European Journal of Crime, Criminal Law and Criminal Justice, 21*(1), 9–35.

Rijken, C. R. J. J., & Koster, D. (2008). A Human Rights Based Approach to Trafficking in Human Beings in Theory and Practice. May. *SSRN Electronic Journal*.

Rijken, C. (2017). Trafficking in persons: a victim's perspective. In R. Piotrowicz, C. Rijken, & B. H. Uhl (Eds.), *Routledge Handbook of Human Trafficking*. New York: Routledge.

Shoham, S. G., Knepper, P., & Kett, M. (2010). *International Handbook of Victimology*. Boca Raton, FL: CRC Press.

Spencer, D. C., & Walklate, S. (2016). *Reconceptualizing Critical Victimology: Interventions and Possibilities*. Lanham, MD: Lexington Books.

Stoyanova, V. (2012). Dancing on the Borders of Article 4: Human Trafficking and the European Court of Human Rights in the Rantsev Case [Online]. https://papers.ssrn.com/sol3/papers.cfm?abstract_id=2282442.

Stoyanova, V. (2016). L.E. v. Greece: Human Trafficking and the Scope of States' Positive Obligations Under the ECHR. *European Human Rights Law Review, 3* [Online]. https://papers.ssrn.com/sol3/papers.cfm?abstract_id=2773670.

Turner, I. (2015). Human Rights, Positive Obligations, and Measures to Prevent Human Trafficking in the United Kingdom. *Journal of Human Trafficking, 1*(4), 296–317.

Vijeyarasa, R., & Bello y Villarino, J. M. (2013). Modern-Day Slavery—A Judicial Catchall for Trafficking, Slavery and Labour Exploitation: A Critique of Tang and Rantsev. *Journal of International Law and International Relations, 8*(1), 36–61.

Westen, P. (2006). An Attitudinal Theory of Excuse. *Law and Philosoph, 25*(3), 289–375.

Worley, W. (2009). Explain the Relevance of the Phrase "A Concession to Human Frailty" When it Comes to the Defence of Duress. [Online] http://www.peterjepson.com/law/LA2-8%20Worley.pdf.

Wit, D., & Wa, T. (2013). Criminality, Judgment and Eschatology. *Dutch Reformed Theological Journal, 54*, 109–119.

Zornosa, F. (2016). Protecting Human Trafficking Victims from Punishment and Promoting Their Rehabilitation: The Need for an Affirmative Defense. *Washington and Lee Journal of Civil Rights and Social Justice, 22*(1), 177.

4

Non-liability in European and International Law

Introduction

This chapter sets out the existing provisions on non-liability as found in European and international law. The chapter will present the text of Article 26 of the *2005 Council of Europe Convention on Action Against Trafficking in Human Beings* and Article 8 of the *Directive 2011/36 on preventing and combating trafficking in human beings and protecting its victims*, which are then dissected in subsequent chapters.

The European legal regime is probably the most forward-looking and progressive system in the world with regard to protecting trafficked persons. However, it will be interesting to see what the Australian Modern Slavery Act and The Honk Kong anti-slavery law will look like. The European frameworks are also far reaching; the *2005 Council of Europe Convention on Action Against Trafficking in Human Beings* has been ratified by nearly all member states and all European Union (EU) member states.

Whilst *Directive 2011/36 on preventing and combating trafficking in human beings and protecting its victims* and the *2005 Council of Europe Convention on Action Against Trafficking in Human Beings* have features in common, they are not identical. This will be highlighted in this

© The Author(s) 2019
J. M. Muraszkiewicz, *Protecting Victims of Human Trafficking From Liability*, Palgrave Studies in Victims and Victimology, https://doi.org/10.1007/978-3-030-02659-2_4

and subsequent chapters. Regrettably, neither document has a Travaux Préparatoires, which we can refer to, to understand the negotiations that preceded the agreement of each article. However, with respect to the *Council of Europe Convention on Action Against Trafficking in Human Being* there are some documents we can rely on to gain a bit of a historical perspective. The Council of Europe's Committee of Ministers had mandated the Ad hoc *committee on action against trafficking in human beings*, (known as CAHTEH) to prepare the text for the Convention; this took place in steps with multiple drafts. Fortunately, we are able to access the various revised drafts of the Convention.

Along with presenting the European law, the chapter will provide readers with knowledge on aspects of international law that do, or as in the case of the UN Palermo Protocol do not, address the non-liability principle for trafficked persons. Subsequently, the chapter will draw parallels with other similar provisions such as Article 31(1) of *Refugee Convention* and Article 31(d) of the *Rome Statue* (dealing with duress). Lastly, the chapter looks at how the law is currently protecting victims of other crimes who are committing crimes, specifically victims of domestic violence and child soldiers.

Article 26 of the 2005 Council of Europe Convention

Article 26 of the 2005 Council of Europe Convention and Its Drafting

As mentioned in the introduction, no Travaux Préparatoires is available with respect to the drafting process of the *Council of Europe Convention on Action Against Trafficking in Human Beings*. This is unfortunate for it would have been beneficial for scholars to easily gain insight into what the discussions focused on, what was a point of disagreement or what inspired the provision. It is possible, however, to make an informed guess as to why Article 26 came about. Firstly, as is shown below at the time of drafting the Convention there was a deficiency in terms of hard law and binding responsibility. The *UN Palermo Protocol* does not make any obligations on states in terms of non-liability. There was, however, since the adoption of the *UN Palermo Protocol*, a developing acceptance of the importance of such a principle. For instance, the UNODC Model Law 2009, which was drafted to deliver guidance on how trafficking laws can be implemented at a domestic level, includes Article 10 entitled *non-liability of victims of trafficking in persons*.[1] Below we come back to further soft law[2] provisions that were developed post the *UN Palermo Protocol*, the key point for now is that there was a growing recognition that trafficked persons are compelled to commit crimes and a recognition that they ought to be protected from prosecution and punishment. Against this discourse, it was only natural that European legislators sought to codify the principle. Moreover, this is consistent with Convention's aim to put a special focus on the human rights of victims of trafficking. The Explanatory Report to the Convention states that the document aims to achieve "a proper balance between matters concerning human rights and prosecution."

The *2005 Council of Europe Convention on Action Against Trafficking in Human Beings* was a fertile answer to the criticisms of the UN document. A suggestion for a Convention was raised in 2002, and although the primarily interest was in women and prostitution, the final version of the document applies to all forms of human trafficking. It was adopted on 3 May 2005 and entered into force on 1 February 2008. Despite there being no Travaux Préparatoires, researchers will find of interest the publicly available documents from the Ad hoc *committee on action against trafficking in human beings (CAHTEH)*. This includes the various versions of the *Revised draft Council of Europe Convention on action against trafficking in human beings* (2004). The mandate given to CAHTEH required that, in their work, "the CAHTEH put a special focus on the human rights of the victims of trafficking, design a comprehensive framework for the protection and assistance of victims and witnesses, take into account gender equality aspects, as well as on the effective prevention, investigation, prosecution and on international cooperation and improve on the protection afforded within the Palermo Protocol" (Amnesty International and Anti-slavery 2004). The mandate also included drafting a provision that would protect trafficked persons again being held liable (now contained in Article 26 of the Convention).

In February 2004, following the 3rd meeting, CAHTEH proposed the following version of Article 26:

Article 26—Non-punishment clause
Each Party shall provide in its internal law for victims a non-punishment clause for violation of immigration laws or for the illegal acts they are usually involved in as a direct consequence of their situation as victims, such as illegal border crossing, illegal stay in the territory, use of forged documents, destruction, falsification and alteration of documents, illegal employment.

By July 2004, following the 5th meeting, this protective wording had changed and CAHTEH proposed three versions of Article 26:

Option 1
Each Party shall provide in its internal law for the possibility of not punishing victims for their involvement in unlawful activities to the extent that such involvement is a direct consequence of their situation as victims.
Option 2
Each Party shall ensure in its internal law that victims are not punished for their involvement in unlawful activities to the extent that such involvement is a direct consequence of their situation as victims.
Option 3
Trafficked persons shall not be detained, charged or prosecuted for the illegality of their entry into or residence in countries of transit and destination, or for their involvement in unlawful activities to the extent that such involvement is a direct consequence of their situation as trafficked persons.

Option one was the least protecting, option two was in the middle, and option three was most protective as it expressly prohibited more than just punishment. Such an option it was argued by NGOs (e.g. La Strada International and the Church's Commission for Migrants in Europe) avoided discrimination and best avoided the criminalisation of trafficked persons. In the light of the three options, Amnesty International and Anti-Slavery International urged CAHTEH to adopt a modified version Option 3, which they suggested should read as follows:

Article 26:

1. Trafficked persons shall not be detained, charged or prosecuted for the illegality of their entry, into or residence in countries of transit or destination, or for their involvement in any unlawful activities that are a direct consequence of their situation as a trafficked persons.

2. Each Party shall ensure that all authorities who are likely to come into contact with trafficked persons, (including police, immigration officials, members of judiciary, lawyers (including prosecutors), NGOs, doctors, social service professionals labour inspectors), are adequately trained and sensitised about this Article and the status and needs of trafficked persons as victims of human rights abuses and crime. Particular attention shall be paid to the special needs of children and other vulnerable groups.

By the time of the 6th CAHTEH meeting, two options remained:

Option 1

Each Party shall, in accordance with the basic principles of its national legal system, provide for the possibility of not imposing penalties on victims for their involvement in unlawful activities, to the extent that they have been compelled to do so, as a direct consequence of their situation as victim.

Option 2

Each Party shall, under the conditions provided by its internal law, ensure that no penalty is imposed on victims for their involvement in unlawful activities when they have been compelled to do so by their situation as victims.

On reading the revised options, it would appear that the urges of NGOs had been disregarded, and in fact, the degree of protection offered to victims had regressed. The Article started with an obligatory wording of "shall provide" and moved towards more discretionary options of "ensuring" "providing possibilities" in accordance with the basic principles of its national legal system. This weakened language found its way into the final version of the article (see below). However, some progress was made. The final version regards victims who have been compelled rather than just victims who breached laws "as a **direct** consequence of their situation as victim"; as discussed in this chapter and chapter 5, relying on compulsion as a criteria allows a wider net of victims to benefit from the protective measure.

The Content of Article 26 of the 2005 Council of Europe Convention

Article 26 of the *Council of Europe Convention on Action Against Trafficking in Human Being* "constitutes an obligation on Parties to adopt and/or implement legislative measures providing for the possibility of not imposing penalties on victims, on the grounds indicated in the same article" (The Explanatory Report to the Convention, 2005: para. 272). That Article states:

> Each Party shall, in accordance with the basic principles of its legal system, provide for the possibility of not imposing penalties on victims for their involvement in unlawful activities, to the extent that they have been compelled to do so.

The Explanatory Report to the Convention (2005: para. 273–274) clarifies that: "In particular, the requirement that victims have been compelled to be involved in unlawful activities shall be understood as comprising, at a minimum, victims that have been subject to any of the illicit means referred to in Article 4, when such involvement results from compulsion. Each Party can comply with the obligation established in Article 26, by providing for a substantive criminal or procedural criminal law provision, or any other measure, allowing for the possibility of not punishing victims when the above mentioned legal requirements are met, in accordance with the basic principles of every national legal system."
The Article is scrutinised in detail in the next chapter.

Article 8 of the 2011 EU Directive on Human Trafficking

Directive 2011/36 on preventing and combating trafficking in human beings and protecting its victims was adopted by the European Parliament on 5 April 2011 and entered into force on 15 April 2011. The Directive, inter alia, approximates amongst EU member states measures to prevent human trafficking, punish the perpetrators and protect the victims. It applies to both EU and non-EU citizens. The Directive was to be transposed by all member states by 6 April 2013. Again, there is no document that describes the discussions surrounding the provisions within. The relevant legal provision in the EU is contained in Article 8 of the 2011 EU Directive on Human Trafficking:

> Member States shall, in accordance with the basic principles of their legal systems, take the necessary measures to ensure that competent national authorities are entitled not to prosecute or impose penalties on victims of trafficking in human beings for their involvement in criminal activities which they have been compelled to commit as a direct consequence of being subjected to any of the acts referred to in Article 2.

The provision is supported by the Recital, which at paragraph 14 states that:

> Victims of trafficking in human beings should, in accordance with the basic principles of the legal systems of the relevant Member States, be protected from prosecution or punishment for criminal activities such as the use of false documents, or offences under legislation on prostitution or immigration, that they have been compelled to commit as a direct consequence of being subject to trafficking. The aim of such protection is to safeguard the human rights of victims, to avoid further victimisation and to encourage them to act as witnesses in criminal proceedings against the perpetrators. This safeguard should not exclude prosecution or punishment for offences that a person has voluntarily committed or participated in.

Although subsequent chapters will dichotomise the two European provisions, it is important to already emphasise that the protection is not conditional on the type of crime. In other words, it does not matter if the trafficked persons committed a migration offence, grievous bodily harm or shoplifting, provided they can show compulsion and a relation to their trafficking situation they ought to be protected. The emphasis is thus on the victims, rather than their offence. This goes back to the reason for having the principle of non-liability in the first place and acknowledges that "when an individual's free will has been overcome, he is not focusing on what crime he is being asked to commit; he is not focused on anything except responding to the free will destroying threat that has been levelled against him. Whether or not an individual's free will has been overcome is not necessarily dependent on what crime he is being asked to commit. Coerced individuals are not free actors and as such they act without moral culpability" (Risacher 2014: 1408).

Non-liability in International Law

Turning our attention to international law and soft law, the most logical place to start is the, mentioned in chapter 1, *UN Protocol to Prevent, Suppress and Punish Trafficking in Persons, Especially Women and Children*. It was the first international instrument addressing state obligations vis-à-vis the crime of human trafficking. In the *2000 UN Protocol on Human Trafficking*, there is no provision that mirrors Article 8 of the *Directive 2011/36 on preventing and combating trafficking in human beings and protecting its victims* or Article 26 of the *2005 Council of Europe Convention on Action Against Trafficking in Human Beings*. However, it is interesting to note that countries were encouraged to include some version of a non-liability clause within the *2000 UN Protocol* but they opted not to. According to Gallagher (2010: 282), this renders any claim that non-liability is implied in the document rather weak.

Nevertheless, the inclusion of the phrase "by means of the threat or use of force or other forms of coercion" in the definition is important, for it is a basis and the ethos for the later developed principles of non-liability for trafficked persons. Indeed, the two European articles (mentioned above) incorporate the underlying logic of the definition of human trafficking. Victims are subjected to various means that result in their will and responsibility being capitulated. The non-liability clause is thus a justifiable progression from the means element of the definition.

Hoshi (2013) notes that "the absence of a binding non-criminalisation provision in international law is significant because it means that there is no unified vision to which regional and national legislators may (or must) adhere." This is not necessarily true, for we do note other sources of international law that concern the non-liability principle. Indeed, the UN body was quick after the Protocol to recognise the importance of supporting the principle of non-liability. The *2001 United Nations General Assembly Resolution on Traffic in Women and Girls* is the earliest international legal document that asks states to ensure that the victims of human trafficking are not penalised. Following suite, in 2002 a version of the principle was asserted within *the UN Recommended Principle and Guidelines on Human Rights and Human Trafficking* (2002; Principle 7), which states: "Trafficked persons shall not be detained, charged or prosecuted for the illegality of their entry into or residence in countries of transit and destination, or for their involvement in unlawful activities to the extent that such involvement is a direct consequence of their situation as trafficked persons." The Commentary to the Recommended Principles and Guidelines on Human Rights and Human Trafficking (2010: 130) validates the importance of the principle by saying the issue is given "given particular and detailed consideration owing to the prevalence of this practice and its serious implications for the rights of trafficked persons, in particular, women and children." In addition, we ought to also acknowledge the principle with respect to children; here, the *UN OHCR Guideline 8.3* adopts a wider approach, and conditions that "there is an obligation to ensure that children who are victims of trafficking are not subjected to criminal procedures or sanctions for offences related to their situation as trafficked persons."

Likewise, in 2002 *The Organisation for Security and Co-operation in Europe (OSCE) Ministerial Council Declaration on Trafficking in Human Beings* stated that "Trafficked victims must be recognised as victims of serious crime. Therefore they should not be re-victimised, further stigmatised, criminalised, prosecuted or held in detention centres for offences that may have been committed by the victim as part of the trafficking process." *The 2014 ILO Forced Labour Protocol* also includes a non-liability clause at Article 4: "Each Member shall, in accordance with the basic principles of its legal system, take the necessary measures to ensure that competent authorities are entitled not to prosecute or impose penalties on victims of forced or compulsory labour for their involvement in unlawful activities which they have been compelled to commit as a direct consequence of being subjected to forced or compulsory labour." Piotrowicz and Sorrentino are right to point out that the obligation found in the ILO is unique when compared to the other documents, for it specifically focuses on forced labour. The ILO Convention thus "explicitly acknowledges that victims of forced labour may involuntarily commit a range of offences as a direct result of their forced labour status. This clause is also important from the perspective of avoiding discriminatory treatment of victims of forced labour versus victims of trafficking - effectively prescribing equality of treatment for both" (Piotrowicz and Sorrentino 2016: 174).

The commitment to the principle at a regional level is not only limited to Europe and the above-described instruments, but is also acknowledged by the *Association of Southeast Asian Nations (ASEAN) Convention Against Trafficking in Persons, Especially Women and Children.* In this 2015 document, we find an obligation for parties to not hold "victims of trafficking in persons criminally or administratively liable." Moreover, numerous soft law instruments and official communications underline the importance and of the principle; a sample of these is detailed in Table 4.1.

This section has presented the numerous hard and soft law provisions that place a duty on states not to hold victims of human trafficking liable for offences related to their trafficking situation. Yet, it is important to emphasise that none of the provisions grant blanket immunity. Indeed, the preamble to the 2011 EU Directive at paragraph 14 states that: "This safeguard should not exclude prosecution or punishment for offences that a person has voluntarily committed or participated in." The use of the word "voluntarily" goes to the heart of what the principle seeks to address. Thus, although when "a person has been trafficked, there is a good likelihood that they are not responsible because they are not acting with free will" (Piotrowicz and Sorrentino 2016: 693), it is not always the case that a trafficked person should be given immunity from liability on the sole basis that they were victims of human trafficking. This author has volunteered in a safe house where she has come across victims who commit crimes, usually battery or theft, the same however is not connected to having been trafficked.[3] It would thus be unjust to exempt them from responsibility.

Table 4.1 Soft law and communications regarding the non-liability of trafficked persons principle

Instrument/Policy	Content
UN General Assembly, "Trafficking in Women and Girls" UN Doc A/RES/63/156, 30 January 2009, at Paragraph 12	Urges Governments to take all appropriate measures to ensure that victims of trafficking are not penalized for being trafficked and that they do not suffer from revictimization as a result of actions taken by government authorities, and encourages Governments to prevent, within their legal framework and in accordance with national policies, victims of trafficking in persons from being prosecuted for their illegal entry or residence
UN Human Rights Council, "Trafficking in Persons, Especially Women and Children," UN Doc. A/HRC/RES/11/3, 17 June 2009, at Paragraph 3(e)	Urges Governments To take all appropriate measures to ensure that victims of trafficking are not penalized for being trafficked and that they do not suffer from revictimization as a result of actions taken by Government authorities, bearing in mind that they are victims of exploitation, and encourages Governments to provide trafficked persons with access to specialized support and assistance, regardless of their immigration status
"Trafficking in Women and Girls: Report of the Secretary-General," UN Doc. A/63/215, 4th August 2008, at Paragraph 62	…Victims should be protected from re-victimisation, including protection from prosecution for illegal migration, labour law violations or other acts
UN Committee on the Rights of the Child, "Concluding Observations: Kenya" UN Doc. CRC/C/KEN/CO/2, 19 June 2007, at Paragraph 66	The Committee recommends that the State party: … (b) Prevent the criminalization of child victims of sexual exploitation;
UN Committee on the Elimination of Discrimination Against Women: "Concluding Observations: Lebanon," UN Doc. CEDAW/C/LBN/CO/3, 1st February 2008, Paragraphs 28–29	…It is further concerned that women and girls who have been trafficked for the purpose of sexual exploitation and forced domestic labour may be prosecuted and penalized under immigration laws and are therefore subject to revictimization
UN Committee on the Elimination of Discrimination Against Women: "Concluding Observations: Singapore," UN Doc. CEDAW/C/SGP/CO/3, 10th August 2007, at Paragraphs 21–22	The Committee is concerned at the narrow definition of trafficking employed by the State party. It is further concerned that women and girls who have been trafficked may be punished for violation of immigration laws and be treated as offenders rather than victims

(continued)

Table 4.1 (continued)

Instrument/Policy	Content
"Further Actions and Initiatives to Implement the Beijing Declaration and Platform for Action," UN DOC. A/RES/S-23/3, 16th November 2000, at Paragraph 70	Consider preventing, within the legal framework and in accordance with national policies, victims of trafficking, in particular women and girls, from being prosecuted for their illegal entry or residence, taking into account that they are victims of exploitation
European Union and African States, "Ouagadougou Action Plan to Combat Trafficking in Human Beings, Especially Women and Children," adopted by the Ministerial Conference on Migration and Development, 22–23 November 2006	Adopt specific measures to avoid criminalisation of victims of trafficking, as well as stigmatisation and the risk of re-victimisation
Organisation for Security and Co-operation in Europe (OSCE) Ministerial Council, "Declaration on Trafficking in Human Beings," OSCE Doc. MC(10). Jour/2, Annex II, 7th December 2002, at 3, Section II	We will strive to render assistance and protection to the victims of trafficking, especially women and children, and to this end, when appropriate, to establish effective and inclusive national referral mechanisms, ensuring that victims of trafficking do not face prosecution solely because they have been trafficked…
UNODC Model Law, Article 10	1. A victim of trafficking in persons shall not be held criminally or administratively liable [punished] [inappropriately incarcerated, fined or otherwise penalized] for offences [unlawful acts] committed by them, to the extent that such involvement is a direct consequence of their situation as trafficked persons
	2. A victim of trafficking in persons shall not be held criminally or administratively liable for immigration offences established under national law
	3. The provisions of this article shall be without prejudice to general defences available at law to the victim
	4. The provisions of this article shall not apply where the crime is of a particularly serious nature as defined under national law

Relation to Similar Provisions

The non-liability principle can be said to have joined a small albeit accepted family of provisions in international law that seek to provide an excuse for those who may have committed a wrong. Provisions once monopolised by national law, in particular criminal law, are now spilling out beyond; an example of this is Article 31(d) of the *Rome Statue*. The Article states that a person shall not be criminally responsible if, at the time of that person's conduct the crime was "caused by duress resulting from a threat of imminent death or of continuing or imminent serious bodily harm against that person or another person, and the person acts necessarily and reasonably to avoid this threat, provided that the person does not intend to cause a greater harm than the one sought to be avoided." The provision excludes liability as to crimes within the jurisdiction of the International Criminal Court, namely war crimes, crimes against humanity and genocide. Of course, this article will not be much help to victims of trafficking, for they are far more likely to be victims than perpetrators of the offences covered by the Rome Statue. However, it is interesting to note that Article 31(d) allows full exonerations, even in the case of the most serious crimes. When discussing the non-liability provision, particularly in the context of domestic law, arguments can be heard that the provision needs to be limited and ought not to provide protection to those who committed serious offences. In some way, echoing the philosophy of Blackstone (2007, 1447) who explicitly stated that a man under duress "ought rather to die himself, than escape by the murder of an innocent."

Recently, this is exemplified in Section 45 of the *Modern Slavery Act*, in England and Wales, which states that the defence for slavery or trafficking victims who commit an offence does not apply to an offence listed in Schedule 4. Schedule 4 is made up of 37 paragraphs and includes crimes such as robbery, burglary, manslaughter, murder, offences against the person (e.g. threats to kill, wounding with intent to cause grievous bodily harm, abandoning children), assisting unlawful immigration and sexual offences, to name but a few examples. *The Modern Slavery Act* and indeed many discussions around the non-liability provision do not reflect the ethos of Article 31(d) of the *Rome*

Statue, and whilst it may be a hard pill to swallow that one ought to be excused for committing a serious offence, it is now in fact the case that international allow makes allowances when one's autonomy is compromised. This follows the civil law approach, contrasted with the common law, where "the general theme of the civil law countries regarding duress is whether or not the free will of the actor has been overcome" (Risacher 2014: 1408).

It is also interesting to note that earlier in history the International Criminal Tribunal for the Former Yugoslavia took a different viewpoint. In the case of *Erdemovic* (1997), the Tribunal held (by a majority) that: "[D]uress does not afford a complete defence to a soldier charged with a crime against humanity and/or a war crime involving the killing of innocent human beings." Yet by the time of the *Rome Statue* of the International Criminal Court, which came into force in 2002, the perception had changed. Potentially showing the maturing of the general understanding of how a person's autonomy can be curbed and an acknowledgement that there is a possibility of a suppression of freedom and autonomy, thus affecting the *mens rea* of the culprit. However, apparently it is also true that the drafters spent little time on the matter. *N:B* The defence enclosed in the *Rome Statue* is not perfect (Risacher 2014), but it is an important recognition of the role that moral culpability plays.

Article 31(1) of Refugee Convention (1951) is another example of an international law provision on non-liability; it obliges member states not to impose penalties on refugees on account of their irregular presence. The provision reads: "The Contracting States shall not impose penalties, on account of their illegal entry or presence, on refugees who, coming directly from a territory where their life or freedom was threatened in the sense of article 1, enter or are present in their territory without authorisation, provided they present themselves without delay to the authorities and show good cause for their illegal entry or presence." As this Article is from 1951, it is one of the first international precedents of an obligation not to use domestic law to sanction individuals who have a special status and require protection. There is commonality between Article 31(1) of *Refugee Convention* and the non-liability provision as found in the European texts that are discussed in this book. For one, both form a key part of a wider commitment to protect the subjects and ensure they have access to their rights, in the case of the *Refugee Convention* that right concerns asylum. Secondly, both refugees and victims of trafficking are forced, by measures outside of their control, to undertake an act which is unlawful. Trafficked victims are compelled to commit crimes, whilst refugees are forced by a situation at home to undertake irregular journeys and illegal border crossings, which themselves are a product of the voluminous measures obstructing access to asylum. However, and this will be discussed in subsequent chapters, it is clear that Article 31(1) of *Refugee Convention* is stricter on states. Its language of "shall not impose penalties" makes a stark contrast again the weak wording of the European document which read that "Member States shall, in accordance with the basic principles of their legal systems, take the necessary measures to ensure…" The margin of appreciation afford in cases of victims of trafficking is far wider than when it comes to refugees.

Beyond the Refugee Convention and Rome Statue, there is another analogous notion, as found in the UN Smuggling Protocol at Article 5, which provides that migrants shall not become liable to criminal prosecution under this Protocol for the fact of having been the object of the conduct of smuggling.

Defences for Other Special Category Victims

Victims of human trafficking are not the only special category of subjects who are caught in the dichotomy of a victim-offender status. In this section, we look at two other victims: those in abusive relationships and child soldiers.

Comparison with Persons in Abusive Relationships

There are parallels to be drawn between victims of human trafficking and victims of domestic violence. Notions of voice, agency and blame are inherent to both groups. There are other similarities between the situation of trafficked persons and those trapped in abusive relationships: the experience of physical and/or psychological harm, intimidation, blackmail, exploitation, the feeling on entrapment without a way out. Both trafficked persons and victims of domestic abuse also experience a dichotomy of agency. In both cases, it would be wrong to say that they had no physical choice; rarely are they tied down. Rather it is a case that their choice is a product of the coerced situation they find themselves in. "Women abused by their partners are not usually physically restricted and prevented from leaving the home, but they are none the less controlled. They have limited access to money, to support networks – including family and friend, and they are threatened that if they try to leave they will be found and subjected to further, usually more serious violence" (Hoyle et al. 2011: 323). The same is true of trafficked persons.

There is also another overlap, committing an offence. Victims of human trafficking and those in an abusive relationship can experience a feeling of no choice, but to resort to a breach of the law. For victims of human trafficking, it may be an immigration offence, cultivating drugs or causing harm to their trafficker. For a person in an abusive relationship, this may be grievous bodily harm to their partner or even homicide. For both victims, relying on traditional defences has not always ended in a success. Consequently, securing fair outcomes for battered persons or victims of human trafficking who were compelled to commit a crime required an evolution beyond traditional defence law.

For those in abusive relationship, the revolution came with the Canadian case of *Lavalle* ([1990] 1 SCR 852)—where an abused woman shot her abusing partner—here, the law recognised the "battered woman syndrome" and the fact that victims may resort to a crime of violence instead of leaving a relationship. As summarised by Sheehy: "[F]irst, the Court held that the lack of 'imminent' harm posed by the threatened would no longer bar self-defence (*R v Lavallee [1990] 1 SCR 852*: 883). Second, the Court clarified that the right to self-defence does not impose a 'duty to retreat' before using lethal force (*R v Lavallee [1990] 1 SCR 852*: 890). Third, the Court ruled that 'Battered Women Syndrome' evidence may be used to dispel erroneous but widely held misconceptions about wife battering and to show the reasonableness of a women's beliefs regarding the danger she faced and her options (*R v Lavallee [1990] 1 SCR 852*: 890)" (Sheehy 2016: 82).

This judgement and subsequent battered woman rhetoric perfectly understand the ethos that also lies at the heart of the non-liability principle for trafficked persons. In the context of narratives that defy agency, we need more than the traditional defences for they do not accommodate the nuances surrounding these types of breaches of law. The compulsion experienced by trafficked persons and the coercion, fear and level of abuse felt by those in an abusive relationship cannot always be excused or justified by reference to, e.g., self-defence or duress. As rightly summarised by Clough (2016: 280) with regard to battered women: "[T]heir plight would mostly fall short of the rules of self-defence, because battered women who kill their abuser tend to act when no immediate physical threat is present. Diminished responsibility would deem them irrational beings, which is an erroneous label to apply to such situations."

Against this background, it is interesting to note the changes happening in legislation. For instance in Australia, Queensland created a partial defence for battered women who commit homicide for self-preservation, introduced by Criminal Code (Abusive Domestic Relationship Defence and Another Matter) Amendment Act 2010. In England and Wales, the debates around a defence of battered persons found some reflection in the *Coroners and Justice Act 2009*, where the defence of provocation has been transformed into a loss of control defence. "Up until this reform, the emphasis of the defence of provocation had been on anger leading a person to loose their control because of things said or done. Now, the emotion of fear as well as anger can be the basis for the new defence of loss of control. A key reason for introducing this reform was to achieve justice for battered women who killed their abusive partners" (Elliott 2015: 231).

Duress is often cited as the domestic law equivalent of the non-liability principle. However, it is problematic for victims of human trafficking on similar grounds for why it is challenging for battered persons. Duress in its multiple requirements includes showing that the threat was unavoidable, that there were no feasible alternatives. Pham's work is particularly interesting for the purpose of this book. In the context of the *Domestic Violence, Crime and Victims Act 2004*, she looks at why victims of domestic violence do not leave. A question that is often asked of trafficked persons, including those who are forced to commit crimes. She analyses the *Domestic Violence, Crime and Victims Act 2004* and S.5 of the act, which criminalised "causing or allowing the death or a child or vulnerable adult." In her argument Pham (2015: 9) notes that it is too simplistic to imagine that victims of domestic violence would leave their house or call the police when their violent partner kills a vulnerable member of their household. The same can be said of trafficked person. They may see no realistic alternative. Similar understanding of the difficulty in leaving needs to be extended to trafficked cases.

It is easy to expect victims to run away from their traffickers, but we must pay attention to how they perceive possibilities of running to safety. If they believe that on running away they will be deported or harmed by the authorities or that they will become injured due to a juju curse, then is it so realistic to expect them to runway? As highlighted by Schloenhardt and Markey-Towler (2016: 23): "traffickers tell their victims that the authorities will not assist victims, will punish them, and that officials are corrupt and cannot be trusted. These statements by the traffickers serve to frighten the victims and prevent them from making any attempts to escape." Like in cases of domestic violence, even though physically the victims may be able to escape, there may be an array of other reasons which means they do not. In addition, we have to also take into account that there may be practical obstacles, not knowing where they are, language barriers, lack of information sources and questions of how to survive economically. Furthermore, some victims may fear that the traffickers know where their families live and would harm them. The expectation of a realistic alternative may be alien to trafficked persons.

Child Soldiers

Child soldiers exhibit another example of a victim-offender intersection. Recruited through force, deceit or other means, they are also subjected to harmful substances and psychological and/or physical violence. They are then required to commit crimes, including the most heinous atrocities such as taking part in genocide. "The vulnerability of child soldier members of State and non-State armed forces that commit systematic grave IHL violations is manifest daily in the severely harsh treatment that these child soldiers endure during training and once engaged in the hostilities by their own side..." (Grover 2012: 88). To protect these children from prosecution, the *Rome Statute* of the International Criminal Court sets the minimum age of criminal culpability at 18; Article 26 states that the court shall have no jurisdiction over any person who was under the age of 18 at the time of the alleged commission of a crime. This follows a history of other courts, such as the ICTR, not investigating or prosecuting children despite the fact that many were detained on suspicion of participation in the Rwanda genocide. Article 26 as observed by Grover "obviates the necessity for each individual child defendant making out a case for his or her lack of culpability under Article 31 of the Rome Statute (concerning the defence of duress or in regards to the issue of the mental element of the crime). The latter fact highlights the point that the drafters of the Rome Statute did not wish to leave the outcome (whether or not a particular individual who perpetrated the international crime(s) when he or she was under age 18 would be found to have mounted a successful defence under Article 31 of the Rome Statute) to the vagaries of judicial process and the particularities of who constituted the judicial panel at each stage of the proceedings. Article 26 eliminated that concern by incorporating an age-based exclusion of ICC jurisdiction based in substantive principles of criminal law" (2012: 87).

Child soldiers, like trafficked persons, act under a level of compulsion. Their actions are not truly theirs. Child soldiers however have an additional reason for why they ought not to be held liable and that is the fact that their age obviates them from forming the necessary *mens rea*. In cases of the crime of genocide, it is argued that a child will not and cannot form the required intentions of eliminating part or all of an ethnic group.

This section aimed to show that child soldiers have their own unique pathway to non-liability with regard to crimes committed over which the *Rome Statue* has jurisdiction. However, it is important to note that the odious but widespread use of children as soldiers is in fact a manifestation of human trafficking. As the individuals in questions are children, they only need to fulfil two of the three elements of the trafficking

98 J. M. Muraszkiewicz

definitions: the act and the intent of exploitation, both which can always be established in cases of child soldiers.

Conclusion

In both domestic law and international law, we find provisions that protect individuals who although are victims also commit crimes. Child soldiers, refugees, those subjected to violence in a relationship often come to the attention of the authorities firstly as offenders. Yet, their experiences and vulnerabilities mean they should fall within the protective scope of the state's actions. Consequently, the law tries to refrain from perceiving them solely as an offender, which would erase their victimhood and thus access to the special rights and assistance they may need.

There are thus provisions examined in this chapter that protect a special category of persons (e.g. children) or persons who find themselves in particular circumstances (e.g. loss of control as in the case of those in abusive relationships). Since 2005, we can add to these legal provisions the non-liability principle for trafficked persons. The question afore us however is whether the protection contained in the European trafficking framework is efficient. We now turn this question.

Notes

1. Article 10 states:
   (1) A victim of trafficking in persons shall not be held criminally or administratively liable [punished] [inappropriately incarcerated, fined or otherwise penalised] for offences [unlawful acts] committed by them, to the extent that such involvement is a direct consequence of their situation as trafficked persons.
   (2) A victim of trafficking in persons shall not be held criminally or administratively liable for immigration offences established under national law.
   (3) The provisions of this article shall be without prejudice to general defences available at law to the victim.

(4)   The provisions of this article shall not apply where the crime is of a particularly serious nature as defined under national law.
2.   The term soft law regards normative instruments developed by states or intergovernmental organisations that lack full legal force.
3.   The author has volunteered for over 32 months in a safe house for victims of human trafficking in Manchester. In the course, she has met over 50 victims.

References

Amnesty International and Anti-slavery. (2004). *Memorandum on the Draft European Convention on Action Against Trafficking in Human Beings: Protection of the Rights of Trafficked Persons* [Online]. https://www.amnesty.org/download/Documents/96000/ior610112004en.pdf.
Blackstone, W. (2007). Commentaries on the Laws of England: In Four Books, Book 1. London: The Lawbook Exchange.
Clough, A. (2016). Battered Women: Loss of Control and Lost Opportunities. *Journal of International and Comparative Law, 3,* 279–316.
Council of Europe. (2005). *Explanatory Report on the Convention on Action Against Trafficking in Human Beings,* ETS 197, 16 May 2005.
Elliott, J. (2015). Victims or Criminals: The Example of Human Trafficking in the United Kingdom. In M. J. Guia (Ed.), *The Illegal Business of Human Trafficking.* Cham, Switzerland: Springer.
Gallagher, A. (2010). *The International Law of Human Trafficking.* New York: Cambridge University Press.
Grover, S. C. (2012). *Child Soldier Victims of Genocidal Forcible Transfer Exonerating Child Soldiers Charged with Grave Conflict-Related International Crimes.* Berlin and Heidelberg: Springer.
Hoshi, B. (2013). The Trafficking Defence: A Proposed Model for the Non-criminalisation of Trafficked Persons in International Law. *Groningen Journal of International Law, 1*(2), 54–72.
Hoyle, C., Bosworth, M., & Dempsey, M. (2011). Labelling the Victims of Sex Trafficking: Exploring the Borderland Between Rhetoric and Reality. *Social & Legal Studies, 20*(3), 313–329.
Pham, J. (2015). *Protecting Trafficking Victims from Porsecution: Analysis of the Modern Slavery Bill Defence* [Online]. http://files.magdalenecambridge.com/pdfs/Publications/peter_peckard_prize_jp_july_2015.pdf.

Piotrowicz, R. W., & Sorrentino, L. (2016). Human Trafficking and the Emergence of the Non-punishment Principle. *Human Rights Law Review, 16*(4), 669–699.

Risacher, B. J. (2014). No Excuse: The Failure of the ICC's Article 31 "Duress" Definition. *Notre Dame Law Review, 89,* 1403–1426.

Schloenhardt, A., & Markey-Towler, R. (2016). Non-criminalisation of Victims of Trafficking in Persons—Principles, Promises, and Perspectives. *Groningen Journal of International Law, 4*(1), 10–38.

Sheehy, E. (2016). Defending Battered Women in the Public Sphere. *Crime, Justice and Social Democracy, 5*(2), 81–95.

5

Dissecting Article 26 of the 2005 Council of Europe Convention

Introduction

There is no shortage of victim rights advocates amongst scholars and NGOs defining how best to offer trafficked persons a holistic protection mechanism. Yet legislations, particularly regional ones, balance such recommendations with state sovereignty and diverse legal traditions and practices. These and other factors, e.g. philosophical differences in state legal traditions, can explain a regional legislator's hesitation to fully implement the recommendations of NGOs and other stakeholders into law. There is thus a hypothesis put forward in this book that because of this balancing exercise, victim rights might be thwarted.

This chapter undertakes a summative evaluation of Article 26 of the *2005 Council of Europe Convention on Action Against Trafficking in Human Beings*. In particular, the aim is to increase our knowledge on what the Article means and what it asks of states. Not complying with the non-liability provision could be argued as a violation of human rights and a violation of regional law. It is thus in the interest of states to comply. At the same time however, states may intend to minimise their obligations and an unclear legal provision gives them the ability to

© The Author(s) 2019
J. M. Muraszkiewicz, *Protecting Victims of Human Trafficking From Liability*, Palgrave
Studies in Victims and Victimology, https://doi.org/10.1007/978-3-030-02659-2_5

do this. As Gallagher (2009: 793) writes with regard to the definition of human trafficking: "as long as the law remained unclear, they [the states] could keep arguing about it; as long as the law remained unclear, they would not be brought to task for failing to uphold it." Thus, this and the subsequent chapter begin from a premise that a failure to understand the substantive matter of the provision can influence the ability to hold states accountable to the obligations contained thereto. In reality, there is a lack of understanding of the law, thus the need for inquisition. As such, a justification for the analysis, in addition to ensuring that trafficked persons are protected, is rooted in a one's desire for clarity.

Equally, this chapter also begins consideration whether the protection offered to the victims is likely to be effective, and thus in line with the overall aim of the *2005 Council of Europe Convention on Action Against Trafficking in Human Beings*, which is "to protect the human rights of the victims of trafficking, design a comprehensive framework for the protection and assistance of victims and witnesses, while guaranteeing gender equality, as well as to ensure effective investigation and prosecution" (Article 1). This aim, which applies to all elemements of the Convention, allows us to extract indicators to judge whether the provision (Article 26) is effective. In other words, Article 1 concretises the legal requirements, which we can resort to, when assessing Article 26 on non-punishment of trafficked persons. The requirements are: ensuring the safeguard of human rights of victims and protecting gender equality. Enabling the preventing of human trafficking by undertaking effective investigations is not used as a benchmark for reasons explained in previous chapters. When evaluating the fulfilment of these requirements, expert opinions are taken into account, and we can undertake comparative exercises, e.g., with similar provisions of soft law discussed in chapter 4 or with Article 8 of the *Directive 2011/36 on preventing and combating trafficking in human beings and protecting its victims* (discussed at length in chapter 6 but also referred to here). The conclusions on whether the Article is effective will be drawn in the subsequent chapters, after Article 8 is dissected.

As a reminder, Article 26 of the *2005 Council of Europe Convention on Action Against Trafficking in Human Beings* reads: "Each Party shall, in accordance with the basic principles of its legal system, provide for the possibility of not imposing penalties on victims for their involvement in unlawful activities, to the extent that they have been compelled to do so."

First Component of Article 26: "Each Party Shall, in Accordance with the Basic Principles of Their Legal System…"

The Article begins with an unsurprising nod to state sovereignty: "Each Party shall, in accordance with the basic principles of their legal system…." In essence, this wording means that the provision is written "in nonbinding terms, and therefore ratifying states can decide exactly how they wish to proceed on this particular matter" (Elliott 2015: 109). States will thus make choices on how the obligation is transposed, e.g. through relying on the existing defence law, implementing a new specific defence clause or by publishing a guide to prosecutors.

Why is this unsurprising? Because the provision predominantly concerns criminal law, which historically is seen as a domain over which solely states have authority. Traditionally, domestic criminal law imitates the specific interests of the state and what is deemed as deserving protection and punishment coupled with being a tool to respond to a nation's psychological make-up, i.e. fears and emotions. In brief, criminal law is deeply rooted in a nation's character. The wording of Article 26, and indeed Article 8 of the *Directive 2011/36 on preventing and combating trafficking in human beings and protecting its victims*, appreciates that states have different legal systems and will have distinctive methods of dealing with culpability and protecting trafficked persons. The Articles specify the end result to be achieved but not the means. Consequently, there is a broad discretion for member states as to how to enforce Article 26, which can, incidentally, have negative effects on harmonising the approach across Europe. It can also make for a difficult cooperative playing field.

Could the Article have been more robust in specifying the methodology that states should use? A strict guideline may have caused conflict with national legislation. This is especially true as the prosecution system is so varied across states. As summarised by Tak (date unknown): "Prosecution agencies do not have similar organisational structures and are not vested with identical prosecutorial powers and tasks. Moreover, the place of the prosecution services in the constitutional state organisation differs considerably." There are states that apply the legality principle where all offences that come to the attention of the state must be prosecuted. Kyprianou (2010: 33) summarised the legality principle and notes that it: "commands that every case in which there is enough evidence and in which no legal hindrances prohibit prosecution has to be brought to court. Adherence to the legality principle in the procedural sense means that the prosecution service cannot exercise any discretion over the prosecutorial decision." Poland provides an example of a country with a strict tradition of the principle of legality; the prosecuting authority has "neither the discretion to drop a case nor the ability to impose conditions / sanctions upon an offender; in accordance with a strict principle of legality the prosecuting authority merely has the function of preparing a case for court" (Jehle et al. 2006: 21). In countries like Belgium or France, the principle of opportunity governs prosecution. This means that the state may refrain from prosecution if the general interest entails it to do that. According to Hirsch Ballin (2012: 42), prosecution may be determined to serve the public interest when "considering the nature of the crime, it will be obvious that a prosecution serves the public interest or when policy guidelines and/or general directions prescribe that prosecuting a particular type of offence is indicated." For Sanders (1996: xi), systems that adhere to the opportunity principle "allow enforcement agencies almost unfettered discretion over whether or not to prosecute, which allows prosecutors to take account of factors other than evidence in making their decisions." Under the principle of opportunity not every offence in respect of which there is evidence that the individual is guilty must go before the court. Instead, the prosecution may at times decide that no action is better due to a number of factors such as, but not limited to: public interest, the victim, resources and the nature of the offence.

An interesting question regards the impact that the specific legal system, legality principle v. opportunity principle, has on the enforcement of Article 26 of the *2005 Council of Europe Convention on Action Against Trafficking in Human Beings*, or equally Article 8 of *Directive 2011/36 on preventing and combating trafficking in human beings and protecting its victims*. In this regard, there is little case law or literature that directly relates to this issue. However, on analysing broader works we can find that, on the one hand, the opportunity principle may offer more protection to victims as it "allows the prosecution service discretion over the prosecutorial decision, even when proof exists as to the occurrence of the criminal offence and the identity of the offender, and when there is no legal hindrance bar proceeding with the matter" (Tak, date unknown: 53). In comparison, under the principle of legality a trafficked person who committed an offence should be prosecuted. This is because the role of the prosecuting body is limited to legal assessment of the sufficiency of the evidence against the suspect.[1]

On the other hand, states where there is already a wide prosecution discretion may maintain that they do not have to take additional steps to implement Article 26 of the Convention or Article 8 of the 2011 EU Human Trafficking Directive. In turn, this could be to the detriment of trafficked persons. As Stoyanova (2015: 240) highlights "in these legal systems, however, the prosecutor might not necessarily be duty bound to withdraw the case or else see to that the trafficked person is acquitted." Furthermore, because of the reliance on discretion, there is no indication to the trafficked persons that they can "exit their trafficking situation and freely cooperate with law enforcement agencies without fear. Discretionary non-prosecution and non-punishment may give many victims too little certainty that they will be believed and not face consequences for offences they had to commit" (Schloenhardt and Markey-Towler 2016: 33). Finland, for example, communicated, with respect to the EU Directive, that: "Legislative amendments are not considered necessary based on Article 8 of the Directive as competent national authorities are entitled not to prosecute or impose penalties on victims of trafficking in human beings within the framework of the legislation in force. There are general provisions on possibilities for judges and prosecutors not to convict or prosecute a person if they do not consider it appropriate in a specific case" (European Commission 2012). Accordingly, by relying on the flexibility of the opportunity principle and not taking active steps to transpose the non-liability principle into national legislations, states will not actively be considering the content of the articles. In contrast, states that follow the legality principle may acknowledge that without special provisions their prosecutors will have little choice but to prosecute trafficked persons. This in turn may lead them to adopt special legislative measures or take other active steps to protect trafficked persons. Spain, for example, adheres to the principle of legality, and indeed, it has adopted the following provision in Article 177 paragraph 11 of its Criminal Code:

> …victims of trafficking in human beings shall be exempt from punishment for the criminal offences that might have been committed while suffering exploitation, as long as participation therein has been a direct consequence of the situation of violence, intimidation, deceit or abuse to which they may have been subjected to and provided there is an adequate proportionality between that situation and the criminal act perpetrated.

What conclusions can we draw from this section? States will transpose Article 26 of the *2005 Council of Europe Convention on Action Against Trafficking in Human Beings* (or Article 8 of the *Directive 2011/36 on preventing and combating trafficking in human beings and protecting its victims*) in accordance with the basic principle of their legal systems. In turn, this means that regional law does not in fact determine the level of protection afforded to trafficked persons. The law only gets us as far as understanding what it is that is to be protected.

It already here becomes questionable whether the Convention's aim of safeguarding human rights is truly met, this is because the obligation seems low. What therefore is very significant is national criminal systems and understanding how states transpose the obligations. For where law allows discretion, as in this case, states will take that discretion at times to the detriment of the rights of victims. Consequently, what additionally matters is for the regional bodies to foster discussion around the topic, spread best practice and engage in monitoring.

Second Component of Article 26: "Provide for the Possibility..."

The provision obliges states to provide for the possibility of not imposing penalties. This author has a problem with such phraseology. Interpreting the wording in good faith in accordance with the ordinary meaning to be given to the terms, one must logically arrive at the conclusion that it will be enough for states to ensure that somewhere in the law there is a provision or there is a policy that will allow relevant authorities not to execute a punishment. Whether such a punishment is executed or not is not, on such a reading, the main focus of the Convention. In other words, there is no concrete responsibility placed on the authorities to consider whether a trafficked person involved in unlawful activities was compelled to do so, and if so not to punish them. As summarised by Hoshi (2013: 59): "non-punishment is not an imperative requirement." Lasocik (2013: 11) also states that the wording is more of a suggestion to the authorities rather than a positive duty. Consequently, where domestic law does not provide any mechanism or possibility for not imposing a penalty, only then does incompatibility with Article 26 arise. Such a lack of trasnposition will not however be found, for all European criminal justice systems have some form of existing defences that they could argue as fulfilling the requirements, e.g. duress or necessity. There is always a possibility. Yet, these defences are not effective protectors for compelled trafficked persons (discussed later in this book), but technically they fulfil the requirements of Article 26.

The drafters of the Convention, being pioneers in this field, had a chance to truly protect trafficked persons from liability; however, they reverted to a general formulation, perhaps even a safe one with using the word "possibility." The same we will see with respect to Article 8 of *Directive 2011/36 on preventing and combating trafficking in human beings and protecting its victims.* The choice of language was probably invoked to pacify state's worries that any stronger wording would equate to immunity from prosecution. This of course is unreasonable, and this book will in its conclusion make suggestions for alternative versions of the non-liability provision that are more demanding without granting immunity.

For now, it is suggested that greater protection could have been afforded to trafficked persons by using wording such as that contained in the already mentioned Article 31(1) of Refugee Convention, namely "States shall not impose penalties…." Alternatively, the Convention and subsequent *Directive 2011/36 on preventing and combating trafficking in human beings and protecting its victims* could have followed the UN Model Law against Trafficking in Persons (Article 10) which states: "trafficked persons shall not be detained, charged or prosecuted…." If further security against immunity was needed, the wording suggested by Amnesty International and Anti-slavery International (2005) could have been considered: "trafficked persons are not detained, charged or prosecuted for illegal entry or residence and unlawful activities, **unless it is shown that the unlawful activities were not a consequence of their situation as a victim**" [emphasis added].

Third Component of Article 26: "Of Not Imposing Penalties"

The first thing to note about the phrasing "of not imposing penalties…" is that the principle focuses on penalties and does not include prosecution. This in stark contrast to the later version of the principle contained in Article 8 of *Directive 2011/36 on preventing and combating trafficking in human beings and protecting its victims*, as will be seen in the subsequent chapter.

How can we understand the term penalties? In accordance with general principles of interpretation, penalties can include a wide variety of punishments: cautions, fines, administrative detention and imprisonment. There are many others. For victims who are forced to commit immigration offences—for human trafficking often occurs within the regulated context of migration, which is controlled by provisions of immigration law—we can also add to the list prohibition of re-entry to a state, deportation and an expulsion order. With punishments such as deportations, it is worth recalling the principle of refoulement, which is the forcible return of refugees or asylum seekers to a country where his or her life would be threatened. This right constitutes one of the basic Articles of the 1951 UN Refugee Convention, to which no reservations are permitted. In an instance where a trafficked person who is a refugee or qualifies for subsidiary protection is forcibly returned, his or her human rights are abused.

By focusing on penalties, and not prosecution, the Convention's attention is on the later stages of criminal law; it thus primarily concerns judges and similar figures, for they are most often the ones dealing with penalties. Such a focus is damaging, and against the ethos of protecting the human rights of trafficked persons (as per Article 1 of the Convention) for, in theory, it does not stop the prosecutor (or equivalent body where the matter is outside of criminal justice) from conducting a trial. Non-punishment will thus be something for the defence team to argue for during trial. The victim must thus endure a full trial, which may lead to secondary victimisation. Secondary victimisation would be evoked through the trauma that a victim may face when re-living the trafficking experiences during trial. Re-experiencing the event in the form of repeated memories, thoughts and reflections brought on by questioning. This can create a level of opprobrium, damage a person's character and physical well-being. Secondary victimisation deepens the effects of primary victimisation.

For Hoshi, the full principle of non-liability should include non-prosecution, as only then it prevents the exacerbated traumatisation of a victim when treated as criminal (Hoshi 2013). He notes that: "minimally, the process of criminalisation is likely to involve being arrested and interviewed by law enforcement officers, at least one court appearance, some form of penalty and the imposition of a permanent criminal record. Maximally, it may additionally involve pre-trial detention, a series of court appearances including an extended trial, which would probably require the trafficked person to give evidence (including cross-examination of their claim of being at trafficked person) and a lengthy sentence of imprisonment. Each stage of the process of criminalisation disempowers and re-traumatises trafficked persons and, fundamentally, fails to recognise that they themselves are victims of crime" (Hoshi 2013: 54). In addition, we can add to that that the social stigma attached to being a defendant in a trial, even if proven innocent, can taint victims of trafficking for a long period thereafter, if not for life. It is thus imperative that if a law truly wishes to protect trafficked persons and safeguard their human rights, it ought to protect them from prosecution (or the equivalent). On balance, allowing a trafficked person to go through a trial shows a lack of understanding and diminishes the availability of support and as a result leads to secondary victimisation, i.e. when the victim is suffering again, this time at the hands of the state.

Some, like Piotrowicz and Sorrentino (Piotrowicz and Sorrentino 2016: 681), may claim that a "[f]ull application of the non-punishment principle means that, ideally, no prosecution should be initiated or other punitive measure taken. If a prosecution has commenced, it should be disconnected as soon as possible; other measures and/or penalties should be cancelled once it is evident that the offence was committed in the course, or as a consequence, of being trafficked." Whilst Piotrowicz and Sorrentino's position is favourable, it risks being too idealistic. For we must remember that the law, in particular criminal law, is such a serious matter, that it requires great caution, and rules are rarely applied by analogy. Instead, many abide by strict constructionism. In turn, on a strict reading of the wording we have little choice but to understand Article 26 of the *2005 Council of Europe Convention on Action Against Trafficking in Human Beings* as solely concerning punishment and being silent on prosecution or commencing a trial. This has been supported by other academics, such as Hoshi (2013: 59): "Three features of this provision are problematic. First, it provides only for the non-punishment of trafficked persons; the prosecution of such persons is not prohibited...." Consequently, if a relevant authority decides that it is in the public interest to go forth with a hearing/prosecution, the victim is not shielded against the re-traumatisation and long-lasting damage that the hearing may entail. The reference to only penalisation is thus an adverse omission in the system of protections for trafficked persons, a central aim of the Convention.

Fourth Component of Article 26: "On Victims..."

Article 26 provides that there will be a possibility of not imposing penalties on victims for their involvement in unlawful activities, to the extent that they have been compelled to do so. In this section, we focus on who is the subject of this provision, victims.

A victim of human trafficking is defined in Article 4(e) of the 2005 Convention as "any natural person who is subject to trafficking in human beings as defined in this article." Thus, the scope of who is a victim is as wide as the definition of human trafficking, which as shown in previous chapters covers a range of eventualities, from trafficking for the purpose of sexual exploitation to trafficking for the purpose of forced labour. Moreover, as human trafficking is a crime of intent, for one to be clarified as a victim one does not have to in fact endure exploitation.

This definition of a victim is however somewhat vague; it does not state whether to be a classified as a victim one needs to be formally recognised as such by competent authorities. It therefore remains ambiguous when the right to non-punishment is triggered. Is it when one is a presumed victim or only once he/she has been formally identified and received the victim status, e.g., in the UK this is when one receives a conclusive ground decision. Stoyanova (2015: 227) suggests that the rights are only enforceable upon formal recognition "since wherever the Convention extends benefits to presumed victims, this is made explicit in the text of the treaty itself. Accordingly, only victims who have been formally identified can benefit from non-punishment." An illustration of her point is Article 10(2) of the 2005 Convention, which states that if the competent authorities have reasonable grounds to believe that a person has been victim of trafficking in human beings, that person shall not be removed from its territory until the identification procedure has been concluded. Of note however is Article 13, which states that each party shall provide in its internal law a recovery and reflection period of at least 30 days, when there are reasonable grounds to believe that the person concerned is a victim. Thus, if a presumed victim—i.e. when there are reasonable grounds to believe that one is a victim—is entitled to a reflection period, it would be very counterproductive to that reflection period to permit the punishment of such persons. It thus follows that a proper application of Article 26 of the 2005 Convention ought to be extended to individuals from when there is a reasonable ground to believe that they are victims.

Yet without doubt Article 26 relies on some form of recognition of the victim. At this juncture, we face possible hurdles when it comes to protecting gender equality. As chapter 7 will show, traditionally more women are recognised and then formally identified as victims of human trafficking. This is because of the existing stereotypes of who is a victim (a frail female forced into sex work) combined with insufficient training and lack of adequate inspections. Thus, males, e.g. who can be victims of trafficking for forced labour as well as sexual exploitation, are often not recognised. This impacts their opportunity to benefit from the non-punishment provision. Elliott (2015: 113) writes that: "the identification of victims and the criminalisation of victims are intrinsically linked i.e. if a trafficked victim is not identified as such (or even as a putative trafficked victim) then the corollary is that they may well be subject to criminal sanction due to the commission of offences as a direct result of the trafficking situation. The identification point is essential, as there is the potential for wealth of difference in treatment between a trafficked victim who has committed offences, and the offender who may be viewed as just another smuggled migrant."

In conclusion of this subsection, Article 26 is abstruse as to who exactly it applies to. Is it for recognised victims or only for those officially identified? Reading it in conjunction with other provisions found in the Convention allows us to adopt a broader reading. At the same time, it is without doubt that the actual application and use of the provision—and thus the true protection of human rights—is dependent on a competent authority recognising a person as a potential victim.

Fifth Component of Article 26: "...for Their Involvement in Unlawful Activities, to the Extent That They Have Been Compelled to Do So"

Moving onto the next part of the Article: "for their involvement in unlawful activities...." Such a wording ensures that the focus is not simply reduced to the area of criminal law. As summarised by Stoyanova (2015: 246) "even measures beyond the boundaries of the national criminal legislation could be considered within its framework." As will be seen in the subsequent chapter, this is in stark contrast with the 2011 EU Directive which only addresses the victims' involvement in criminal activities. By having such a broad scope, the 2005 Convention does a better job at ensuring the safeguard of human rights of all victims. A sole reference to criminal law (like in the case of the EU Directive) leaves trafficked persons unaware of the consequences of wrongful acts committed outside of the criminal justice system and potentially leaves them outside the sphere of protection.

These unlawful activities have to however be committed as a result of compulsion. In comparison with Article 8 of the *Directive 2011/36 on preventing and combating trafficking in human beings and protecting its victims*, it is noted that compulsion is not explicitly linked to the human trafficking experience. This is surprising for it could be read that any victim of human trafficking who experience compulsion, even outside of their trafficking experience, is entitled to protection. This would be too broad of an obligation for many states to swallow. In any case, such a reading is wrong. This is made clear by reference to the Explanatory Report (2005: para. 273), which states: "...the requirement that victims have been compelled to be involved in unlawful activities shall be understood as comprising, at a minimum, victims that have been subject to any of the illicit means referred to in Article 4." There is an established relationship between the trafficking definition, the trafficking occurrence and the non-punishment principle. "It could therefore be argued that although not explicitly stated, the CoE [Council of

Europe] Trafficking Convention assumes that the source of compulsion is related to the trafficking" (Stoyanova 2015: 231).

However, what is compulsion? Law enforcement authorities and policy makers will want to know at what point it is necessary to refrain from punishing a person. The search for the parameters of compulsion is thus important and inevitably should focus on the effect on someone's autonomy. In other words, the ability of an individual to make choices rooted in personal liberty (freedom from controlling influences) and agency (ability for deliberate action). As shown in earlier chapters, much of the justification for the principle in question hinges on capability and responsibility. This law understands the frailty of human nature, and our moral weakness is such that we can be compelled into wrongdoing.

In the context of human trafficking, it is possible to agree that compulsion is a prima facie wrong. When a victim is compelled to commit a crime, they are the subjects of someone's command. There could also be a temptation to equate compulsion with coercion, especially as the trafficking definition refers to coercion. Van der Rijt (2012: 6) writes about coercion and notes that: "though many (according to some, even all) cases of coercion involve a genuine choice made by the coerced, the context of that choice has been deliberately manipulated by someone else to ensure that the 'correct' choice is made." This seems to be aligned with what happens to victims of human trafficking. On compulsion, Leiser (2008: 33) writes: "one who is compelled to act in a certain way has no choice, but because of some physical or psychological force over which he has no control, must behave as he does." There is an obvious similarly in the two terms. Nevertheless, despite some undeniable overlaps, compulsion and coercion are not one and the same. We must therefore separate the two and precisely understand the word used within both Article 26 of the Convention and Article 8 in the EU Directive. The word compel is rather infrequent within European criminal discourse and more used as a term of court power to make an individual give evidence or be subjected to an examination. Interestingly, in New Zealand or South Africa compulsion is more common and is more analogous to what the principle in questions is striving to achieve (Burchell 2011: 455–487).

In undertaking our scrutiny of the term, we can begin with a dictionary reference. The Oxford dictionary defines compel as: "to force or oblige (someone) to do something." In contrast, coerce is defined as: "to persuade (an unwilling person) to do something by using force or threats." The inclusion of "oblige" in the definition of compel gives it a lesser threshold than coercion. It could thus be interpreted that by using compelled rather than coerced, the European legislators designed a broader principle. The OSCE (2013: 12) makes a comparable case and states that compulsion includes: "the full array of factual circumstances in which victims of trafficking lose the possibility to act with free will; not only under threat of physical violence or emotional abuse, but also in the devastatingly prevalent scenarios wherein traffickers exploit victims by abuse of a position of vulnerability."

In understanding the full meaning of compulsion, we come back to the trafficking definition—as referred to above by the Explanatory Report—and note that compulsion can be established when some of the means provided in the trafficking definition are used against the victim to get him/her to commit an unlawful activity. The UK Law Society (2015) practice note adopted a similar interpretation of compulsion: "in considering whether a trafficked victim has been compelled to commit a crime, prosecutors should consider whether any of the means has been employed so that the victim has effectively lost the ability to consent to his / her actions or to act with free will." This broad understanding seems fair, for it is not just harm or threat of harm that can make a person do things. Emotions, vulnerabilities and deceptions all shape a person's behaviour and will affect criminal responsibility. Compulsion can therefore be a psychological act; the trafficker can take advantage of a psychological vulnerability, which frustrates the trafficked victim's ability to reason effectively. That vulnerability may branch from poverty, socio or economic difficulties, fear, isolation, lack of knowledge, to name just some examples.

Understandably, "some states might find it unacceptable that individuals are not criminally punished because, say, they have been deceived or their position of vulnerability has been abused" (Stoyanova 2015: 234). Such an approach would lead national authorities to interpret compulsion narrowly. For instance, they may take it to require physical harm of a threat to one's life. This however is contrary to the intention of the European legislators, who purposely used the word "compelled." In parallel, this book will in later chapters argue that reference to the defence of duress is not a true reflection of the non-liability principle for it is too narrow. As stated above, the purpose of the non-punishment provision is to increase the protection offered to trafficked persons and secure their human rights in a non-discriminative manner. Undeniably, interpreting "compulsion" broadly is more in line with a human rights-based approach. Central to utilising compulsion is thus an understanding of the "means" and "exploitation" element. Yet, as highlighted in chapter 1, these concepts themselves are not free from ambiguities, and thus difficulties will undoubtedly arise.

Missing Element: Children

As was highlighted in chapter 1, a child can be trafficked without the presence of the action element. This was summarised in a UN Office on Drugs and Crime report (2009): "Even if a child is not threatened, no force is used against him or her, or he or she is not coerced, abducted or deceived, the child cannot give consent to the act of trafficking for the purpose of exploitation." Article 26, which relies on compulsion, makes no mention of a child victim who has committed a criminal offence. However, noting the particular vulnerability of children in trafficking situations a law on non-liability should specifically address minors. In May 2016, the EU Observer (an independent online newspaper) reported that the EU is struggling with the increase in number of children trafficked. Moreover: "Denmark, Lithuania, Sweden, and Slovakia have all reported an increase in children forced into committing crimes." The UN Principles and Guidelines on Human Rights and Trafficking (2010: 137) state that "[a] critical source of vulnerability for children lies in their lack of full standing – as a matter of act as well as in law. A lack of agency is often made worse by the absence of a parent or legal guardian who is able to act in the child's best interests. Such absence is typical in trafficking cases, since the deliberate separation of children from parents or guardians is a common strategy for facilitating exploitation." Children can be more vulnerable than adults, and so the obligation to protect them is particularly stark. We cannot dispute the centrality of the needs and rights of children, including protection from the state from prosecuting or punishing them for crimes they were compelled to commit as part of their trafficking situation. It follows that prosecution bodies should not question a child's capacity to avoid conducting criminal activities. Consequently, UNICEF (2006) advises that "[t]he judicial authorities shall ensure that child victims are not subjected to criminal procedures or sanctions for offences related to their situation as trafficked persons including violations of migrations laws." The argument is also brought forth by the OSCE report (2013: 20): "[h]ence, when non-punishment provisions are being applied to the case of a child, States should adopt a broad, not literal, interpretation of the word "compelled" which appears in both Article 26 of the Council of Europe Convention and Article 8 of the EU Directive on trafficking. This would involve a consideration of whether the offence committed by the child was related to the trafficking. In cases where this link is present, the prosecution should not be brought or it should be discontinued at an early stage or an appeal against conviction should be allowed."

It is argued in this book that both Article 26 of the Convention and Article 8 of the Directive missed an important opportunity to specifically address trafficked children who are made to commit crimes.

Conclusion

Having been recognised as a victim of human trafficking and proved that one was compelled to commit an unlawful activity, under Article 26 of the *2005 Council of Europe Convention on Action Against Trafficking in Human Beings* a person falls within the scope of the non-punishment protection. The Convention is silent on the nexus between the unlawful activity and the human trafficking experience. Or to put differently is does not tell states when that compulsion ought to have happened and by whom. Potentially, the victim does not therefore need to prove that the activity was directly linked to the human trafficking, e.g. was part of the exploitation. In theory, a victim who escaped their trafficker but still out of fear of their perpetrator committed a crime could benefit from protection. In reality, and because the provision is implemented within the basic principles of a state's legal system the situation may look different. The discussion on the nexus is important; however, we defer this to the subsequent chapter, for contrastingly *Directive 2011/36 on preventing and combating trafficking in human beings and protecting its victims* makes a clear reference to the nexus.

Note

1. Nonetheless, despite the theoretical contrast the practicalities can look different. Kyprianou (2010: 34) writes that "these days most of those [States] traditionally regarded as legality systems, especially due to rising caseloads and scarce resources, allow the prosecutors to also take into account other reasons apart from evidential ones when deciding to prosecute or drop a case." Jörg-Martin (2006: 24) supports this and concludes that: "There is almost no country in Europe which follows the principle of legality without any exception. Almost nowhere are all criminal offenders prosecuted in order to be convicted by a court. Mostly one finds either diversion from the criminal justice system or discretion at police and/or prosecution service level." Germany, traditionally associated with the *legality principle*, introduced a statutory basis for discretionary non-prosecution under § 153 German Code of Criminal Procedure, so that the authorities could cope with the rising caseload. Notwithstanding, the court's consent is essential in gaining approval for dismissal of cases that regard certain kinds of offences. In addition, only a very small numbers of senior decision-makers are empowered to take the most serious decisions.

References

Amnesty International and Anti-slavery. (2005). *Council of Europe: Don't Compromise on the Rights of Trafficked Persons* [Online]. https://www.amnesty.org/download/Documents/80000/act840052005en.pdf.

Burchell, J. (2011). South Africa. In K. J. Heller & M. D. Dubber (Eds.), *The Handbook of Comparative Criminal Law*. Stanford, CA: Stanford Law Books.

Council of Europe. (2005). *Explanatory Report on the Convention on Action Against Trafficking in Human Beings*, ETS 197, 16 May 2005.

Elliott, J. (2015). Victims or Criminals: The Example of Human Trafficking in the United Kingdom. In M. J. Guia (Ed.), *The Illegal Business of Human Trafficking*. Cham, Switzerland: Springer.

European Commission. (2012). *Ad-hoc Query on Transposition of Article 8 of Directive 2011/36/EU* [Online]. http://emn.ee/wp-content/uploads/2016/02/433_emn_ad-hoc_query_on_transposition_of_article_8_of_directive_2011-36_widerd_en.pdf.

EU Observer. (2016). *Child Trafficking in EU on the Rise* [Online]. https://euobserver.com/justice/133482.

Gallagher, A. (2009). Human Rights and Human Trafficking: Quagmire or Firm Ground? A response to James Hathaway. *Virginia Journal of International Law, 49*(4), 789–848.

Hirsch Ballin, M. F. H. (2012). *Anticipative Criminal Investigation: Theory and Counterterrorism Practice in the Netherlands and the United States*. The Hague: Asser Press.

Hoshi, B. (2013). The Trafficking Defence: A Proposed Model for the Non-criminalisation of Trafficked Persons in International Law. *Copyright Groningen Journal of International Law, 1*(2), 54–72.

Jehle, J.-M., Wade, M., Aubusson de Cavarlay, B., & Fritz Thyssen-Stiftung. (2006). *Coping with Overloaded Criminal Justice Systems: The Rise of Prosecutorial Power Across Europe*. Berlin and Heidelberg: Springer.

Jörg-Martin, J. (2006). The Function of Public Prosecution within the Criminal Justice System Aim, Approach and Outcome of a European Comparative Study. In J. Jörg-Martin & M. Wade. (Eds.), *Coping with Overloaded Criminal Justice Systems*. New York: Springer.

Kyprianou, D. (2010). *The Role of the Cyprus Attorney General's Office in Prosecutions: Rhetoric, Ideology and Practice*. Berlin and Heidelberg: Springer.

Lasocik, Z. (2013). *Niekaralność ofiar handle ludźmi – wstepna diagnoza problem*. Warsaw: Warsaw University.

Leiser, B. M. (2008). On Coercion. In D. Reidy & W. Riker (Eds.), *Coercion and the State*. New York: Springer.

OHCHR. (2010). *Recommended Principles and Guidelines on Human Rights and Human Trafficking*. Geneva: OHCHR [Online]. http://www.ohchr.org/Documents/Publications/Traffickingen.pdf.

OSCE Office of the Special Representative and Co-ordinator for Combating Trafficking in Human Beings. (2013). *Policy and Legislative Recommendations Towards the Effective Implementation of the Non-punishment Provision with Regard to Victims of Trafficking.* Vienna [Online]. http://www.osce.org/secretariat/101002?download=true.

Oxford Dictionaries [Online]. http://www.oxforddictionaries.com/definition/english/compel?q=compELLED.

Oxford Dictionaries [Online]. http://www.oxforddictionaries.com/definition/english/coerce?q=coerced.

Piotrowicz, R. W., & Sorrentino, L. (2016). Human Trafficking and the Emergence of the Non-punishment Principle. *Human Rights Law Review, 16*(4), 669–699.

Sanders, A. (1996). Introduction. In A. Sanders (Ed.), *Prosecution in Common Law Jurisdictions.* Aldershot: Dartmouth.

Schloenhardt, A., & Markey-Towler, R. (2016). Non-criminalisation of Victims of Trafficking in Persons—Principles, Promises and Perspectives. *Groningen Journal of International Law, 4*(1), 10–38.

Stoyanova, V. (2015). *Human Trafficking and Slavery Reconsidered: Conceptual Limits and States' Positive Obligations.* Lund: Lund University.

Tak, J. P. (Date Unknown). *Methods of Diversion Used by the Prosecution Services in the Netherlands and Other Western European Countries* [Online] http://www.unafei.or.jp/english/pdf/RS_No74/No74_07VE_Tak.pdf.

The Law Society. (2015). *Criminal Prosecutions of Victims of Trafficking* [Online]. http://www.lawsociety.org.uk/support-services/advice/practice-notes/criminal-prosecutions-of-victims-of-trafficking/.

United Nations Children's Fund (UNICEF). (2006). *Guidelines on the Protection of Child Victims of Trafficking* [Online]. http://www.unicef.org/ceecis/0610-Unicef_Victims_Guidelines_en.pdf.

United Nations Office on Drugs and Crime (UNODC). (2009). *Trafficking in Persons* [Online]. http://www.unodc.org/documents/human-trafficking/HTleafletA5EnglishupdatedAugust09.pdf.

Van der Rijt, J.-W. (2012). *The Importance of Assent.* Dordrecht: Springer.

6

Dissecting Article 8 of the 2011 EU Human Trafficking Directive

Introduction

Whilst the previous chapter examined the non-liability principle as found in the *2005 Council of Europe Convention on Action Against Trafficking in Human Beings* (Article 26), this chapter considers the non-liability principle as contained in the legislation of the European Union. It will look at the wording of Article 8 of the *Directive 2011/36 on preventing and combating trafficking in human beings and protecting its victims*, and it will continue the work started in chapter Five, of comparing and contrasting the two provisions.

First, however one ought to ask what the purpose of the Directive is, so as to have a benchmark against which to examine Article 8, coupled with the overarching human rights-based approach. The document has a number of purposes, including the aim to establish minimum rules concerning the definition of criminal offences and sanctions in the area of trafficking in human beings. Furthermore, it seeks to introduce common provisions to prevent human trafficking and protect victims. It also seeks to be part of a global action against trafficking in human beings.

© The Author(s) 2019
J. M. Muraszkiewicz, *Protecting Victims of Human Trafficking From Liability*, Palgrave Studies in Victims and Victimology, https://doi.org/10.1007/978-3-030-02659-2_6

With regard to the non-liability provision, the Directive aims to safe-guard the human rights of victims, to avoid further victimisation and to encourage trafficked persons to act as witnesses in criminal proceedings. Consequently, the safeguard of human rights is not just a concern for NGOs but is also expressed in EU legislature.

First Component of Article 8: "In Accordance with the Basic Principles of Their Legal System"

As stated in the preceding chapter, Article 8 of the *Directive 2011/36 on preventing and combating trafficking in human beings and protecting its victims* opens in the same way as Article 26 of the *2005 Council of Europe Convention on Action Against Trafficking in Human Beings*. It appreciates that states have different legal systems and will have distinctive methods of dealing with culpability and protecting trafficked persons. The opening words thus frame the entire provision within an acknowledgement of the importance of state sovereignty. This is in coherence with EU law; Article 4(2) TEU (Treaty on European Union) states that any instrument must respect the national identities of member states. In similar vein Article 67(1) TFEU (the Treaty on the Functioning of the European Union) makes it clear that the Union respects the different legal systems and traditions of member states.

Notably, the EU legislator was only able to enact Article 8 after the Treaty of Lisbon. Prior to Lisbon "criminal law, strictly speaking, remained an exclusive competence of Member States, and consequently this excluded the legitimacy of any European legal act introducing criminal offences or a measure of criminal nature. This situation remained essentially unchanged until the recent adoption of the Treaty of Lisbon, introducing an express competence of the EU in criminal matters" (Sicurella 2016: 49).

The wording "in accordance with the basic principles of their legal system" was most likely seen as necessary by the drafters, because defences are understood and applied in different ways across different legal traditions. Gallant, with regard to international criminal law, writes that the "issue of inculpation, the definition of command responsibility, is a good example of how difficult politically it is to represent the defence perspective in international criminal law" (Gallant 2003: 322). The same is true of EU criminal law (Hodgson 2011). To put differently, there is no overarching defence law theory that is applicable globally or even across the 28 member states. In her work on the need for common rules of criminal procedure in the EU, Longridge finds that: "[d]espite a trend towards deeper cooperation in the area of criminal law, Member States remain hesitant to harmonize rules of criminal procedure as a result of a fear that harmonization will bulldoze important differences between the adversarial and inquisitorial criminal justice traditions" (Longridge 2013/2014: 14). The same could be true for substantive criminal law, of which defences are a part of.

Furthermore, understanding EU's competence to legislate on matters of human trafficking requires us to bear in mind that member states are reluctant to give up the power over their criminal jurisdiction. This is because, as fittingly argued by Herlin-Karnell (2012: 115) "criminal law is hugely sensitive as it concerns the right to punish and the governing of dangerous behaviour." For Max Weber (1965), criminal law is a true reflection of sovereignty; the right to use violence is the enforcement of law and is the right of the state. Since criminal law is perceived as a hallmark of national sovereignty, the European Union has moved with extreme caution in advancing approximation. Consequently, it is logical to speculate that in drafting Article 8 the authors had to accommodate state sovereignty and divergence of criminal law traditions. Indeed, an intrusive non-liability provision might have inflicted with the above-mentioned Article 4(2) TEU, which regards the need to respect national identities, and could have led states to pull the emergency break.[1]

Second Component of Article 8: "Take Necessary Measures to Ensure Competent National Authorities Are Entitled Not to...Prosecute or Impose Penalties"

The Article states: "Member States shall...take necessary measures to ensure competent national authorities are entitled not to prosecute or impose penalties." In EU legislation, the word "shall" aims to convey a hard obligation and denote mandatory action. Article 8 seeks to place a direct obligation on member states, who are obliged not to just "consider" but to in fact "take the necessary measures." Consequently, the provision is far more robust than, for example, the various obligations to protect victims that are found in the 2000 UN Protocol on Human Trafficking. Writing on the Protocol, Obokata (2015: 177) notes: "Articles 6 and 7 contain phrases such as 'to the extent possible', 'shall consider implementing measures' and 'shall endeavour to provide'. This in effect means that states will not be generally held accountable under international law if they cannot or do not take action, as long as they try to implement or think about implementing protection measures."

Article 8 of the EU Human Trafficking Directive then specifies what it is member states are obliged to do: take necessary measures to ensure competent national authorities[2] are entitled not to prosecute or impose penalties. It is here that denigrations with regard to the extent of the obligation should be made; for the wording implies a very discretionary language.

In evaluating the potency of the EU Trafficking Directive, one can compare Article 8 to its equivalents, particularly to see how far international standards have evolved. As such we revisit Article 26 of the *2005 Council of Europe Convention on Action Against Trafficking in Human Beings* and as mentioned in the previous chapter, it can be noted that the Convention only mentions imposing penalties whilst the Directive goes further and also regards not prosecuting. Thus, "the Anti-Trafficking Directive shifts the attention to earlier stages in the criminal law chain thereby involving different actors (such as police and public prosecutor service)" (Jovanovic 2017: 47). However, what progress the Directive makes in this regard it then quickly disenchants. This is because of the low level of obligation placed on states. The use of the wording "ensure" waters down responsibilities. With respect to the Directive, the High Court of Ireland stated that (P v. Chief Superintendent Garda National Immigration Bureau & Ors 2015: para. 184): "all that is required is that there must be a discretion on the part of the prosecution authorities not to prosecute. The Directive does not seek to interfere with the exercise of that discretion." The High Court then went on to say: "The Directive enjoins the state to provide for prosecutorial discretion but does not require a particular outcome. It does not, therefore, confer an enforceable right on a victim of trafficking not to be prosecuted" (para. 200). This book is in agreement with the court's assessment and finds that there is no concrete obligation.

Interestingly, the UK Charity Anti-slavery (2014) challenges this perspective: "[t]he non-prosecution provision under the EU Directive is not a discretion, but a prohibition on prosecution where the person/defendant was compelled to commit a criminal offence as a direct consequence of their trafficking. The non-prosecution provision(s) are binding on member states and provide for a positive obligation on states not to prosecute victims of trafficking. It is not optional." However, a careful and strict reading of the Article disputes such an understanding. Even if we rely on interpreting Article 8 by taking account of the objective and the purpose of the legislation, we still have to proceed and deduce that the obligation is limited. The focus on only entitling national authorities makes it so, and this author does not stand alone in her criticism. Obokata and Payne criticise Article 8 for having weak language. In particular, they highlight the term "entitled not to prosecute" as giving states a too wide margin of appreciation (Obokata and Payne 2012: 310). Similarly, Sitarz (2015: 64) criticises the limited obligations placed on States by the Article.

Although the position of Anti-Slavery finds some backing in the Recital, which states "[v]ictims of trafficking in human beings should, in accordance with the basic principles of the legal systems of the relevant Member States, be protected from…" (the word should is more obligatory then what is found in the Article), recitals are not legally binding, nor under the principle of legal certainty should they be. Their role is more to set the scene and to provide interpretative guidance. The Court of Justice of the European Union does not give effect to recitals that are drafted in normative terms and "they do not have any autonomous legal effect" (Baratta 2014). Even if the Recital in *Directive 2011/36 on preventing and combating trafficking in human beings and protecting its victims* is more obligatory, it "cannot displace the operative provisions of a legal instrument" (Baratta 2014). It is thus contended that it would have been better if the Article itself focused more on the rights-holder. In such an instance, the trafficked victim would have been the recipient of human rights protection. The current wording and in particular the use of the phrase "are entitled" make it difficult for Article 8 to achieve its goal of safeguarding the human rights of victims and avoiding further victimisation. How can it, when it makes the state the focus and places meek obligations. To maximise potential for protecting trafficked persons, the European legislator could have been more robust in how it phrased its obligation. We come back to an alternative in the concluding chapter of this book.

Third Component of Article 8: "Prosecute or Impose Penalties...for Their Involvement in Criminal Activities"

The phrase "prosecute or impose penalties on victims of trafficking in human beings for their involvement in criminal activities" is restrictive. Following strict interpretation rules, the meaning of this phrase is understood as regarding solely criminal law. Prosecution is recognisably a term used within the sphere of the criminal justice, and involvement in criminal activates already contains the word "criminal." Examples include: forgery, violation of laws in relation to prostitution (depending on member state), keeping a brothel (depending on member state), thefts, illicit production of drugs and engagement in violent crimes such as battery. A key question for consideration is whether Article 8 can be applied beyond criminal activities. For example, how can we protect trafficked persons forced to work in agricultural and construction industries without a work permit, or irregular migrants? Of some assistance is paragraph 14 of the Recital, which states that criminal activities include "the use of false documents, or offences under legislation on prostitution or immigration...." Reading the full Directive—the Article and the Recital—leads to the conclusion that although strictly civil law matters (e.g. Tort) are unlikely to fall within the remit of the provision, immigration and potentially breach of state regulations does. However, in practice victims commit a more varied array of offences. Moreover, as already stated recitals are not legally binding.

To better, more clearly and with legal certainty reflect the reality of the trafficking experience and the range of offences that victims are compelled to commit, Article 8 ought to have better resembled Article 26 of the *2005 Council of Europe Convention on Action Against Trafficking in Human Beings*. The Convention uses the phrase "...for their involvement in unlawful activities...." Here, the use of the phrase "unlawful activities" means that the Convention is not restricted to activities defined by criminal law. Equally, the phrase "not to prosecute" could be substituted or elaborated so that it has broader scope. Indeed, the counterpart provision in the *ASEAN Convention against Trafficking in Persons, Especially Women and Children* adopted in 2015 uses the following phrase: "not holding victims of trafficking in persons criminally or administratively liable." It is argued that such a provision is better suited and prepared for the eventualities where traffickers force victims to engage in unlawful activities beyond traditional criminal law boundaries. Such an approach is not discriminatory to those compelled to commit other breaches and is more in tune with a human rights approach that seeks to protect all victims. A human rights approach means putting victims at the centre of our thinking, policies and actions. The human rights approach takes into account the complexities surrounding holding trafficked persons not liable for crimes they were committed, seeking not only legal solutions but also social and political.

Fourth Component of Article 8: "On Victims of Trafficking in Human Beings"

Correspondingly to Article 26 of the *2005 Council of Europe Convention on Action Against Trafficking in Human Beings*, Article 8 of *Directive 2011/36 on preventing and combating trafficking in human beings and protecting its victims* concerns victims of human trafficking. The same conclusions as made in Section 4.4 are applicable here. However, additional points should be made.

Firstly, of note are questions about communication between the different relevant national authorities, namely the prosecution and the identification body. Currently, there is an existing problem of miscommunication, as clearly demonstrated by the case of *L., H.V.N., T.H.N and T. v. R (The Children's Commissioner for England and Equality and Human Rights Commission)*. In this case, a competent authority had made a reasonable grounds decision that H.V.N was a victim; this was done before the sentencing. This, however, was not communicated to the defence lawyer, the prosecutor or the judge. What if it was communicated? Is the prosecution bound by decisions of authorities that decide on a person's victim status? In the Irish case of *P v. Chief Superintendent Garda National Immigration Bureau & others* (2015), the Director of Public Prosecutions held that "...the identification of the applicant under the Arrangements would not have the effect of preventing her trial on the offences with which she is charged, nor any offences." The UK Court of Appeal also gave time to the question in *R v. N* and *R v. LE* (2012). In this case, the UK Border Agency [UKBA] accepted that L had been trafficked. In the light of this, the Court of Appeal had to decide whether the convictions of the appellants were safe. The court held (para. 81–82): "Self-evidently, in making the decision to prosecute in this case, the CPS [Crown Prosecution Service] did not have the advantage of the findings after conviction by UKBA. However even if those findings had been available, **they would not have bound the CPS**, whether they supported or did not support the appellant. Assuming in the present case that the UKBA report had been available before conviction, the CPS would have noted and would have been justified in noting first, that UKBA itself entertained reservations about "credibility" issues, and second, that its conclusion ignored (because it was unaware of it) the more or less contemporaneous material available for consideration by the CPS when making its decision. In reality, UKBA and CPS are exercising different responsibilities. Neither can bind the other. What is essential is that if at all possible in the relatively constricted timetable, that each should be provided with all the material made available to the other and that both should approach the exercise of their responsibilities on the basis of mutual respect and comity" [emphasis added].

The judgement provides support for the view that the prosecutor does not have to be bound by the findings of the national authority responsible for identifying victims. Such an approach ought to be condemned. The knowledge and experience of prosecutors in identifying trafficked persons and understanding the circumstances surrounding trafficking may be inadequate, which implies that the prosecution ought to seriously take into consideration the views of more experienced colleagues.

Perhaps more importantly, both judgements also emphasise the point made in the prior section. As the obligation in Article 8 of the 2011 EU Human Trafficking Directive is so limited—states are only obliged to ensure that competent national authorities are entitled not to prosecute or punish—the state can prosecute a victim even when they are aware of the victim's status and past experiences. In bringing such a case, the state does not violate Article 8. Yet as is argued in this book, it violates the ethos of fundamental rights. To quote the OSCE: "not only does it fail to take into account the serious crimes committed against the victim by the traffickers, and which should be investigated, it fails to recognise trafficked persons as being victims and witnesses of those serious crimes and exacerbates their victimisation and trauma by imposing on such persons State-sanction, unjust punishment" (OSCE Office of the Special Representative and Co-ordinator for Combating Trafficking in Human Beings 2013: para. 4). The result of this analysis adds strength to the argument that the aim of *Directive 2011/36 on preventing and combating trafficking in human beings and protecting its victims* is not achieved, and so the EU ought to have put further obligations on states.

Fifth Component of Article 8: "For Their Involvement in Criminal Activities Which They Have Been Compelled to Commit as a Direct Consequence of Being Subjected to Any of the Acts Referred to in Article 2"

In Article 8, like in Article 26 of the *2005 Council of Europe Convention on Action Against Trafficking in Human Beings*, there is a focus on victims who committed a crime because they were compelled. As this was discussed in the preceding chapter, it will not be repeated here. In the already cited words of the UK Law Society (2015) "in considering whether a trafficked victim has been compelled to commit a crime, prosecutors should consider whether any of the means has been employed so that the victim has effectively lost the ability to consent to his / her actions or to act with free will." As with the Convention, the broader term of compulsion is in line with a human rights approach for it relies on a nuanced understanding of what happens to trafficked person and in turn is truly about protecting victims who are in need of protection from being held liable and enduring secondary victimisation. Using other words such as coerced or forced would have risked directly or indirectly violating victims' fundamental rights because it would have made it impossible to protect a majority of victims who in fact commit crimes because of more subtle pressures.

Whilst the wording "have been compelled" is of benefit to trafficked persons, subsequent phraseology is kerbing. The phrase "the act was a **direct consequence** of being subjected to any of the acts referred to in Article 2" [emphasis added] is particularly worrying. This prerequisite of direct consequence is rightly absent from the wording of the *2005 Council of Europe Convention on Action Against Trafficking in Human Beings*. Sadly, neither the Directive nor any guidance from the EU explains the exact meaning of "direct consequence" and it is contended in this book that the wording is problematic and confusing. It would have been much simpler to simply require that the crime was a result of compulsion.

The lack of clarity as to direct consequence can be viewed as a problem of *lex certa*. Kaifa-Gbandi (2011: 7) reminds readers that "criminal law is admittedly the harshest mechanism states employ to achieve social control. Criminal sanctions themselves…constitute counter-breaches of inter alia the liberty and property of those convicted." Such a description of criminal law shows that it can impact key rights of persons. That is why any provision related to criminal law should abide by the principle of *lex certa*, or legal certainty. As summarised by Faure et al. (2012: 28): "the idea that individuals can only face *criminal* punishment by a dully-enacted, publicly promulgated, clear and open law continues to hold a central place in our notions of the rule of law." This is also embedded in human rights law: Article 11 UNDHR and Article 15 ICCPR. The logic that criminal law should be certain also extends to excuses; they too should be plainly set out in law. This is because they help foresee what is and is not punishable.

Consequently, elements regarding non-prosecution or non-punishment of trafficked persons compelled to commit a crime prescribed by a legislator, including any European legislator, should not be so vague that when implemented they infringe on the *lex certa* principle. With regard to the provision contained in EU law, a lack of a precise demarcation of the non-prosecution or non-application of penalties risks negative consequences. To again borrow from Kaifa-Gbandi (2011: 27), "[r]equiring the EU to clearly delimit a minimum core of the conduct to be proscribed consists in two important parameters. First of all, lack of such clear delimitation would pose a dilemma to national legislators: either to unilaterally adopt a precise [provision] and risk diverging from the actual objective of the EU, which the European legislator did not adequately describe; or fail to give a clear description of the offense, thereby violating the principle of n.c. s. l. certa, which would amount to a breach of the Constitution in a number of Member States. It becomes evident that the 'lex certa' requirement is addressed to the European legislator as well, inasmuch as the latter may bind Member States to adopt minimum elements of an offense."

What could "direct consequence" mean? Reason dictates that it links the proximity of the crime to the trafficking situation. The use of the word direct seems to imply that there is a need for immediacy, for the crime to be committed as a result of an impending and near at hand situation. Supposedly, the justification for the direct consequence requirement is to ensure that the victim's crime was necessary. The requirement of a degree of immediacy has led literature to equate "direct consequence" with duress (Derenčinović 2014).

How does a direct consequence manifest in real life? A trafficked person who is transported by their trafficker into a country and who uses a false ID is evidently committing a crime through direct consequence. There is a close connection between the offence and being subjected to human trafficking. Unambiguous examples of direct consequence also include when the purpose of exploitation is a criminal activity. For example, persons who have been forced to shoplift or produce and/or sell drugs. When the wrongdoing is part of the exploitation, the proximity is immediate. In these situations, "the victims merely serve as agents or instruments while the traffickers are the directing minds behind the offending but without any direct involvement in the commission of individual offences" (Schloenhardt and Markey-Towler 2016: 14).

A more complex situation arises when a trafficked person is not with the trafficker and commits a crime that is related to the trafficking situation but is not direct per se. For example, the victim commits a crime in trying to escape from their oppressor. This is illustrated in Adam Weiss's story of a victim. He writes about Luminata, who as part of her trafficking experience was forced to have sex with fifteen men a day. She, however, managed to escape by assaulting one of her clients and stealing his wallet. She was caught by the police when she was shoplifting (Weiss 2016: 41). The direct consequence here is less obvious. Likewise in situations where a victim commits a crime (e.g. cultivates cannabis) without direct supervision of the trafficker. In both these situations, we have to acknowledge that the trafficker is no longer standing over the victim forcing or obliging them to commit a crime. Indeed, in Luminata's case the trafficker would not support the crime. Nonetheless, the victim's trafficking situation/status is still the underlying cause of the offence. Should they be allowed to rely on the exemption from liability? Certainly, the notion of "direct" no longer applies in this case as the proximity between the crime and the trafficking situation is no longer immediate.

To further illustrate the lack of immediate proximity, we can rely on a case that came before the Criminal Case Review Commission (the CCRC), an independent organisation concerned with cases of miscarriages of justice in England, Wales and Northern Ireland. Holiday (2012) writes: "The case already referred by the CCRC - the *T* case - involved a female victim of human trafficking who in 2007 was found trying to fly out of Heathrow with a passport that did not belong to her. She was convicted of possession of an identity document with intent under section 25(1) of the Identity Cards Act 2006. In the course of the proceedings, T came into contact with the police as well as defence and prosecution lawyers, but no one asked the right questions or recognised her situation for what it was. T, who was then aged 17, was arrested at Heathrow Airport trying to escape her trafficked situation. A duty solicitor was present at the police interview which lasted only ten minutes. The CPS was satisfied that all key evidence was available; it identified the public interest as relating to 'the likely penalty and nature and seriousness of the offence'; and even noted that there were 'no victim issues'." In this case, the gap between the victim's escape and her arrest at the airport was 12 weeks. There was no immediacy, and depending on how narrowly we interpret it, probably no direct consequence. Yet on looking into the facts, the CCRC found that there was a nexus of compulsion.

Is there space to interpret "direct consequence" more broadly? In international law, the *Vienna Convention* on the law of treaties teaches to interpreters of law to begin with a strict construction of the words and give *them their strict plain meaning*. Where matters are vague, it is possible to consider the purpose of a legislation, in this case *Directive 2011/36 on preventing and combating trafficking in human beings and protecting its victims*.[3] Having regard to the objective and the purpose of the Directive, which is a system for the protection of human rights, lends weight to broadly interpreting the phrase "the act was a direct consequence of being subjected to any of the acts referred to in Article 2" so that it includes crimes that were not only directly linked to trafficking but were also related to it.

Conceivably by using the words "**any** of the acts referred to in Article 2" [emphasis added], the EU legislator could mean that any of the three components of the crime (action, means and purpose) must be present but they do not all have to be present. Thus, in theory the absence of, for example, the purpose element would not prevent the victim from relying on Article 8, provided that the means and/or action elements were there and directly related to the crime. Accordingly, a victim who was harboured in a house (action) through the means of abuse of vulnerability and who broke out of the house, causing damage, and then stole a car to get away (provided there were no other reasonable means of getting away safely) should not be held accountable. This is because their responsibility in committing the said liberation offence was diminished due to the presence of the acts referred to in Article 2 and thus a direct consequence. Similar logic can be extended to situations where victims strive to improve their well-being and thus collaborate with the trafficker, e.g. by helping with the recruitment of new victims. In these instances, however "[a] distinction has to be drawn between, on the one hand, (former) victims collaborating as equals with their trafficked as 'partners in crime', participants, managers (such as brothel madams), and, on the other, victims acting under compulsion or out of necessity" (Schloenhardt and Markey-Towler 2016: 15). That is why, as is stressed in this book, there is an onus on the trafficked victim to prove on a case-by-case basis that they were acting under compulsion.

Things become more complicated in cases of victims who have escaped the trafficking situation and then sometime later go onto commit crimes, for example stealing food or using false ID in order to move to a new country, as in the case of the above-described T or Luminata. These victims can be referred to as historical victims; "the term used to describe those trafficked persons who are no longer in a situation of exploitation (or at risk of it) at the time when they come to the attention of the authorities" (Jovanovic 2017: 64). Technically, at this point they are not subjected to any of the acts referred to in Article 2 and so there is no direct consequence. The person is technically choosing committing or participating in the crime. In this case, we have to agree that there is no direct consequence, even on broad interpretation of the phrase.

The summary is as follows:

1. When a person commits an offence under the direct influence of the trafficker (e.g. during exploitation or during "transportation" and thus breaching migration law), they can benefit from Article 8.
2. When a person commits an offence, without the trafficker being in the immediate proximity, but nevertheless the means and action elements exist, as in the case of escape, they can on broad interpretation of the law benefit from Article 8.
3. When a person commits an offence in order to protect himself or herself, following from what happened during the trafficking situation, then they cannot benefit from Article 8. In other words, where the wrongdoing falls short of the yardstick of direct consequence, the defendant is left "without any prescribed regard to the circumstances of trafficking" (Pham 2015: 8).

The lack of protection in the third instance is regrettable, for there is in fact still a nexus of compulsion. It is suggested that EU law should protect trafficked persons such as T, without the need for national courts to reach for very broad interpretations. In other words, Article 8 should be clear and highlight that when compulsion exists, trafficked persons should be protected because there is "a connection between [the victims'] offence and the circumstances of being a victim of human trafficking" (Holiday 2012). In determining the degree, authorities should take into account things such as age, psychological and physical experiences, migration status, fears of "juju" and other threats made by the exploiters, to name but a few examples. In addition, the authorities should also consider the victim's perceived absence of real alternatives, and that perception is also linked to their historical trafficking status.

Such a broader understanding of the principle contained in Article 8 is more in tune with the human rights approach and allows fundamental rights to constitute general principles in this. It is naïve and simplistic to assume crimes by trafficked persons will always be caused due to direct consequence. Moreover, we have to be aware that the boundaries between direct consequence and not direct-consequence are too blurry, and so a better phraseology/approach is needed.

A better approach would entail what this book calls a true causation approach. In English criminal law, causation is understood as the causal relationship between conduct and result. Traditionally causation is used to determine if a person is guilty of an offence. The basic test for establishing causation is the "but-for" test in which the question is asked "but for the actions of the defendant, would the result have occurred?" In the case of non-liability of victims of human trafficking, this is turned around and we ask "but for the trafficking situation of the defendant, would the result have occurred?" If the answer is no, then the trafficked person ought to be granted an excuse. A causation approach thus refers to the trafficking still being the underlying cause of the offending; however, the degree is less strict than in cases of "direct consequence" or duress. There is larger range of application. Of course, here it becomes harder to decipher which crimes warrant a defence, and we will need to do this on a case-by-case basis. Certainly, our scrutiny of compulsion will be stricter. It would seem unreasonable to offer non-liability to a victim who escapes their trafficking situation and is living safely for ten years but then decides to use a false ID to gain entry into another country. However, we may be more willing to accept a victim who escapes their trafficking situation and in that same month, due to immense fear of the traffickers and due to serious psychological impacts, uses a false ID to gain entry into a different country. In this case, non-liability should be allowed or at least strongly considered because the trafficked person is "acting to protect or assist himself on account of his trafficked status" (Pham 2015: 7).

In implementing Article 8, countries should ensure that both eventualities are covered: those arising as a direct consequence (in the literal meaning of the phrase) and those that are connected to the trafficking status. A good example is found in American legislation, the Victims of Trafficking and Violence Protection Act of 2000: "Penalties for the crime of unlawful conduct with respect to documents in furtherance of trafficking, peonage, slavery, involuntary servitude, or forced labour do not apply to the conduct of a person who is or has been a victim of a severe form of trafficking in persons, [...] if that conduct **is caused by, or incident to, that trafficking**" [emphasis added]. This wording takes into consideration the fact that some crimes may be in relation to or incident of trafficking and not necessarily a direct consequence, e.g. in the case of a trafficked victim using a false ID to get away from the country where the trafficker is. Here, it is recognised a victim should not be prosecuted or punished because their vulnerable position and the frailty of the humanity still stand.

The trafficking situation impedes the capacity to accurately perceive and evaluate. In other cases, compulsion may arise from a need to free oneself, e.g. when a trafficked person steals a sum of money in order to run away from the place of exploitation. Thus, if we understand "direct consequence" in a strict sense, then a provision that uses such wording becomes unsuitable for various cases involving trafficked persons. Sorrentino and Piotrowicz usefully summarise that "[w]here the victim is compelled to commit an offence one must take into account all of the circumstances which have resulted in the victim losing their free will and having no option but to act as they did…" (Piotrowicz and Sorrentino 2016: 677). However, in practice Sorrentino and Piotrowicz's aspiration does not always transform to reality. It is argued in this book that the lack of clarity as to "direct consequence" has allowed member states to apply strict solutions to holding victims non-liable (e.g. relying on duress), which has been to the detriment of the victim.

Using a strict constructionism approach leads us to a situation where the wording of Article 8 gives with one hand in using "compulsion" rather than "coercion" but takes away with the other by requiring compulsion to be a result of direct consequence. As such the wording "direct consequence" ought to be improved upon or removed.

Conclusion

Article 8 of *Directive 2011/36 on preventing and combating trafficking in human beings and protecting its victims* was drafted circa five years after Article 26 of the *2005 Council of Europe Convention on Action Against Trafficking in Human Beings* came into force. Against this time lapse, we could expect that the approach to non-liability would have evolved. We might expect that advances in knowledge on human trafficking, including better knowledge of the compulsion felt by victims to commit crimes, during these years would provide a better context for policy development. Especially against the backdrop of work done by NGOs, court rulings and publications. On the latter, there was the Background paper on *Non-punishment and non-prosecution of victims of trafficking in persons: administrative and judicial approaches to offences committed in the process of such trafficking*, produced by the UN Working Group on Trafficking in Persons (UN Working Group on Trafficking in Persons 2010). The EU response, we would presume, ought to have built on prior solutions—that of the *2005 Council of Europe Convention on Action Against Trafficking in Human Beings* or even soft law—such that the non-liability principle would have emerged as a piece of legislation with the hallmarks of human rights and understanding of victim's experiences.

However, the reality is somewhat different. Under Article 8, victims are not rights holders. The 2011 EU Human Trafficking Directive's is aimed to have a victim-cantered approach; this, however, is compromised by the words "competent national authorities **are entitled** not to prosecute or impose penalties" [emphasis added]. There is no direct provision that will protect trafficked persons. This is the first shortcoming of Article 8, and there are others, which in turn mean the protection is not adequate enough. As mentioned, on the one hand the provision is applauded for relying on the word "compel" rather than "coercion" or referring strictly to duress. Indeed, the provision "is not merely a re-statement of the established defence of duress" (Schloenhardt and Markey-Towler 2016: 35); instead, it is associated with the means elements in the human trafficking definition. On the other hand, our enthusiasm is constrained by the presence of the phrase "direct consequence." A strict reading of the latter phrase can annul what good is achieved by the word compulsion. Ultimately, there is a lack of clarity as to how to interpret "direct consequence," which probably relates to the proximity between the offence committed by the trafficked person and their trafficking situation. This ambiguity can (and does, as will be shown in subsequent chapters) lead to a lack of uniformity in the implementation and use of the principle of non-liability. This diminishes the harmonised protective function it is designed to play as there may be a lack of equal treatment of trafficked persons amongst member states.

The EU legislative response lacks the nuance and sensitivity to deal effectively with protecting victims from being held liable for crimes they were compelled to commit. This is despite the European law's aim of safeguarding the human rights of victims, avoiding further victimisation and encouraging victims to act as witnesses in criminal proceedings against the perpetrators. The collateral damage of a frail system includes the continuation of holding trafficked persons liable and thus a further erosion of their rights, endurance of secondary victimisation and sustained mistrust of authorities.

However, this assessment, which although negative is made against the acknowledgement that protecting trafficked persons against liability, particularly in the criminal context, is difficult to do when one must account for the sovereignty of 28 member states. The 2011 EU Human Trafficking Directive, including Article 8, is a product of the communitarisation of EU criminal law; it is the first legislation in this domain. Discretionary language is unavoidable in the context of EU criminal law Directives; possibly, it is the broad language that even made an agreement on this Article possible. It is also acknowledged that Directives will always be state-centred, almost by their very own definition. However, after Lisbon and its emphasis on human rights and the competence granted in Article 83 TFEU,[4] it is feasible for a Directive that aims to protect trafficked persons to be worded in a more "victim-centred" way, without becoming disproportionate. This book will suggest an alternative wording in the concluding chapter.

Notes

1. Article 82(3) and 83(3) of the TFEU, respectively, stipulate that a State can request that the draft directive be referred to the European Council if it considers that the proposed directive would fundamentally affect aspects of its own criminal justice system. In that case, the ordinary legislative procedure is suspended. However, despite this provision, it is still possible for the remaining member states to move forwards and establish enhanced cooperation (Article 20(2) of the TEU and Article 329(1) of the TFEU), provided that at least nine MS wish to do so. These States

need to notify the Parliament, Commission and Council. The use of emergency breaks has to be justified by a damaging effect of the proposed directive on the fundamental aspects of a state's criminal justice system, e.g. if it were to affect areas of the sentence for life or offences concerning religion. In summary, the emergency break is a system of check and balances and serves to increase control over criminal law. A similar view has been taken of the entry into force of the European Charter of Fundamental Rights which can have a regulatory effect on the ECJ.

2. With regard to this part of the Article, we can also ask: Who are competent national authorities? There is no listing of national authorities; however, this does not pose great difficulties. Effectively, these will be persons/bodies who make decisions on prosecution and penalties; police, prosecutors, judges. The exact list will depend on the justice system of each member state.

3. The Vienna Convention can be described as an interactive approach, combining a strict textual methodology and one of purpose and intent. However, there is clear supremacy given to strict constructivism. Article 31(1) emerges as the central pillar. In this regard, other methods, such as those in Article 32, are secondary. Article 31 of the Vienna Convention on the Law of Treaties (1969) states:

(1) "A treaty shall be interpreted in good faith in accordance with the ordinary meaning to be given to the terms of the treaty in their context and in the light of its object and purpose.

(2) The context for the purpose of the interpretation of a treaty shall comprise, in addition to the text, including its preamble and annexes:

(a) any agreement relating to the treaty which was made between all the parties in connection with the conclusion of the treaty;

(b) any instrument which was made by one or more parties in connection with the conclusion of the treaty and accepted by the other parties as an instrument related to the treaty.

(3) There shall be taken into account, together with the context:

(a) any subsequent agreement between the parties regarding the interpretation of the treaty or the application of its provisions;

(b) any subsequent practice in the application of the treaty which establishes the agreement of the parties regarding its interpretation;

(c) any relevant rules of international law applicable in the relations between the parties.

(4)   A special meaning shall be given to a term if it is established that the parties so intended.

Article 32 then compliments the broad interpretation canon by giving recourse to supplementary means of interpretation:

"Recourse may be had to supplementary means of interpretation, including the preparatory work of the treaty and the circumstances of its conclusion, in order to confirm the meaning resulting from the application of article 31, or to determine the meaning when the interpretation according to article 31:

(a)   Leaves the meaning ambiguous or obscure; or

(b)   Leads to a result which is manifestly absurd or unreasonable."

4. Lisbon expanded EU competencies in the domain of criminal law; in particular Article 83(1) TFEU allows the EU legislator to adopt rules concerning the definition of criminal offences and sanctions in the area of particularly serious crime. Indeed, human trafficking is listed in Article 83(1) TFEU as a crime that falls within the EU competence for harmonisation.

Article 83(1) states:

The European Parliament and the Council may, by means of directives adopted in accordance with the ordinary legislative procedure, **establish minimum rules** concerning the **definition of criminal offences** and **sanctions** in the areas of particularly serious crime with a cross-border dimension resulting from the nature or impact of such offences or from a special need to combat them on a common basis.

These areas of crime are the following: terrorism, **trafficking in human beings** and sexual exploitation of women and children, illicit drug trafficking, illicit arms trafficking, money laundering, corruption, counterfeiting of means of payment, computer crime and organised crime.

On the basis of developments in crime, the Council may adopt a decision identifying other areas of crime that meet the criteria specified in this paragraph. It shall act unanimously after obtaining the consent of the European Parliament. [Emphasis added]

References

Anti-slavery. (2014). *Trafficking for Forced Criminal Activities and Begging in Europe.* RACE in Europe Project [Online]. http://www.antislavery.org/includes/documents/cm_docs/2014/t/trafficking_for_forced_criminal_activities_and_begging_in_europe.pdf.

Baratta, R. (2014). Complexity of EU Law in Domestic Implementing Process. In *19th Quality of Legislation Seminar: 'EU Legislative Drafting: Views from Those Applying EU Law in the Member States'* [Online]. http://ec.europa.eu/dgs/legal_service/seminars/20140703_baratta_speech.pdf.

Derenčinović, D. (2014). Comparative Perspectives on Non-Punishment of Victims of Trafficking in Human Beings. *Annales, XLVI*(63), 3–20.

Faure, M., Goodwin, M., & Weber, F. (2012). The Lex Certa Principle in Criminal Law: Reconciling Economics and Human Rights? *SSRN Electronic Journal* [Online]. https://www.researchgate.net/publication/256012631_The_Lex_Certa_Principle_in_Criminal_Law_Reconciling_Economics_and_Human_Rights.

Gallant, K. S. (2003). Politics, Theory and Institutions: Three Reasons Why International Criminal Defence Is Hard, and What Might Be Done About One of Them. *Criminal Law Forum, 14*(3), 317–334.

Herlin-Karnell, E. (2012). *The Constitutional Dimension of European Criminal Law.* London: Bloomsbury.

Hodgson, J. (2011). 'Safeguarding Suspects' Rights in Europe: A Comparative Perspective. *New Criminal Law Review, 14*(4), 611–665.

Holiday, Y. (2012). Victims of Human Trafficking and the CCRC. *Law Gazette.* Retrieved from https://www.lawgazette.co.uk/law/victims-of-human-trafficking-and-the-ccrc/67995.article.

Jovanovic, M. (2017). The Principle of Non-punishment of Victims of Trafficking in Human Beings: A Quest for Rationale and Practical Guidance. *Journal of Trafficking and Human Exploitation, 1*(1), 41–76.

Kaifa-Gbandi, M. (2011). The Importance of Core Principles of Substantive Criminal Law for a European Criminal Policy Respecting Fundamental Rights and the Rule of Law. *European Criminal Law Review, 1*(1), 7–34.

Longridge, C. (2013/2014). In Defence of Defence Rights: The Need for Common Rules of Criminal Procedure in the European Union. *European Journal of Legal Studies, 13*, 136–156.

Obokata, T. (2015). Human Trafficking. In N. Boister & R. J. Currie (Eds.), *Routledge Handbook of Transnational Criminal Law* (pp. 171–186). Oxon: Routledge.

Obokata, T., & Payne, B. (2012). Implementing Action Against Trafficking of Human Beings Under the TFEU: A Preliminary Analysis. *New Journal of European Criminal Law, 3*(3–4), 298–319.

OSCE Office of the Special Representative and Co-ordinator for Combating Trafficking in Human Beings. (2013). *Policy and Legislative Recommendations Towards the Effective Implementation of the Non-punishment Provision with Regard to Victims of Trafficking*. Vienna [Online]. http://www.osce.org/secretariat/101002?download=true.

Pham, J. (2015). *Protecting Trafficking Victims from Porsecution: Analysis of the Modern Slavery Bill Defence* [Online]. http://files.magdalenecambridge.com/pdfs/Publications/peter_peckard_prize_jp_july_2015.pdf.

Piotrowicz, R. W., & Sorrentino, L. (2016). Human Trafficking and the Emergence of the Non-punishment Principle. *Human Rights Law Review, 16*(4), 669–699.

P v. Chief Superintendent Garda National Immigration Bureau & Ors [2015] IEHC 222.

R v. N and R v. LE [2012] EWCA Crim 189.

R v. L and Others (The Children's Commissioner for England and Equality and Human Rights Commission intervening) [2013] EWCA Crim 991.

Schloenhardt, A., & Markey-Towler, R. (2016). Non-criminalisation of Victims of Trafficking in Persons—Principles, Promises, and Perspectives. *Groningen Journal of International Law, 4*(1), 10–38.

Sicurella, R. (2016). EU Competence in Criminal Matters. In V. Mitsilegas, M. Bergstrom, & T. Konstadinides (Eds.), *Research Handbook on EU Criminal Law* (pp. 49–77). Chelteham: Edward Elgar.

Sitarz, O. (2015). O problemie niekaralnosci ofiar handle ludzmi raz jeszcze. In Z. Lasocik (Ed.), *Niekaralnosc ofiar handle ludźmi – nowe perspektywy* (pp. 63–71). Warsaw: Warsaw University.

UN Working Group on Trafficking in Persons. (2010). *Non-punishment and Non-prosecution of Victims of Trafficking in Persons: Administrative and Judicial Approaches to Offences Committed in the Process of Such Trafficking* [Online]. https://www.unodc.org/documents/treaties/organized_crime/2010_CTOC_COP_WG4/WG4_2010_4_E.pdf.

Weber, M. (1965). *Politics as a Vocation*. Philadelphia: Fortress Press.

Weiss, A. (2016). The Application of International Legislation: Is the Federalisation of Anti-trafficking Legislation in Europe Working for Trafficking Victims? In M. Malloch & P. Rigby (Eds.), *Human Trafficking* (pp. 41–62). Edinburgh: Edinburgh University Press.

7

How States Have Implemented the Non-liability Provision

Introduction

Previous chapters considered the meaning of, and the obligations imposed by Article 8 (*Directive 2011/36 on preventing and combating trafficking in human beings and protecting its victims*) and Article 26 (the *2005 Council of Europe Convention on Action Against Trafficking in Human Beings*). This chapter moves the discussion forward, and through a positive discourse analysis describes the different methods taken by states in implementing the non-liability provisions into national law. By seeing how states understand the obligation, the address in this chapter aids in determining whether the existing frameworks on non-liability should be improved. Moreover, the aim of this chapter is to deduce which method of transposition has the biggest potential to protect trafficked persons. In particular, this chapter looks at three methods:

- The use of guidance directed at relevant authorities;
- A specific non-liability provision;
- Reliance on existing defences.

© The Author(s) 2019   **145**
J. M. Muraszkiewicz, *Protecting Victims of Human Trafficking From Liability*, Palgrave
Studies in Victims and Victimology, https://doi.org/10.1007/978-3-030-02659-2_7

In the discussion of these three approaches, reference is made to countries that have implemented them, in particular: Poland, England and Wales, Lithuania, Spain, Cyprus, Germany, France and Moldova.

Unsurprisingly, this book is not the first to raise the question of transposition of the non-liability principle. In 2012, the Slovakian authorities issued an ad hoc query on Transposition of Article 8 of *Directive 2011/36 on preventing and combating trafficking in human beings and protecting its victims*. The Republic of Slovakia was in 2012 amending its Criminal Code and was seeking guidance on how other member states have transposed Article 8. 19 Member States replied to the query. The answers revealed that in many cases the national law regarding non-prosecution or non-punishment of human trafficking victims remained the same as it was before the entry into force of *Directive 2011/36 on preventing and combating trafficking in human beings and protecting its victims*. In other words, little had changed since the regional obligation on non-liability was introduced. We have to thus wonder about the extent of the obligation, which as shown in previous chapters is seen by this book as minimal. The primary and emerging conclusion has to be that neither Article 8, nor the requirements of the *2005 Council of Europe Convention on Action Against Trafficking in Human Beings*, placed new obligations on states. However, the question thus remains: what is the better method of transposition to achieve the best results for victims?

The Use of Guidance Directed at Relevant Authorities

This section reviews the use of guidelines as a possible method of transposing the non-liability principle. This is the approach taken by Belgium. England and Wales also used this method prior to the enforcement of the *Modern Slavery Act* (MSA), *2015*. Is the use of guidelines an effective form of protecting trafficked persons from being held liable? Does such a method safeguard their dignity and other human rights?

Generally, guidelines to public prosecution services are predefined strategies. They serve to direct prosecutors and, in some cases, to inform the community, about the approach that prosecutors should take when making evaluations in relation to cases where it is purported that a criminal offence has been committed. They also provide the necessary information on prosecutorial discretion. As argued by Kyprianou (2010: 37) "[p]rosecutors are, theoretically at least, obliged to follow all these guidelines, although practice showed that there has been a considerable degree of variation regarding their approaches and their understanding of the code." Kyprianou's deduction casts a shadow of doubt as to the guidelines ability to protect the rights of trafficked persons.

Yet not all is bleak. Guidelines, in comparison with statutory legislation, can be adapted more swiftly to reflect emerging trends and understandings of the crime. They can ensure that the implementation of the law remains modern. Moreover, it is more likely that a guideline will cover more, i.e. be more encompassing. It can in detail encourage prosecutors to seek the assistance of civil society bodies or communicate with authorities responsible for identifying trafficked persons. A further advantage is that they are less rigid than legislation, as the name suggests they are guidelines and allow for the use of discretion and common sense. This can be particularly useful as no two cases are likely to be the same, thus the prosecution can use the guidelines in determining the appropriate course of action. At the same time, too much discretion can be dangerous. We can rightly worry about prosecutors acting under the influence of political motives, e.g. meeting quotas or supporting a government's policy on hostility to migrants (the so-called hostile environment). The high degree of discretion can also be problematic when an atypical situation arises, as the prosecution may not recognise or may not wish to recognise the applicability of the guidelines. Indeed, guidelines undeniably lack a level of certainty. The Anti-Trafficking Monitoring Group (ATMG 2013) quoted in their report a legal practitioner who asserted that: "It is inevitable that this [guideline on non-prosecution of trafficked persons] will incorporate an amount of subjectivity. The same set of facts may lead one prosecutor to prosecute and another to take a different view. Of course, lawyers are not machines into which data is fed and the same result is produced on each and every occasion. The tests and guidelines referred to above provide discretion. It is perhaps fair to observe that in those circumstances some prosecutors take a more rigid view than others."

In such an instance, there is room to argue that the possibility of discretion leads to uncertainty. A prosecutor's discretion could be exercised in a way that is incorrect or unpredictable. Consequently, trafficked persons may not be sure as to whether a prosecutor would act in accordance with the principle of non-liability. O'Neil (2004: 1439) documented the discrepancies amongst prosecutorial decisions for a number of criminal charges, and noted that: "understanding why prosecutors select certain cases for prosecution and disregard others is one of the greatest enigmas of the criminal justice system." This lack of consistency could be used as a reason for why the law ought to rely on something more certain, such a statutory defence.

The lack of certainly has also been recognised as a weakness by the Court of Justice of the European Union (CJEU). *Case 102/79* considered an application for a declaration that Belgium failed to fulfil its obligations under the then EEC treaty, by failing to bring into force, within the prescribed period, the provisions necessary to comply with *Council Directive 77/780/EEC on the Coordination of Laws, Regulations and Administrative Provisions Relating to the Taking Up and Pursuit of the Business of Credit Institutions.* The court criticised Belgium because it used "mere administrative practices, which by their nature can be changed as and when the authorities please and which are not publicized widely enough" (Case 102/79 Commission v. Belgium 1980: point 11). Such practice does not adhere to the principle of certainty and, as highlighted by the court, "each member state must implement Directives in a manner which fully meets the requirement of legal certainty and must consequently transpose their terms into national law as binding provisions."

The statements by the court subside the argument that guidelines to relevant authorities are an effective and appropriate method of implementing Article 8 of the *Directive 2011/36 on preventing and combating trafficking in human beings and protecting its victims*, or Article 26 of the *2005 Council of Europe Convention on Action Against Trafficking in Human Beings.* Certainly, their lack of statutory standing and the ability to change guidelines without the same level of scrutiny as a change in a legislative Act or a Criminal Code demands does make them uncertain. Hoshi (2013: 69) expresses concern with regard to guidelines to prosecutors. He states: "[t]his does not provide adequate protection because the power is placed entirely in the hands of the prosecutor. Trafficked parties do not have the right to defend themselves by asserting that the offence was committed as a result of the trafficking situation; rather, they must ask the prosecutor (who, it must be remembered, represents the opposing party in the litigation and, thus, has interests and motivations that diverge manifestly from those of the trafficked person) for mercy. If the prosecutor refuses, as long as the decision to continue with the prosecution is not so unreasonable that no reasonable prosecutor acting reasonably could have come to it, a court has no power to intervene."

A further disadvantage of using guidelines is that they are directed at the prosecution. Yet the issue of non-liability similarly concerns law enforcement agencies such as the police, judges and also defence lawyers. In England and Wales, for example, "decisions are not the exclusive responsibility of prosecutors. Most non-prosecution decisions are still made by a relatively large number of police officers and, thus, are difficult to control. Police are empowered to take no further action, give an informal warning, or administer a caution without notifying the CPS [Crown Prosecution Service]" (Kyprianou 2010: 36). It follows, that any guideline should also be disseminated to the police, this, however, is not always the case in practice. Any guidelines should certainly be disseminated to defence lawyers, as it is noted that defence lawyers are unaware of the non-liability principle and advise their clients to plead guilty.

Of course, some of the apprehensions around guidelines could be addressed. For instance, it could be an option to give guidelines the force of law and make them binding. Legal certainty could also be improved by strict wording of guidelines that do not allow prosecutors to diverge away too much, or if the guidelines obliged non-liability, unless it was strictly necessary and in the public interest. However, for this author, it is more preferable to have clear legislation that to rely on the discretion of prosecutors that can be by their very nature inconsistent in application.

Undeniably, much also depends on the particularities of a given legal system. Where the principle of legality operates—in which every case without a legal obstacle has to be prosecuted—the use of guidelines may be less useful. In contrast, in jurisdictions where the principle of opportunity is followed—where there is unconstrained discretion on whether to prosecute—guidelines may seem more applicable. Indeed, a legal culture that follows the principle of opportunity is more suited because prosecutors will require as much assistance and direction as possible to make the desired choice. These guidelines, however, as stated above have to be certain, clear and, in order to protect trafficked persons adequately, must be followed. On the whole, there seems to be a lack of convincing arguments for solely relying on guidelines. It is possible to argue that to insure against the dangers of potentially arbitrary decisions to prosecute (or not) the best chance of justice lies with a defence.

A Specific Non-liability Provision

Is including the non-liability principle in a legal act a preferable means of safeguarding the rights of victims? Potentially yes. Certainly, the principle would no longer be an option but a statutory right. Moreover, the codified law is more visible than guidelines. In turn, visibility means that trafficked persons may be more confident in escaping from the traffickers and coming to the authorities for help. It may also mean that traffickers are more restricted in using threats of authorities as a means of controlling the victims. Thus, having a separate non-liability provision, which solely deals with trafficked persons, may grant more visibility and usability. Such a clause could also ensure that law enforcement authorities are not faced with numerous possible defences and guidelines, which can be confusing. Indeed, lawyers may be unsure which defence, duress or necessity, they should use. As is shown below, it is not always straightforward which existing defence is suited.

Lastly, and perhaps most importantly for advocates of a victim-centred approach, having a statuary defence recognises the particular vulnerability of the victims and signposts that the legislator is serious about protecting them. However, this argument may not be strong enough for some to justify introducing more criminal law. Ultimately we should empirically research if a non-liability provision does in fact work better in practice.

We also have to recognise the arguments made by some scholars that a non-liability clause might source more problems than solve. Gallagher has argued in front of the UK Parliament (2014) that a defence may be dangerous. She stated: "…it would be both unnecessary and dangerous to grant persons identified as victims of trafficking some kind of special defence or immunity from prosecution without tying this to the fact and situation of their trafficking. What would be the parameters of such a defence / immunity? Within what time frame would it operate? What steps would be taken to address the potential consequences of such a law (e.g. increased use of victims of trafficking for the commission of serious offences)? Persons who are or have been trafficked can and do commit serious crimes. They may kill their employers / exploiters. More commonly they may traffic / exploit others. The State must retain the flexibility to decide whether the circumstances justify non-prosecution or non-punishment but should not be compelled, through law or policy, one way or another." Gallagher's standpoint reflects the fear that a defence may be too automatic and leave no room for consideration of the facts. In addition, trafficked victims may commit crimes of the highest severity, which, depending on the circumstances, may not warrant a defence. Yet, on balance none of these arguments seem to present significant challenges. They are good questions to ask, but not decisive arguments against introducing a statutory provision. A well-worded defence clause could warrant that the risks raised by Gallagher are insured against. Importantly, a non-liability provision does not equate to immunity. Like with any defence, the defendant victim will have to satisfy the evidential burden, i.e. produce enough evidence to be permitted to raise the defence at trial. After which the prosecution can try to disprove the defence. Moreover, the existence of a defence does not remove the role of the police and/or prosecutor in undertaking relevant investigations. Rather, the prosecutor can still decide that it is not in the public interest to prosecute. If, however, the prosecutor decides to go forth with the prosecution then the victim will have access to a relevant defence.

Frank Mulholland QC (2014) also argues against a statutory defence clause, amongst the arguments he presented to the Parliament was that "not every allegation by an accused facing a criminal prosecution that he or she is a victim of trafficking will be truthful and made in good faith. When dealing with the prosecution of serious and organised crime it is important to note that perpetrators are inventive as to the defences they adopt and the arguments they advance in attempting to avoid or frustrate prosecution." This point has some merit but could be applied to almost any defence. For example, not every allegation by an accused facing a criminal prosecution that he or she is a victim of historic abuse will be truthful. In this context, we have to revert to the architecture of the criminal system, where a jury or judge is entrusted with the ability to judge whether a defence is artificial or truthful. As was summarised by the OSCE (2013: 27): "The state must make a judgment as to whether an offence was in fact linked to trafficking. If the offence is not linked, then the trafficked person may be liable to a penalty, like anyone else."

HHJ Edmunds QC (2014) noted, also before the Parliament, that a defence might not stop prosecutors from prosecuting; instead, it will be something for the defence team to prove during trial. Consequently, the trafficked victim would remain in the criminal justice system longer. Certainly "dragging" a trafficked person through the criminal justice system will contribute to secondary victimization. Moreover, it goes against the notion of non-prosecution. To appease the concerns raised by HHJ Edmunds QC, we can revert to the notion that the defence does not exist in isolation. Instead, it can be coupled with a methodology such as guidelines to relevant law enforcement persons as well as a prosecution's discretion. Thus, ideally the victim would be protected before a trial, through the wisdom of the prosecuting bodies' decision not to initiate a case, yet in the absence of this wisdom the victim can rely on a defence.

Two questions still remain. Firstly, will the defence be visible enough to those that need to rely on it? Much here will hinge on the state's dissemination of the defence, incorporation in practitioner's textbooks and the provision of relevant training. Secondly, how should such a provision be famed? At a minimum, it should be four-dimensional. Firstly, it should provide an excuse. Thus an offence, which satisfies the *actus reus* and *mens rea* and is generally unlawful, will not lead to criminal liability. Secondly, such a provision should not be offence-specific. In other words, it would recognise the reality that trafficked persons can commit an array of offences as a consequence of having been trafficked. Empirical research in Spain conducted by Villacampa and Torres (2015) showed that crimes committed by trafficked women vary and include amongst others drug-trafficking offence, theft, and document and bankcard forgery. Thirdly, a defence should be clear and unambiguous. Lastly, the provision should be flexible enough to assist victims of trafficking who experience different forms of compulsion that leads them to commit crimes. With regard to this last point, we can observe two diverging approaches amongst states.

The first approach focuses on the victim and their lack of choice. In such an instance, there are no requirements for the crime to have taken place as a direct consequence of exploitation. Instead the trafficked victim only needs to show that their trafficking situation, and the compulsion that came with it, was in some way responsible for the crime. The second approach only provides an excuse to victims who committed a crime as a direct consequence of being a victim of human trafficking. In that sense, it is more restrictive and of a higher threshold.

Moldova uses the first type of a defence clause. Article 165(4) of the Moldavian Criminal Code stipulates that: "a victim of trafficking in human beings shall be exempted from criminal liability for any crimes committed by him/her in **relation to this procedural status**" [emphasis added]. In contrast, Lithuania adopted the second type of provision. This is contained in the Lithuanian Criminal Code Article 147 (3): "The victim of trafficking in human beings may be released from criminal liability for the criminal act which (s)he has been compelled to commit as a **direct consequence** of being subjected to any of the acts referred in this Article" [emphasis added]. Likewise Cypriot law 60(I)2014 in Article 29 "provides that victims of THB [trafficking in human beings] are not to be prosecuted and subject to sanctions for their involvement in criminal activities, if they were a direct consequence of the fact that the persons were victims of THB" (Council of Europe's Group of Experts on Action Against Trafficking in Human Beings 2015). Similarly, the Spanish Criminal Code at Article 177, paragraph 11 provides that: "Without prejudice to application of the general rules of this Code, the victims of trafficking in human beings shall be exempt of punishment for the criminal offences that might have been committed while suffering exploitation, as long as participation therein has been a **direct consequence** of the situation of violence, intimidation, deceit or abuse to which they may have been subjected to and provided there is an adequate proportionality between that situation and the criminal act perpetrated" [emphasis added].

There is a key difference between the laws of Cyprus, Spain and Lithuania on one hand and Moldova on the other. In the Moldavian approach, the victim will not have to produce evidence as to the proximity of the crime to the status of the victim. The focus is on the victimhood, the loss of autonomy and the impact that the trafficking situation had on the person's psychology. In contrast, the other models refer to a direct consequence. As mentioned afore, a direct consequence requirement might not assist persons who are "acting to protect or assist [themselves] on account of [their] trafficked status" (Pham 2015: 7). The Moldavian approach understands that trafficked persons can be in a compelled state for an array of reasons related to their trafficking situation but not necessarily as a direct consequence thereof.

The Moldavian approach is also superior to the defence clause found in the MSA of the Parliament of the UK for it does not include an exemption clause. The MSA at s. 45 includes a defence for slavery or trafficking victims who commit an offence, which states that a person is not guilty of an offence if:

(a) the person is aged 18 or over when the person does the act which constitutes the offence,
(b) the person does that act because the person is compelled to do it,
(c) the compulsion is attributable to slavery or to relevant exploitation, and
(d) a reasonable person in the same situation as the person and having the person's relevant characteristics would have no realistic alternative to doing that act.

The defence also makes it clear that a person may be compelled to do something by another person or by the person's circumstances. It then elaborates that compulsion is attributable to slavery or to relevant exploitation only if—

(a) it is, or is part of, conduct which constitutes an offence under section 1 or conduct which constitutes relevant exploitation, or
(b) it is a direct consequence of a person being, or having been, a victim of slavery or a victim of relevant exploitation.

However, the victim will not be entitled to the defence if they commit an offence listed in Schedule 4. Noting the length of the Schedule (37 paragraphs) it can be argued that the defence in many instances will not be applicable. This is contrary to the rationalisation of having a principle of non-liability, which seeks to protect all trafficked persons. Importantly, no exclusions are provided in any of the regional documents. Furthermore, having so many exemptions reinforces the requirement for the victim to be innocent, vulnerable and as passive as possible. In other words, the ideal victim (we come back to this in subsequent chapters). Committing minor crimes seems to be tolerable but those listed in Schedule 4 interfere with our ability to accept someone as a victim. Yet it is precisely because of the prevalence of the ideal victim theory that the law needs to break away from this and provide protection for vulnerable persons that may not fit the ideal victim image. As said afore, more on this in the next chapter.

When thinking about possible exceptions to the principle of non-liability we must also reflect on human trafficking victims who commit the crime of human trafficking. This is a seminal issue and acknowledged in literature. The United Nations Office on Drugs and Crime (UNODC 2009) describes cases from Eastern Europe, where trafficked women go on to become recruiters. Similarly, well documented are cases of Nigerian women who have been trafficked and subsequently become involved in the crime of human trafficking, the so-called madams (Kleemans 2007: 184). On the one hand, the state has a legitimate interest in prosecuting and penalising these persons, for they are committing a serious crime. However, it is in this instance that vulnerabilities and lack of autonomy are zenith. In such situations, traffickers manipulate their victims so that they become perpetrators and engage in human trafficking. It is a conscious strategy that allows one to maintain control over the new victims while maintaining control over the primary victim. As such instead of having a Schedule 4 type list "[c]onsideration should be given to the extent to which the offence is connected with the trafficking of the victim and their lack of autonomy. Where such a connection exists, the State, it is suggested, should acknowledge this through the non-punishment principle: it must keep them immune from prosecution, detention and the application of penalty" (Piotrowicz and Sorrentino 2016: 686).

The Use of Existing Legislation

For some there is little doubt that states fulfil their obligations vis-à-vis the *2005 Council of Europe Convention on Action Against Trafficking in Human Beings* and *Directive 2011/36 on preventing and combating trafficking in human beings and protecting its victims*, by relying on the defences that already exist in national law, in particular necessity and duress. This section explores whether it is enough to trust existing defences to adequately protect trafficked persons.

The Use of Existing Legislation: Necessity

Necessity provides a legitimate exemption from being punished for committing an offence. In some countries, it is worded as a defence to an emergency. Poland predominantly cites the defence of necessity as a means of satisfying the international obligations with respect to protecting trafficked persons from punishment (Council of Europe's Group of Experts on Action Against Trafficking in Human Beings 2013). The legal basis for the defence of necessity is found in Article 26 § 1 and § 2 of the Polish Criminal Code.[1] Italy also relies on necessity and stipulates that a person will not be punished if the criminal act was committed in a state of necessity—Article 54 of the Italian Criminal Code. Despite various countries using this defence as a hallmark of their commitment to the non-liability principle, this author struggles to find compelling arguments for the appropriateness of necessity in these particular circumstances.

What is and when does necessity apply? One of the features of this defence "is that the prospective defendant is free to choose which course to take, whether to obey the letter of the law and do nothing and risk damage to all interests involved in the weighing exercise, or damage one and thus protect the other" (Bohlander 2006: 151). Necessity thus applies in situations where the defendant commits a crime in order to protect their own interests or the interests of another. Blackstone (1941: 596) framed necessity as the choice between two evils: "[t]his species of necessity is the result of reason and reflection and obliges a man to do an act, which, without such obligation, would be criminal. This occurs, when a man has his choice of two evils set before him, and chooses the less pernicious one. He rejects the greater evil and chooses the less. As where a man is bound to arrest another for a capital offence, and being resisted, kills the offender, rather than permit him to escape." Situations that would be covered by the defence of necessity would include a person breaking into a parked car that is blocking the path to a burning building and driving it away so as to allow a fire engine to pass. Necessity allows prisoners to escape from a burning jail and not find them guilty for escape. Dennis (2009: 33) rightly highlights that "after 9/11 one scenario that has been said to illustrate such a defence of necessity is shooting down a hijacked aircraft, inevitably killing the passengers and crew, before it will crash into a tower block killing thousands more." Necessity is considered in this book as an excuse, rather than a justification. Those influenced by necessity have their will is subordinated making their actions "morally involuntary" (Fletcher 2000).

Whilst the defence of necessity will vary from state to state, generally it requires three elements:

1. The crime was committed to avoid a significant evil.
2. There was no other adequate means of escape.
3. The act was proportionate to the evil being avoided.

Would an irregular entry into a country, or any of the other crimes committed by trafficked persons, fall within the ambit of the defence? A lot will depend on deciding whether, according to the judging society, the value claimed was greater than the value denied. "The Model Penal Code recognized that any formulation of the defense of necessity will be imprecise because there are disagreements over what constitutes an evil and over which of two evils is greater and because deep disagreements are bound to exist over some moral issues, such as the extent to which values are absolute or relative and how far desirable end may justify otherwise offense means" (Arnolds et al. 1974: 296).

The assessment in cases of human trafficking may pose problems as it will not always be obvious whether the act committed was necessary to avoid a greater evil and whether the trafficked persons could have escaped, the latter being the second requirement. Juries or courts may even fail to comprehend the evils at play. Take for instance a case where a trafficked victim recruits new victims (thus committing human trafficking themselves) because they believe that they are under a juju curse. It is unclear whether the defence of necessity is equipped to protect such persons from prosecution or punishment.

As mentioned, the defence requires that committing the crime must be the only option, and there was no possible option to escape (as is shown below this is similar to duress). Thus, Article 26 of the Polish Criminal Code requires that if it is possible to flee rather than sacrifice a legal interest, than the defendant should flee. This again may be problematic for trafficked persons. Common is the mantra "why did you not run away from the cannabis farm?" or "why did you not tell the authorities?" Firstly, any efforts to resist or escape typically further infuriate the trafficker. Secondly, whilst on paper there may be alternative solutions, subjectively this may not be the case. Yet the defence requires that the danger must be real. The imagination or state of mind of the defendant is not enough. This narrows the scope of the defence. Moreover, such a requirement risks expecting the victim to have superpowers. Here it is possible to borrow Stringer's (2013: 160) words who writes about rape, "one must be able to render oneself as an agent whose agentic capacity was expressed as physical resistance and who momentary deprivation of agency was physically enforced by the wrongdoers." This is an unrealistic expectation trafficked persons are first and foremost interested in surviving and enduring as least harm as possible. They are not trying to figure out alternative solutions.

Certain jurisdictions, like Poland, also require that the danger was immediate/imminent. For the same reasons why "direct consequence" may be limiting, the condition of imminence will also significantly reduce the number of trafficked persons that this defence will be applicable to. Schloenhardt and Markey-Towler (2016: 19) note that "by focusing on an individual's choice to act at a particular moment in time, these theories potentially fail to consider the broader context in which some of these actions occur. For example, in the case of victims of trafficking their decision to act may be coloured by the history of abuse they have been exposed to." Similar reservations with regard to the required of immediacy are relevant to the defence of duress discussed below.

Engaging with understanding the trafficked persons' experience can offer jurisprudence a sort of intellectual insight to recognising that persons who commit crimes are very differently situated. What is appropriate for one offender won't be for another. Certain trafficking victims commit crimes even where the evil they are avoiding is lesser than their crime, and/or where there is a route to escape, yet their autonomy is curbed and so they deserve an excuse, and the defence of necessity is not appropriate. We must argue that the defence of necessity is not neutral, nor is it equipped to understand cases of compulsion, which subordinates victims to another and violates their integrity and denies them ability to resist committing a crime. The very nature of that compulsion makes it almost impossible for many victims to safety remove themselves from the situation they exist in. When the criminal justice systems were evolving, issues affecting vulnerable persons—women, trafficked persons, the disabled—were not well understood of even acknowledged. Accordingly, the existing defences such as that of necessity are not well designed to respond to the specific and perplexed situation that victims of human trafficking find themselves in. The strict factual requirements of the defence make it ill-suited for victims of human trafficking who were compelled to commit a crime.

One way to support the use of the defence of necessity would be to show it works. However, and as argued by Zielińska and Namysłowska-Gabrysiak (2013) in practice it is difficult to assess to what extent the judicial authorities and, above all, the prosecutor's office, apply the defence of necessity and immediately discontinue proceedings against victims who committed a crime in connection with their situation. Certainly, there has not been enough empirical research on the use of the defence of necessity and its success. However, it would appear that this law is better suited for other crimes than those committed by trafficked persons. The OSCE's Special Representative and Co-ordinator for Combating Trafficking in Human Beings (2013: 28) also expressed concern as to the use of the defence of necessity, stating that: "such general provisions are narrowly interpreted by courts and hitherto have been rarely used in trafficking cases. Therefore, the SR [Special Representative] takes the view that a specific non-punishment provision applying to victims of trafficking - and to victims of other related crimes such as forced labour - must be introduced in national criminal legislation to comply with the legal obligations stemming from the Council of Europe Convention and EU Directive 36/2011."

It is important not to confuse the defence of necessity with that of duress, which is discussed below. Duress is raised when the accused has committed a crime under explicit threats of death or grievous bodily harm made to him by another person.

The Use of Existing Legislation: Duress

Duress is an existing defence, which some states claim fulfils their obligations with respect to protecting trafficked persons. Prior to the MSA, England and Wales relied on the defence of duress. Germany and Denmark still do. It is a defence that is provided in many criminal justice systems and is also recognised at an international legal level.

In its simplest terms, the defence of duress is applicable for those who commit an illegal act but are not guilty because they acted out of a well-founded fear of death or serious bodily injury rooted in the unlawful threat of another. The exact definition of duress will vary across states, but regardless of geographical location duress has a high threshold. The requirements of a threat of imminent death or serious injury are omnipresent as is the lack of a reasonable escape. As highlighted by Heim, in international law: "[a] defendant can raise an affirmative defence of duress when the person, faced with an imminent danger to life, limb, or freedom that cannot otherwise be averted, commits an unlawful act to avert the danger away from himself or herself, a relative, or a person close to himself or herself. To constitute duress...the threat must emanate[ ] from a human being. The threat must be imminent such that the fear caused by the threat must be operating on the mind of the actor at the time of the criminal act. The law also requires that the person under duress have no way to avoid the impending harm.... Most courts also require that the coerced actor is not responsible for the circumstances of his duress" (Heim 2013: 168).

The defence of duress is problematic, however, because like necessity it does not understand the situations in which vulnerable persons find themselves. This was evidenced in the case of Dao & Ors (2012); here the defendants were convicted of cultivating cannabis and possessing criminal property. They argued that having been tricked into entering the premises they then wanted to leave but were threatened. They were locked in the building with no means to escape and were forced into cultivating cannabis. The defence argued that duress should also be applicable in cases of threats to falsely imprison a person, i.e. not just a threat to kill or cause grievous injury. The courts did not accept this argument and upheld the high threshold of the duress defence.

There must be a specific threat to kill or cause grievous injury. This will often not be the case for trafficked persons. Consequently, it is argued in this book that the defence of duress does not recognise the means through which victims are controlled. Traffickers are continually developing new methods of controlling their victims and do not solely rely on threats to kill or injury. They use for instance:

- Debt bondage
- Threat of disclosure of the position to friends or families
- Threat of disclosing the victims to the authorities combined with building a negative image of the authorities

- Victims are filmed in a pornographic context and the video is used as blackmail
- Using an emotional bond; for example, an intimate relationship
- Fraud and deception.

A victim who committed a crime because of one of the aforementioned or other forms of compulsion would not be protected from liability if he/she had to use duress.

Another important concern with duress is the "no fault requirement." In other words, we need to ask if the defendant willingly participated in a situation, which they should have reasonably expected would result in breaking the law. In this context, the theories from victimology are of particular importance. Trafficked persons, like some other types of victims, are blamed for what happens to them. They are told, for example, that they should not have sought out a smuggler. If a trafficked person knew that by engaging with a smuggler they may break the law, but they went ahead anyway and then subsequently ended up being trafficked, should we still allow them the benefits of the defence of duress? Some would undoubtedly respond in the negative. Yet such an approach is wrong, it engages in victim blaming and misidentifies vulnerability that has led to the situation. It does not see vulnerability as a complex social, personal and psychological state of being. Moreover, it does not recognise that the defendant had no choice but to take part in the activity because of various forms of suffering, e.g. poverty, inequality, disaster, gendered violence. Victims will struggle to show that these factors prevented them from not engaging in an activity that may have led to them committing a crime. In essence, duress advocates personal responsibility and fails to realise that the system in which we live in likewise has an effect. Again to borrow from Stringer (2013: 161) who writes on rape, "the victim emerges as a self-assailing pseudo-victim, one who in some way "asked for it" and so may be regarded as having actively visited the passivity of victimisation upon herself." To an extent Article 26 of the *2005 Council of Europe Convention on Action Against Trafficking in Human Beings*, challenges the victim blaming construction by not including requirements of no fault. Instead the Convenion focuses on compulsion. By focusing on the compulsion exercised over the victim, who had his/her vulnerability abused, the regional law in theory sets to see the trafficked persons as a victim who is not a blameworthy agent. The same cannot be said for duress.

In addition, and alike in the case of necessity, the threat must be immediate. Yet we know from our discussion of direct consequence, that the circumstances in which trafficked persons commit crimes will not always satisfy the requirement of immediacy. For instance, where victims may be compelled to shoplift from a series of shops during the day, they may not be supervised and so duress would be inapplicable. For Hoshi (2013: 63), the requirement of immediacy is the obvious deficiency within the defence of duress as applied in cases of trafficked persons. Zornosa (2015: 188) argues that: "duress falls short for the many sex trafficking victims who would not be able to prove in court that their criminal behaviour was the result of some imminent threat of death or physical serious bodily injury. In fact, instead of using threats of imminent physical violence to compel their victims to prostitute themselves, sex traffickers oftentimes threaten to the call the police and have their victims arrested if they do not submit to the trafficker's demand."

Duress also requires that there was no reasonable escape from the threat except through compliance with the demands of the coercer. The inadequacy of this was already addressed above.

In conclusion of this section, the defence of duress is not reflective of what a principle of non-liability for trafficked persons seeks to achieve. This book is in agreement with Zornosa (2015: 188) who finds that: "duress is defined narrowly and thus would not encompass a substantial amount of crimes that trafficking victims commit at the direction of their traffickers." Whilst Schloenhardt and Markey-Towler (2016: 21) stress that duress: "does not have broad enough application to excuse all possible offences a victim may have to commit to escape, endure, or survive the trafficking situation. This also – and in particular – relates to offences a victim may be compelled to commit because of means other than force or threat, for example, by manipulation or psychological coercion over an extended period of time." In cases of states that rely on duress as a means of protecting trafficked persons, this is incompatible with the aim to protect victims from harms way, and such law ought to disregard in favour or something more suited.

Conclusion

This chapter looked at a number of methods for transposing the non-liability principle as found in Article 8 of *Directive 2011/36 on preventing and combating trafficking in human beings and protecting its victims* and Article 26 of the *2005 Council of Europe Convention*. Undeniably despite EU and Council efforts to approximate protection against prosecuting and punishing trafficked persons, this has proven challenging. Key contexts such as sovereignty, politics and a range of criminal law frameworks mean that transposition has varied. Perhaps more worrying is that certain methods of transposition are inappropriate, thus risking the protection of trafficked persons. Yet, because the onus on the state is limited (see previous chapters), it is unlikely that the state will be found in breach of the regional obligations. All states will be able to show that one way or another there is a way for competent national authorities not to prosecute or impose penalties on victims. Whether it is through existing defences or through the use of guidelines. However, in practice, these methods may not be adequate enough for trafficked persons. Such a conclusion elucidates the argument that perhaps a different wording of the principle of non-liability was needed, or additional direction from the EU and Council ought to have accompanied the relevant articles. It is of course accepted that an empirical study would give more credence to this point; however, empirical research will be difficult. As emphasised by Jovanovic (2017: 73): "the legal effect of these diverse provision establishing the non-punishment principle on a national level is hard to assess because, in reality, the number of victims who benefit from this principle is negligible."

The OSCE (2013: 26) notes that "[s]tates are obliged to ensure the protection of rights of victims of trafficking, including the right not to be punished for offences committed because of their situation as trafficked persons. States are therefore to secure an effective implementation of the non-punishment principle in their criminal justice systems and practices." In order to fulfil this obligation, this chapter proposes that there is a need for a multi-dimensional approach based on substantive and procedural criminal law. This is achieved through the dual use of guidelines and a non-liability provision.

This conclusion is determined by the fact that such a solution ensures the highest level of protection to trafficked victims and one that is most likely to work in practice. The use of a victim-focused defence clause, like in the case of Moldova, captures all situations in which a trafficked person may find themselves in, and not just the ones where the crime is for instance committed as part of the exploitation (e.g. prostitution in countries where the practice is outlawed). Thus, a trafficked person who relies on false documents when trying to escape their situation would also be covered by such a defence clause. The defence is also certain and visible to a range of relevant stakeholders, and not just the prosecution. The defence clause, however, ought to be supported by guidelines, which have the ability to remain up-to-day and direct relevant law enforcement persons on significant matters before the victim reaches the courtroom.

Such a system has been well summarised by Hoshi (2013: 70): "Of course, the trafficking defence could be invoked only upon the commencement of a criminal prosecution. Therefore, it is proposed that that the trafficking defence would work in tandem with an ordinary causation-based non-criminalisation provision allowing discretionary non-prosecution and non-punishment to continue. However, if a trafficked person is faced with a prosecutor who is determined that the public interest lies with prosecution, then the trafficking defence would empower them to protect themselves against criminalisation (if not arrest, interview and prosecution). Importantly, the primary role in assessing the credibility of the trafficked person would be removed from the prosecutor and vested in the court."

Thus, a combination of a statutory defence and guidelines to relevant law enforcement persons is the optimal solution, and it is advised that member states should consider such a method of implementation if protection of trafficked persons is really a priority.

Note

1. **Art. 26.**

   § 1. Anyone whose actions are carried out in order to avert an immediate danger threatening any legally protected interest, if the danger cannot otherwise be avoided and the interest sacrificed is less valuable than the interest saved, is not deemed to have committed an offence.

   § 2. Anyone who saves any legally protected interest under the circumstances defined in § 1, or who sacrifices an interest not significantly greater than the interest being saved, will also not be deemed to have committed an offence.

References

Anti-trafficking Monitoring Group (ATMG). (2013). *In the Dock* [Online]. http://www.antislavery.org/includes/documents/cm_docs/2013/i/inthe-dock_final_small_file.pdf.

Arnolds, E. B., Garland, N. F., & Garlandt, N. F. (1974). The Defense of Necessity in Criminal Law: The Right to Choose the Lesser Evil. *Journal of Criminal Law and Criminology, 65*(3), 289–301.

Blackstone, W. (1941). *Commentaries on the Laws of England*. Saint Paul: West.

Bohlander, M. (2006). Of Shipwrecked Sailors, Unborn Children, Conjoined Twins and Hijacked Airplanes—Taking Human Life and the Defence of Necessity. *The Journal of Criminal Law, 70*(2), 147–161.

Case 102/79 Commission v. Belgium [1980] ECR 1980 *–01473*.

Council of Europe's Group of Experts on Action Against Trafficking in Human Beings. (2013). *Report Concerning the Implementation of the Council of Europe Convention on Action Against Trafficking in Human Beings by Poland.* Council of Europe [Online]. https://ec.europa.eu/anti-trafficking/sites/anti-trafficking/files/greta_report_poland_2012_en_0.pdf.

Council of Europe's Group of Experts on Action Against Trafficking in Human Beings. (2015). *Report Concerning the Implementation of the Council of Europe Convention on Action Against Trafficking in Human Beings by Cyprus.* Council of Europe [Online]. https://rm.coe.int/CoERMPublicCommonSearchServices/DisplayDCTMContent?documentId=0900001680631b96.

Dao & Ors v R [2012] EWCA Crim 1717.

Dennis, I. H. (2009). On Necessity as a Defence to Crime: Possibilities, Problems and the Limits of Justification and Excuse. *Criminal Law and Philosophy, 3,* 29–49.

Drichel, S., & Stringer, R. (2013). Vulnerability After Wounding: Feminism, Rape Law, and the Differend. *SubStance, 42*(3), 148–168.

Fletcher, G. P. (2000). *Rethinking Criminal Law.* New York: Oxford University Press.

Gallagher, A. (2014). *Dr Anne Gallagher—Written Evidence.* Submission to the Joint Committee on the Draft Modern Slavery Bill [Online]. http://www.parliament.uk/business/committees/committees-a-z/joint-select/draft-modern-slavery-bill/written-evidence/?type=Written.

Heim, S. (2013). The Applicability of the Duress Defence to the Killing of Innocent Persons by Civilians. *Cornell International Law Journal, 46,* 165–190.

HHJ Edmunds QC. (2014). *HHJ Edmunds—Written Evidence.* Submission to the Joint Committee on the Draft Modern Slavery Bill [Online]. http://www.parliament.uk/business/committees/committees-a-z/joint-select/draft-modern-slavery-bill/written-evidence/?type=Written.

Hoshi, B. (2013). The Trafficking Defence: A Proposed Model for the Non-criminalisation of Trafficked Persons in International Law. *Groningen Journal of International Law, 1*(2), 54–72.

Jovanovic, M. (2017). The Principle of Non-punishment of Victims of Trafficking in Human Beings: A Quest for Rationale and Practical Guidance. *Journal of Trafficking and Human Exploitaion, 1*(1), 41–76.

Kleemans, E. R. (2007). Organized Crime, Transit Crime, and Racketeering. *Crime and Justice, 35*(1), 163–215.

Kyprianou, D. (2010). *The Role of the Cyprus Attorney General's Office in Prosecutions: Rhetoric, Ideology and Practice.* Berlin, Heidelberg: Springer.

Mulholland, F. QC. (2014). *Frank Mulholland QC—Written Evidence.* Submission to the Joint Committee on the Draft Modern Slavery Bill [Online]. http://www.parliament.uk/business/committees/committees-a-z/joint-select/draft-modern-slavery-bill/written-evidence/?type=Written.

O'Neill, M. (2004). Understanding Federal Prosecutorial Declinations: An Empirical Analysis of Predictive Factors. *American Criminal Law Review, 41,* 1439–1498.

OSCE Office of the Special Representative and Co-ordinator for Combating Trafficking in Human Beings. (2013). *Policy and Legislative Recommendations Towards the Effective Implementation of the*

Non-Punishment Provision with Regard to Victims of Trafficking. Vienna: OSCE [Online]. http://www.osce.org/secretariat/101002?download=true.

Pham, J. (2015). *Protecting Trafficking Victims from Prosecution: Analysis of the Modern Slavery Bill Defence* [Online]. http://files.magdalenecambridge.com/pdfs/Publications/peter_peckard_prize_jp_july_2015.pdf.

Piotrowicz, R. W., & Sorrentino, L. (2016). Human Trafficking and the Emergence of the Non-punishment Principle. *Human Rights Law Review, 16*(4), 669–699.

Schloenhardt, A., & Markey-Towler, R. (2016). Non-criminalisation of Victims of Trafficking in Persons—Principles, Promises, and Perspectives. *Groningen Journal of International Law, 4*(1), 10–38.

United Nations Office on Drugs and Crime (UNODC). (2009). *Anti-human Trafficking Manual for Criminal Justice Practitioners, Module 4—Control Methods in Trafficking in Persons* [Online]. https://www.unodc.org/documents/human-trafficking/TIP_module4_Ebook.pdf.

Villacampa, C., & Torres, N. (2015). Trafficked Women in Prison: The Problem of Double Victimisation. *European Journal on Criminal Policy and Research, 21*(1), 99–115.

Zielińska, E., & Namysłowska-Gabrysiak, B. (2013). *Transpozycja do prawa polskiego art. 8 Dyrektywy 2011/36/UE Parlamentu Europejskiego i Rady w sprawie zapobiegania handlowi ludźmi i zwalczania tego procederu oraz ochrony ofiar.* Warsaw: Instytut Wymiaru Sprawiedliwości [Online]. https://www.iws.org.pl/pliki/files/Jednostr.IWS_Zieli%C5%84ska%20E.,%20Namys%C5%82owska-Gabrysiak%20B._%20Zapobieg.%20handlowi%20lud%C5%BAami.pdf.

Zornosa, F. (2015). Protecting Human Trafficking Victims from Punishment and Promoting Their Rehabilitation: The Need for an Affirmative Defence. *Washington and Lee Journal of Civil Rights and Social Justice, 22,* 177–203.

8

What Thwarts the Use of the Non-liability Provision?

Introduction

Trafficked persons have to convince society that they are victims. They need to show that they are virtuous and deserving of state funds and protection and persuade against being labelled as criminals who should be punished.

Much depends on being able to obtain the victim label. Most importantly, that label validates their experience and shows that their story is a springboard for access to assistance, support and a series of rights. Yet the social construction of what is victimhood, including in the space of human trafficking, may have negative impacts on trafficked persons. As recognised by Seibel (2014: 7) "the attributes of ideal victimization characterize many of the news stories about human trafficking. Too often those who write about human trafficking either for news media or non-profit organizations focus on details that make victims seem ideal or attributes that are not ideal are left out." These ideals can help explain why it is hard to identify trafficked persons, few will meet society's expectations of the model victim.

© The Author(s) 2019
J. M. Muraszkiewicz, *Protecting Victims of Human Trafficking From Liability*, Palgrave Studies in Victims and Victimology, https://doi.org/10.1007/978-3-030-02659-2_8

This chapter moves beyond the legal analysis of the right to non-liability and discusses how a victim's incapability to meet the stereotypical human trafficking narrative may thwart their ability to evoke the right to non-liability. This concerns both their personal characteristics—e.g. in the case of strong looking males—but also their trafficking experiences. It is key to also intertwine gender perspectives, to show that gender as a socially constructed notion can also thwart a victim's ability to gain victim status. The chapters thus expose the pressures and difficulties victims face when trying to prove their prerogative to support. In essence, the chapters show what Stringer (2013: 150) has already illustrated with regard to victims of rape. In her writing, she states that "the parameters of victim recognition, rather than the apparent severity of real suffering, decide whether and how a form of victimization is recognized or effaced."

Ideal Victim Theory

Early vicitimologists Von Hentig (1948) focused his work on identifying categories of persons who were susceptible to becoming a victim based on psychological, sociological and biological criteria. A more general victim sketch included the young, women, the elderly, immigrants, minorities, the ill as well as those with psychological problems. Von Hentig also analysed the psychological make up of a victim. The traits included: eager for profit, depressed, sexually agitated, lonely and those with troubled life situations. Acknowledging the contribution of von Hentig's work, it is however the philosophies of Nils Christie that are of special interest to us. The theories of Nils Christie are useful for he presented a typecast of the "ideal victim" (Christie 1986). Christies' work "offers an appropriate lens through which to examine the literal 'poster child' of the anti-trafficking movement" (O'Brien 2013: 315). Thus, having established the legal definition of who is a victim of human trafficking (chapter 2), it is appropriate to look at the prevailing image of human trafficking victims. Importantly, it is not the aim of this book to dissect Christie's work. Instead, it focuses on exploring the manner in which his theoretical tools can help better explain how society views victims of human trafficking, and thus explain why identification and consequently the use of the principle of non-liability continues to be problematic.

According to Christie, the ideal victim has five characteristics and is "a person or category of individuals who, when hit by crime, most readily are given the complete and legitimate status of being a victim" (Christie 1986: 2). The below subsections examine the five characteristics.

Ideal Victim Theory: First Characteristic

The first characteristic is that the victim is perceived to be weak or vulnerable. Society wants the victim to, for example, be an old, very young or a sick person. In the context of human trafficking, this can explain why we are more likely to accept women than men as victims; that is because of notions that the female sex is more vulnerable than male. Del Zotto and Jones (2002) emphasise that in most societies the conception of masculinity interferes with victimhood. Trafficked persons compelled to commit crimes are more likely to be assessed not according to the crime which they have committed, and why, but primary according to societies evaluation of whether they fit the image of a vulnerable person. The law, which is said to be patriarchal by Mawby and Walklate (1994) judges woman and sentences them "not according to the seriousness of their crime but primarily according to the court's assessment of them as wives, mothers and daughters" (Carlen 1985: 10).

In line with Christie's hypothesis, research by Segrave et al. (2009) shows that in identifying trafficked persons, gendered notions guide victim service providers in Australia, Serbia and Thailand. The authors highlight that there is a need to see the trafficked persons as passive. Any illustration of agency can cast doubts on perceiving a person as a victim. As highlighted by Wilson and O'Brien (2016: 41), "this is consistent with the representation of ideal victims of trafficking within the TIP Reports [Trafficking in Persons Reports, published annually by the United States of America's Department of State]; as passive young women who are deceived by deviant others." Elsewhere, O'Brien (2013) examines who is the ideal human trafficking victim using empirical evidence from awareness-raising campaigns. She analyses ten anti-trafficking awareness movements from Europe and North America as well as worldwide campaigns including the United Nations' "Blue Heart" campaign and the Body Shop's "Stop" Campaign. In her research, she finds evidence to support Christie's notion that a victim is perceived as weak. She notes that awareness-raising campaigns "conform to this understanding of victims by selecting predominantly young female victims, exploiting the assumption that they are weak as a result of their gender and age" (O'Brien 2013: 319). The same has been supported by Andrijasevic (2007: 38) who notes "that female figures in trafficking campaigns are often scantily clad and never shown looking towards the audience, reiterating the notion that victims are passive entities and bodies to be gazed at." Such a stance has been adopted to create a more sympathetic character, one that is easily recognised by society.

Jahic and Finckenaeur (2005: 26) explain that early literature and activist work showed victims as "young, usually uneducated, willing to move abroad and attracted by a flashy lifestyle, entertainment, clothes, and the possibilities of their dream destinations. Naiveté and a note of childishness in their thinking characterize their victimization." This picture provided society with an image of a female victim that they could easily accept, and it remains in the mindset until this day. Similarly, Brunovskis and Surtees (2008: 59) found in their empirical research that a woman's modesty, good behaviour and general vulnerability "may be key, in some circumstances, to being seen as a victim." Indeed, such an image does not threaten established patriarchal social order, which till this day upholds our state.

Yet it isn't only strong women that will have a difficult time relying on the non-liability principle. Men too can become a victim of judicial and societal patriarchy and its held assumptions on who is a victim. In her work on gendering violence Gilani (2010) states that "[i]t may be somewhat contentious, but nonetheless accurate, to make the claim that when a woman commits an act of violence she is rarely regarded as an agent of violence, and more often considered a victim herself." Thus, a state may find itself in a situation of discrimination, where women are more likely to be perceived as victims and thus granted protection, including from liability, whilst the men are treated as wrongdoers. Noting the feminisation of victims of human trafficking it is essential that we move away from the perception that males are unlikely human trafficking victims. Walklate has extensively written about the need to correctly stress the gender perspective when it comes to criminal actors and victims, and her arguments can easily be incorporated into the discussions on human trafficking. Moreover, this preoccupation with the female victim is hazardously connected to associating human trafficking solely with the sex industry. This in turn diverts attention away from other forms of human trafficking such as for the purpose of forced labour.

Recognising forced labour is particularly problematic as it requires an acknowledgement that coercion does not always manifest itself in physical violence but is present in more subtle forms such as abusing the victim's lack of knowledge of the local language and/or employment rights or the threat of the authorities. In addition, in the minds of society we struggle to comprehend—or perhaps do not want to—that forced labour takes place in the territories that we frequent on a day-to-day basis. This includes car washes, warehouses, takeaways and farms. What Davidson wrote in 2006 with respect to migrants still, sadly, holds true today, "migrants who have been subject to abuse and exploitation within legal systems of migration are not likely to be caught by police or immigration officials. Indeed, for migrant workers in most sectors in the UK, there is no authority vested with the duty and power to check that they are not being exploited, and if they are, to discover whether their exploitation is linked to the use of force, debt or deception within the migration process" (Davidson 2006: 10). Consequently, the application of a non-liability principle becomes more difficult.

An interesting addition to the discourse on recognising victims outside of the sex industry concerns the role of the media. The narratives of trafficking in human beings that the news present, contribute to society's conceptualisation of the issue. The TRafficking As a Criminal Enterprise (TRACE) project[1] found that news stories are frequently couched in narratives that do little to challenge existing myths about trafficked persons. Indeed, there is an overrepresentation of human trafficking for the purpose of sexual exploitation. The dissemination of information by the news media does not account for exploitation beyond the sex industry. Thus, we have to also recognise the role that the media play in hindering identification.

Ideal Victim Theory: Second Characteristic

The second trait that the ideal victim should have, regards carrying out a respectable project prior to victimisation. Christie gives the example of taking care of a sick relative as a worthwhile project; imaginably spending time in a bar is not. Preceding being subjected to human trafficking victims are engaged in a range of projects. Some are looking for opportunities to better their lives, e.g. looking through online recruitment offers, contacting agencies and generally looking for a job. It can be argued that the person looking for employment and then falling prey to human trafficking is engaged in a respectable project. However, equally there are persons who engage in petty crimes, are homeless or work in the sex industry. Such a project may not be accepted as respectable by society (in particular in countries where prostitution is illegal or deemed as immoral), thus such persons may struggle to be perceived as victims. This point is also made by O'Brien (2013: 323) who notes that: "the social stigma attached to prostitution, even in societies where sex work is legal, seems to taint victims of trafficking who began their journey intending to migrate for sex work. The intent to participate in an industry that is deemed unsavoury and unsafe somehow diminishes the exploitation these women experience, making them less worthy of the showcase status granted to other victims of trafficking." This is supported by O'Connell Davidson (2010: 252) who states that "to stand any hope of being identified and assisted as a victim of trafficking (VoT) by the authorities in most countries, a female migrant working in the sex trade needs to demonstrate that she did not originally consent to work in prostitution, and that she has undergone great physical suffering." However such a perception does not correspond with the legal definition of a victim of human trafficking. Following the definition as contained in all international and regional instruments, even if one knowingly enters a job (e.g. sex work), this does not take away from their victim status if at some point they experienced the means elements listed in the definition. In law, the initial choice should not affect the victim status, however in practice things may be different.

Another unrespectable project is that of migration. "Hundreds of thousands of undocumented migrants are in detention centres around the world, often in appealing overcrowded and dangerous conditions" (O'Connell Davidson 2010: 254). Their crime? They survived dangerous journeys, in rickety boats or cramped in vans, hoping to improve or even just safeguard their lives and resided in countries irregularly. Yet because of the existing hostile environment towards migrants, these persons, even if exploited and abused, may struggle to prove they are "genuine" victims.

Ideal Victim Theory: Third Characteristic

According to the ideal victim theory, the third element that a victim should possess is that they are in the right place, a place that they could not be blamed for being. The peculiarity of blamelessness is linked to the victim's commitment to a respectable project. According to Christie, society is only able to give empathy when the victim is without culpability. The usual hypothetical example is that of a girl in provocative clothes, getting drunk in a bar and flirting with men. She is likely to struggle to be perceived as a victim of rape because she does not clearly fit the described criteria of blameless. Her clothing and attitude stand as "proof" that she wanted a sexual encounter. The result is that such a girl may not be granted the solace she deserves. Why as society are we quick to blame a victim for what has happened to them? It is probably a mechanism developed to help confront what would otherwise appear an unjust world. In other words, we remain calm and carry on because bad things happen to bad people.

According to the blameless criteria, only those who took no part in the lead up to their trafficking situation would acclaim the victim status. However, how often is a victim of human trafficking in a completely neutral situation? Rare are cases where victims are doing nothing and are kidnapped. Such is the stuff that movies are made of.

More often, the victim seeks out the trafficker believing they can offer a better life. Indeed, one can become a victim, according to victimology theories, because of being in proximity to crime. Persons who live in high-crime areas are more likely to have contact with offenders, which escalates their chances of being manipulated by the perpetrator into a status of victimhood.

As argued by Jahic and Finckenaeur (2005: 26–27) "many victims reportedly do have some idea of what they will be expected to do. Many are aware that they will be entering countries illegally...despite this, such [persons] are nevertheless trafficking victims. They are just not those with whom the public will be particularly empathetic and would want to help." Working in the human trafficking field ones hears stories of women who knew that they would be working as sex workers, or migrants knowing they are incurring a large debt to those moving them across borders. These persons make an informed choice to go and start a new life, what they do not know however is the exploitation that awaits them. Their knowledge however can be perceived as a contribution to the criminal act that happens to them, or indeed may be seen as a piece of evidence that prevents them from relying on a defence to a crime they may have committed as a result of their trafficking situation. Particularly, as previous chapters demonstrated if the non-liability principle is applied through the use of the defence of duress.

Ideal Victim Theory: Fourth Characteristic

The fourth characteristic requires that the victim should be weaker than the offender. Christie states that for society to attribute the status of a victim, the offender should be "big and bad." This is mirrored in constitutive criminology, where criminals are calculating persons who use any means to achieve an outcome whilst a victim is an incapacitated person who experiences pain and is denied humanity. However, here too we encounter difficulty. When the offender is an elderly lady who is frail—as in the case of a sickly Tallat Ashar, 68, who was found guilty of trafficking and jailed for five years—can we really speak of a "big" offender? In this particular case, the victim started off as a minor who had learning difficulties. It is thus possible to establish that compared to the victim the offender was "big." However, compared to Albanian mafia gangs Tallat Ashar is less "big and bad."

It is suggested that society is likely to accept even a frail elderly person as a "big and bad" offender, provided that on some level this person is "more bad" than the victim. Or that they are different from us. With regard to human trafficking, it is the power imbalance that is likely to convince "the society" that someone is a victim. Power imbalances include economic disparities. These elements are perhaps more relevant than physical strength with regard to cases of human trafficking. This however is problematic, as will be shown below, the criminal and the victim in cases of human trafficking are not always that much different. They have similarities, which further thwart the societies ability to label one as a victim and another as an offender responsible for their victimhood, curtailing their autonomy and forcing them to commit a crime (more below).

Ideal Victim Theory: Fifth Characteristic

In the fifth criteria, Christie notes that the offender and victim should be unknown to each other. According to Christie (1986: 26–29) in an ideal situation, the offender creates anxiety and comes from far away and is foreign. Cases of human trafficking do not always meet such a requirement. In many instances, a victim of human trafficking seeks out and contacts the trafficker (in order to help find a job or aid with transportation), and often the trafficker is someone who the victim already knows. For instance, a friend, a known person in the village, member of family or a lover. According to Christie, this knowledge of the offender acts as a barrier to being granted victim status. Yet this expectation is in contradiction to what we understand about how victims become victims. According to Cohen et al. (1981) exposure to crime, which is an individual's visibility and accessibility to potential offenders, is a significant contributing factor to victimisation. Many victims of trafficking before they become victims are exposed to crime; they may be homeless and using drugs, or they may work as sex workers. These undertakings increase their visibility to traffickers who will mark them as vulnerable and thus easy to compel into an exploitative situation.

If the above listed five traits are present, society will readily accept someone as a victim. On the whole according to Christie, the victim needs to be weak and vulnerable. The old, sick, young or female fit this category especially well. But young men, those with substance abuse problems, homeless, acquaintances of the traffickers and anyone existing on the margins of society will—in the eyes of society, media or even law enforcement authorities—face challenges in obtaining victim status. There is thus a disparity with how society wants to view victims of trafficking and the legal parameters; the latter produce a more diverse range of victims than that of societies' ideal victim image. Problematically, the construction of a victim as helpless and naïve does not take into consideration the complexities and choices that come into play. As aptly argued by Rijken and Römkens (2011: 82) "[t]he construction of the helpless victim implies a denial of victim's agency on either end of the trafficking route. It not only misconstructs the needs of victims, but also leads to the construction of the real and 'worthy' victim, deserving our support, versus the unworthy victim who does not need or deserve support since she responsible for her predicament of having been trafficked."

Van Dijk's work is also relevant here. Relying on historical accounts—where Jesus Christ was the first victim identified in literature—Van Dijk (1999) states that for the public to accept someone as a victim they should be a forgiving, passive individual who endures their suffering in silence. Van Dijk then shows how the "ideal victim" does not stand up to empirical scrutiny. In other words, rarely are victims what we want/expect them to be. He argues that when a victim rebels against the assigned role—e.g. seeks revenge and is outspoken—they are rejected by society and their status as a victim is challenged or even removed. Van Dijk's writings are useful for trafficked persons who commit crimes. Some of those crimes may be committed as an act of rebellion to their trafficking situation, particularly the crimes connected to escape. Yet any such showcase of agency, aggression and lack of passivity may act against them. The agency will take away from being seen as victims and will potentially lead to the trafficked person being tried in court as an offender of the law, not worthy of an excuse.

Having ideal characteristics is thus a powerful currency. Arguably the state will also prefer such victims for they are model for policy purposes. Such individuals induce sympathy from taxpayers, will attracts attention of the press and media and will legitimatise spending state budgets on assistance. Cynically speaking, their ideal suffering is a commodity on which the state can draw on.

How Do Perceptions About a Trafficked Person Impact the Application of the Non-liability Principle

For a victim to be able to use the non-liability principle he/she must first be identified as a trafficked person. Identification in the context of human trafficking can take two meanings. Firstly, the plain meaning of the word: the process of identifying—or recognising—someone. Secondly, there is the more official identification, as rooted in for example Article 11 of Directive *2011/36 on preventing and combating trafficking in human beings and protecting its victims*. Here a trafficked person is identified when competent authorities have a reasonable grounds belief that the person might have been subjected to human trafficking and thus award that person the status of the victim. Article 11 (4) states: "Member States shall take the necessary measures to establish appropriate mechanisms aimed at the early identification of, assistance to and support for victims, in cooperation with relevant support organisations."

It is argued in this book (see discussion in chapter 4) that for the non-liability principle to be engaged it is enough for a person to be identified within the plain (first) meaning of the word, i.e. recognised. This argument stems from the definition of a victim, which is a natural person who has suffered harm, including physical, mental or emotional harm or economic loss, which was directly caused by a criminal offence. In other words, the definition of a victim does not require a formal awarding of the victim status. Yet, identification is hampered for reasons described above, which have an impact on the use of the non-liability principle. Thus, if a young male picked up at a cannabis farm is not recognised as potentially being a victim of human trafficking for the purposes of forced labour, and engaging in criminal activities, the result is that they may be subject to prosecution and ultimately punishment. It is clear therefore that recognition is crucial, it will make the difference between receiving support and potentially going to prison.

Yet if we operate in a space were stereotypes prevail, there will be an impact on successful recognition and thus the use of a provision like Article 8 of the *Directive 2011/36 on preventing and combating trafficking in human beings and protecting its victims* or Article 26 of the *2005 Council of Europe Convention on Action Against Trafficking in Human Beings*. A case in point of prevailing typecasts is a 2017 Court of Appeal case from England and Wales. In *R v. VSJ, ADC, VCL, NTN, DN, AA and Anti-Slavery International,* one of the appellants, DN, had disappeared and the court noted that he had failed to maintain contact with his solicitors. It then stated (para. 143): "there is no evidence that he has been re-trafficked. He is a mature man in his mid-40s." It is not argued that DN had for sure been re-trafficked, the author does not know enough about DN to conclude that. However, for the Court to say in the same breath that DN was not re-trafficked and that he is a male in mid-40, suggests that middle-aged men could not be re-trafficked. This is a clear example of how having an ideal victim image in our minds can prevent from the granting of protection. What is seen afore us is an overriding factor, leading to a neglect of the victim status. As pointed out by scholars in the context of USA: "Even Justice Department officials who understand stereotypes of gender in trafficking may be locked into an overly constricted conception of victimhood by a regulatory model based on the iconic victim concept" (Srikantiah 2007: 202).

Taking note that stereotypes impact the use of the non-liability provision it is particularly important that law enforcement agents and in particular defence lawyers need constant training to change existing mindsets, and challenge existing stereotypes. It goes without saying that the situation is not always as bleak; there are of course law enforcement persons who look beyond a stereotypical picture and are able to acknowledge the wide variety of victims. However, equally we need to remember that often the victim's protection and refuge may lie, not in the law, but in the voluntary efforts of society who may be compromised by the ideal victim image. Thus, society should also be exposed to the realities of human trafficking and the range of people it affects.

Victim's Perceptions: The Other Barriers for Using the Non-liability Provision

Self-identification, or the lack of, can also have an effect on the use of the non-liability principle. Some trafficked persons do not see themselves as victims. Firstly, a trafficked person may be unaware of the existence of the said crime category. Notwithstanding, in such an instance the trafficked person may report the crime as abuse, rape, kidnapping, etc. This, in turn, emphasises the need for relevant authorities to be able to identify the signals of human trafficking in order to avoid categorising the crime of human trafficking as something else. Secondly, we need to consider that many persons may wish to hide their experiences. Being a victim of human trafficking can make a person feel ashamed. In certain populations exposure to some of the happenings that trafficked persons experience can be deemed dishonourable and can result in being ostracised. The European migration Network Study (March 2014) identified the following factors as obstacles to self-identification:

- Lack of awareness that he/she has been a victim of this particular crime
- Mistrust/fear of the police and asylum authorities
- Fear of being identified as irregular and returned to the country of origin, to face (possible) stigmatisation by society
- Lack of country of destination language skills
- Lack of information on legal rights
- A first claim may have been rejected due to it being false, making it legally problematic for the applicant to make a new claim.

All these elements act as barriers for a victim to receive appropriate care. Furthermore, Rijken and Römkens (2011: 82) correctly write that some victims prefer not to be seen as objects of a crime as they wish to get on with their lives and try earning money for themselves. Alternatively, they may not feel as victims because they received some money, even if was below standards. Moreover, trafficked persons may not wish to be identified as a VoT in human beings because they have experienced worse things in their home country, and in fact may see the working conditions as an advancement of circumstances. Indeed, Neil Howard (2014) writes that labour migration portrayed as "trafficking" is in fact not experienced as such by young migrants in Benin.

We also have to consider that trafficked persons may not trust authorities and this will also impact the use of a non-liability provision, for they may not tell the authorities the detailed account of their story. During trafficking situations, victims are taught to fear law authorities and can be indoctrinated to believe that if caught, they will be deported, imprisoned or subjected to abuse. They can also be "aware of other victims who have been prosecuted for illegal entry or for other offences they may have been forced to commit as victims of trafficking" (UNODC 2009: 4). Hence, they may be hesitant to communicate with the authorities.

In general, a number of barriers stand in the way of the victim making themselves and their story known to the authorities, which will impact identification. The conclusion to draw in this section is that a clear and effectively disseminated principle of non-liability may help to overcome some of these additional barriers. As summarised by Schloenhardt and Markey-Towler (2016: 23), it may "encourage victims to disbelieve their traffickers and take steps to leave their control. It may also prevent traffickers from exerting even further control over their victims by threatening exposure to punishment by the State."

Modern Slavery Can Harm Victims

Today there is a powerful rhetoric of describing human trafficking as "modern day slavery." On the one hand, it is an interesting attempt to broaden the pool of those deserving protection and aims to move away from the constricted definition of human trafficking which requires an action, means and purpose. On the other hand, as this section aims to show, using this new terminology is erroneous, confusing and can harm victims' chances of receiving recognition and support. In essence, it can lead to creating a small pool of victims who are worthy of protection, whilst abandoning the remainder of unworthy persons.

As scholars we ought to continue to rely on the definition of slavery that was developed in 1926 by the League of Nations, for it still remains law. Article 1 of the *1926 League of Nations Slavery Convention* (1926 Convention) defines slavery as: "The status or condition of a person over whom any or all of the powers attaching to the right of ownership are exercised." An additional instrument entered into force in 1957, *The Supplementary Convention on the Abolition of Slavery, the Slave Trade, and Institutions and Practices Similar to Slavery.* "This convention formally enumerated and defined several institutions and practices similar to slavery including: debt bondage, serfdom, servile marriage and child exploitation. The Supplementary Convention also reconfirmed the Slavery Convention's definition of slavery" (Siller 2016: 409). Gallagher finds that "the core element of the 1926 definition […] remains intact. A situation…will be identifiable as slavery only if it has involved, as required by the 1926 Convention, the exercise of any or all of the powers attached to the right of ownership" (Gallagher 2009: 810). Existing case law further confirms that the definition of slavery remains unbroken. In the High Court of Australia case (The *Queen v Tang* [2008] HCA 39), the judges recognised that the 1926 definition applies to both de jure, which is the right of ownership, and de facto, which regards the powers attaching to the right of ownership. The argument that slavery is made up of the de jure and de facto is straightforward, for the definition itself regards the status or condition. In law, the two are separate elements. The "status" refers to the legal whilst the "condition" regards the factual situation. In the latter, there can still be a master-property type relationship even without the master legally owning the slave. As coherently summarised by Turner (2014: 99): "nowadays, the element of ownership or rather 'powers attached to the right of ownership', no longer require the acquisition of a person for money or some other value."

To explain how a person may in law not own another person but can exercise powers attaching to ownership Allain (2009) uses a helpful parallel. He states: "consider the analogy to the drug dealer: he cannot make a claim before a judge against the theft of his heroin – he does not 'own' the heroin in law— but can still be found to exercises powers of ownership over his drugs, such as possession, if brought before a court of law. In the same manner, a person may not – in law – own another human being, but she could exercise powers attaching to ownership – such as buying or selling a person in a de facto manner." To put another way, although the concept of one human owning another is no longer possible, there are a series of powers that can be exercised to establish de facto right of ownership. This was found in *The Queen v. Tang* and *Ho v. The Queen*. Stoyanova (2015: 370) states that both cases: "substantially deepen our understanding of what slavery means since they suggest that the determination comes down to the degree of control exercised over the victim and the comparison with hypothetical de jure slavery, i.e. measuring the factor situation with the powers that would be exercised over the victim, if contrary to the fact, the law recognised the right to own another person. Thus, the degree of control is the primary consideration."

This is also illustrated in the case of *Hadijatou Mani Koraou v The Republic of Niger*. In this case, the plaintiff was sold into the ownership of a tribal chief. "This transaction occurred in the name of the 'Wahiya', a... practice in Niger consisting of acquiring a young girl, generally a slave, to work as a servant as well as a concubine" (para. 9). She was 12 and he was 34 years older. She was made to live with him, perform domestic duties and work in the field. She had four children with him and was regularly abused. In 2005, the tribal chief provided Mrs. Mani with a liberation certificate from Slavery. This claimed to free her, but she was still forced to live in the house, as she was his wife nonetheless. The Economic Community of West African States (ECOWAS) court held that the claimant was "subject for nearly a decade to psychological pressure characterised by submission, sexual exploitation, hard labour in the house and the field, physical violence, insults, humiliation and the permanent control of her movements by her purchaser" (para. 76). She was a slave. Importantly, the court here also took as a starting point the definition of slavery as laid down in Article 1 (I) of the *1926 Slavery Convention* of 1926.

It is easy for us to find proof that shows that the 1926 slavery definition remains unbroken and continues to be used by courts.[2] The crime of slavery is defined by the exercise of powers attaching to the right of ownership. Yet, numerous persons and organisations use the word slavery to mean an array of different abuses. One of the newest pieces of legislation addressing the exploitation of human beings, the UK's *Modern Slavery Act 2015* uses this very phrase in its title. The scholars, Bales (2007), Scarpa (2008) and Kara (2009) have referred to trafficking as modern slavery, whilst the *Polaris Project* (a non-profit, non-governmental organisation that works to combat and prevent modern-day slavery and human trafficking) in their overview of human trafficking, state that "human trafficking is a form of modern-day slavery where people profit from the control and exploitation of others." As highlighted by Chuang (2015): "The United States of America (US) Department of State and powerful philanthropists are key proponents of the slavery makeover, prompting other governments, international organisations, and nongovernmental organisations alike to adopt the 'modern-day slavery' frame. The slavery frame has helped ignite outrage and galvanise political support for modern anti-slavery campaigns."

Undeniably there is value in using the term slavery when talking of trafficking in persons. It makes the audiance aware of the experience of control. Moreover, and perhaps more importantly for activists, using the term slavery raises attention due to the emotional connotation. It also prompts the force of law; slavery is a crime of *jus cogens*. However, the term "Modern Slavery" is not defined in any international or regional legal instrument and so we must ask, what does it mean, and what effect does it have on victims? Bales (2005: 21) argues that the most common types of modern slavery include debt bondage, forced prostitution and child labour. Moreover, Bales and Robbins (2001: 32) advocate the view that modern slavery is "a state marked by the loss of free will where a person is forced through violence or the threat of violence to give up the ability to sell freely his or her own labour power." We have to note however that from a legal perspective this definition is neither one of slavery nor of human trafficking.

From reading the works of the above-named scholars or reports from various civil society organisations, it would appear that the term "modern slavery" has become an all-purpose hybrid classification into which all forms of oppressive labour and exploitation related activities are inserted. However, for legal purists it remains problematic. Firstly, there is nothing modern about slavery. Secondly, it is a confusing term that wrongfully incites the public to equate human trafficking with slavery. Our minds will inevitably jump to the slave trade and the transatlantic heinous activities. By calling human trafficking modern slavery this, even if indirectly, asks judges or jurors to think of the dismays of chattel slavery. This can be an obstacle in determining whether a businessman who recruits a worker, does not pay wages and threatens to call immigration authorities, commits an act of human trafficking. A juror, who has come to understand human trafficking through the term of modern slavery may not think there is anything slave-like in the businessman's act and would thus be inclined to acquit. At the same time, this may be problematic for a victim. If the use of the phrase modern slavery is popularised, a victim who was not in effect a slave but was nevertheless trafficked may not be recognised. In turn, he/she may not receive the deserved protection, including that of the non-liability principle.

The worry is that those relevant to ensuring that the non-liability principle is manifested in practice will possibly be more influenced by the "cultural language of slavery, coercion and (ideal) victimhood, than by the legal language of the protocol" (Hoyle et al. 2011: 317).

Distinguishing Between Victim and Perpetrator: How Do We Move Beyond the Binary Perceptions of Victim Versus the Criminal?

Certain groups of people regularly move between being a victim and committing a crime; e.g. the homeless person who in the morning can be a victim of theft and in the evening may themselves commit theft (Tyler and Beal 2010). This group of offender/victims can also include trafficked persons. Distinguishing vividly between a victim of human trafficking and a perpetrator is not always an easy task. It is hypothe-sised in this book that unless the victim fits the ideal victim theory—is a weak, young female, who was engaging in a worthwhile project—they are more easily to be accepted by society as an offender. Just as there is an ideal victim theory, there is also an ideal offender in human traf-ficking. This person is unknown and big and bad, relative to the victim (in Christie's theory). The offender is male and middle aged, very much in contrast to the weak, young, blameless female victim. Even if the offender is not necessarily big or middle aged, say in the case of young Vietnamese boys working on cannabis farms, their difference may be sufficient for society to label them as a potential offender.

"[V]ictims are framed in contrast to traffickers. In order to paint traf-fickers as most deserving of punishment, prosecutors have an incentive to seek victims who appear innocent and passive" (Srikantiah 2007: 195). Those words written in 2007 still hold true today. Law enforce-ment authorities prefer pursuing cases where the victim is blameless, for it will smooth the road to proving that the trafficker is guilty. "The ideal victim is still 'blameless': a faultless innocent who has had crime visited upon them by a wicked perpetrator. When victims are not fault-less, when they are in some sense 'deviant', they become much more problematic, both as object of public empathy but also in terms of their entitlement to formal compensation on the part of the state" (McEvoy and McConnachie 2016: 115). Thus, an ability to show innocence, purity and blamelessness is what will distinguish them from criminals. A problematic task for trafficked victims who were compelled to com-mit a crime, sometimes including serious crimes, and particularly prob-lematic for those who do not look like the poster child of victimhood.

In practice, in the domain of human trafficking and elsewhere in criminal justice the world is not as black and white. Traffickers are not completely malicious and wicked, and victims are not always fully pure and innocent. In her role as a support worker at a safe house for victims of human trafficking the author comes across numerous cases of victims of trafficking who have past criminal convictions, civil pro-ceedings against them, can appear arrogant or offensive. Victims are not always women from countries where women's rights are supressed and traffickers are not always from discriminatory and oppressive patriarchal states. These stereotypical perceptions overlook the broader reasons for why people either become victims or traffickers. In fact, a 2014–2016 EU funded project—TRACE—found that there can be much overlap between the victim and the trafficker. Part of this can be explained by references to theories such as the principle of homogamy, which implies that the relationship between victimisation and offending is the artefact of shared routine activities and lifestyle types of both victims and offenders. Thus, mutual presence can explain why similar types of people may end up as traffickers and as victims of trafficking. Indeed, there are certain areas that are well known as the home-communities of both traffickers and victims, showing that the victim and offender can come from similar backgrounds. Empirical studies on the relationship between offending and victimisation within the trafficking domain are still scare; however, we can hypothesise that the theory can be complimented by an acknowledgement that socio-economic factors also play a role. In particular issues such as poor health, lack of money, domestic violence and low level of education can be responsible factors that lead to either victimhood or a criminal life. Lack of a stable family or lack of emotional attention is also possible factors to push someone towards criminality or victim status. Traffickers spoken to as part of the TRACE project pronounced that they felt excluded, could not find a job, did not finish school and could not participate in "the real world." They thus became vulnerable to criminal activities, others may become victims. This discredits theories that victims and offenders are rational individual, disconnected from sociopolitical factors. In fact neither is self-made.

If we line up a victim of human trafficking and an offender side by side, they will not necessarily have that much that separates them. How does then society, which tends to operate on preconceived notions, protect victims and punish wrongdoers? There are important lessons to be learnt from this for the purpose of making the right to non-liability work in practice. Firstly, we distinguish between the victim and the perpetrator not by how they appear on the outside, or would even perform afore a jury, but on their actions. In other words, we must engage in the difficult task of removing preconceived stereotypes of victimhood and focus on identifying whether the elements that make up the human trafficking definition are present. The culpability of the trafficker is rooted in him/her having performed one of the actions through the means as described in the human trafficking definition, for the purpose of exploitation. The victim in contrast is, as already explained in chapter 3, a natural person who has suffered harm, including physical, mental or emotional harm or economic loss which was directly caused by the trafficking situation.

Secondly, we must acknowledge that the victim is not solely someone who suffers harm. The victim is also an individual "making a variety of decisions to protect herself or her family, including her [his] children and family in her [his] home country. These decisions are most likely influenced by the victim's socio-political reality and psychological state. A trafficking victim's exercise of choice in this context does not diminish the conditions of exploitation under which she [he] chooses" (Srikantiah 2007: 198). That agency can also be visible in the context of leaving the trafficking situation, often referred to as the escape. The decision to leave is brave, it is also removed from the notion of a passive victim which informs the ideal victim theory. Importantly, the choice to flight should not obviate the person's victim status, nor should it prevent them from being able to enforce the non-liability principle.

Srikantiah (2007) proposes, within the American context, practical solutions that can help better inform who is a victim. Her key proposition is to locate victim identification with trained adjudicators, who could more quickly understand and respond to changes in trafficking patters and methods. She argues that by "de-coupling victim status determinations from prosecutional involvemnt, the proposed model focuses on the credibiloty of victim narratives, not law enforcement assessments of victim suitability to serve as a witness." Such a recommendation is correct, and indeed through system such as the national referral mechanism already exists in Europe. Certainly for the purposes of trafficked persons who were compelled to break the law such a de-coupling is crucial; it would be perverse to have the prosecution try run a case against the victim whilst also be engaged in deciding if they were indeed trafficked.

Take into Account Advice from Civil Societies

As this chapter has shown the correct use of the non-liability provision depends on the victims being recognised and our ability to hear their full story. A story that will in full reveal the compulsion that led to breaking the law. Here the role of civil society should not be understated. Yet, relevant law authorities, such as the defence or prosecution do not take into account the intelligence or recommendations from third parties, in particular the civil society sector. This was clearly the paradigm in the ECtHR case on human trafficking, *L.E. v. Greece* (January 2016).

L.E. was a Nigerian national who came to Greece in 2004; she was accompanied by K.A. K.A. promised the applicant that she would work in bars and nightclubs. To facilitate the deal L.E. promised not to tell the police and was indebted to K.A. for 40,000 Euro. A voodoo priest secured the debt. Once in Greece, K.A. took control of the applicant's passport and forced her into prostitution for two years. In the course of the two years, the applicant was arrested for breaching prostitution laws, but all resulted in acquittals. In April 2006, the applicant was detained and was pending expulsion as her migration status was irregular. In November 2006, she filed a criminal grievance against K.A. and his wife D.J., accusing them of compelling her into sex work. L.E. also asserted that she was a human trafficking victim. The prosecution in the Athens Criminal Court overruled this claim. Importantly, in doing so it did not consider a testimony provided by an NGO (Nea Zoi). In 2007, the applicant requested a re-examination of her complaint, which was successful. In August 2007, the prosecutor recognised that the applicant as a human trafficking victim, and her imminent deportation was suspended.

The ECtHR's ruling in this case affirms that positive obligations include the identification and a formal awarding of victim status to trafficked persons. Moreover, "Greece was also found to have failed to conduct an effective investigation; the national court proceedings were also found to be deficient. There were various aspects that were unsatisfactory: the testimony provided by the director of Nea Zoi, who was in continuing contact with the applicant and reported that she was a VoT, was not initially included in the record; after the inclusion of this testimony, the competent authorities did not initiate a renewal of the proceedings, rather it was the applicant who had to do this; there were long periods of inactivity; the police did not search other addresses mentioned by L.E. where the alleged perpetrator might have been; the police did not try to gather additional information" (Stoyanova 2016). It is likely that had the evidence provided by the director of Nea Zoi been seriously considered at the state, the applicant would not have been held liable and would not have endured secondary victimisation.

Given the unique position of civil society organisations to recognise a trafficking victim and determine whether they were compelled to break the law, it is suggested that a provision dealing with non-liability ought to consider placing an obligation on law authorities to take into account advice from the third sector.

Conclusion

Most people do not experience the level of compulsion and the nuanced situations that induce trafficked persons to break the law. Consequently, society may have a hard time understanding the impact that the psychological and/or physical control has on a victim. This hurdle for victims to overcome is married with the struggle against the ideal victim theory. The foundation of this chapter is that a failure to identify trafficked persons can result in a trafficked person being held liable for crimes they were compelled to commit. In turn, this failure is explained partly by reference to social perceptions. On the one hand, legal definition can be applied broadly; anyone who has been affected by the crime can be considered a victim. On the other hand, the social perception of who is a victim is narrower. Thus, whilst there are international standards obliging states to protect trafficked persons from prosecution and punishment, these obligations do not translate to practice.

Christie's ideal victim theory shows that certain categories of persons may find it difficult to prove their victimhood. Rooted in the notion of the ideal victim are assumptions concerning vulnerability, the body and our activities. The image of the ideal victim produces a level of exclusion for those who do not fit the preconceived mould. We can use the hypothetical example of a trafficked male who is an irregular migrant, physically strong and working in the underground economy. Based on the held stereotype of what a human trafficking victim should look like, it is likely that this male will be excluded from the victim category. Consequently, he will not receive the protection he may require. In this respect, although his victimhood may exist in law, there is little practical relevance. Instead victim mythology portrays a picture of a human trafficking victim as a young woman from a developing country, trafficked for the purpose of sexual exploitation either by deceit or force. Yet, as correctly argued by Sorensen (2003: 11) "today more and more men, and especially children are being trafficked for a whole range of forms of exploitation." Moreover, the expected link between the passivity and helplessness that is associated with trafficked persons, does not accurately capture their agency or even how they may have to commit crimes to survive.

An important conclusion to draw from the discussion is that the right to protection measures, including that of non-liability, are thwarted by societies' disillusions as to who is in fact a victim. This chapter has also argued that there are other elements that can impede a victim's chances or receiving protection through the non-liability principle. Namely, the problems around self-identification and the misguided use of the term modern slavery.

Notes

1. A two year, project on the business of human trafficking, funding from the European Union's Seventh Framework Programme for research, technological development and demonstration under grant agreement no. 607669. http://trace-project.eu/.
2. In cases where the threshold of slavery is not met the Courts can rely on The Supplementary Convention on the Abolition of Slavery, the Slave Trade and Institutions and Practices Similar to Slavery (1956). The Convention calls for the abolition of: (a) debt bondage, (b) serfdom, (c) servile marriage, (d) child servitude. Article 1 states:

Each of the States Parties to this Convention shall take all practicable and necessary legislative and other measures to bring about progressively and as soon as possible the complete abolition or abandonment of the following institutions and practices, where they still exist and whether or not they are covered by the definition of slavery contained in article 1 of the Slavery Convention signed at Geneva on 25 September 1926:

a. Debt bondage, that is to say, the status or condition arising from a pledge by a debtor of his personal services or of those of a person under his control as security for a debt, if the value of those services as reasonably assessed is not applied towards the liquidation of the debt or the length and nature of those services are not respectively limited and defined;

b. Serfdom, that is to say, the condition or status of a tenant who is by law, custom or agreement bound to live and labour on land belonging to another person and to render some determinate service to such other person, whether for reward or not, and is not free to change his status;

c. Any institution or practice whereby:

  i. A woman, without the right to refuse, is promised or given in marriage on payment of a consideration in money or in kind to her parents, guardian, family or any other person or group; or

  ii. The husband of a woman, his family or his clan, has the right to transfer her to another person for value received or otherwise; or

  iii. A woman on the death of her husband is liable to be inherited by another person;

d. Any institution or practice whereby a child or young person under the age of 18 years is delivered by either or both of his natural parents or by his guardian to another person, whether for reward or not, with a view to the exploitation of the child or young person or of his labour.

References

Allain, J. (2009). *A Response to Anne Gallagher by Jean Allain. Opinio Juris* [Online]. http://opiniojuris.org/2009/06/08/a-response-to-anne-gallagher-by-jean-allain/.

Andrijasevic, R. (2007). Beautiful Dead Bodies: Gender, Migration and Representation in Anti-Trafficking Campaigns. *Feminist Review, 86,* 24–44.

Bales, K. (2005). *Understanding Global Slavery: A Reader.* Berkeley: University of California Press.

Bales, K. (2007). *Ending Slavery How We Free Today's Slaves*. Berkley, CA: University of California Press.

Bales, K., & Robbins, P. T. (2001). No One Shall Be Held in Slavery or Servitude: A Critical Analysis of International Slavery Agreements and Concepts of Slavery. *Human Rights Review, 2*(2), 18–45.

Brunovskis, A., & Surtees, R. (2008). Agency or Illness-The Conceptualization of Trafficking: Victims' Choices and Behaviors in the Assistance System. *Gender, Technology and Development, 12*(1), 53–76.

Carlen, P. (1985). *Criminal Women*. Cambridge: Polity Press.

Christie, N. (1986). From Crime Policy to Victim Policy. In E. A. Fattah (Ed.), *From Crime Policy to Victim Policy*. London, UK: Palgrave Macmillan.

Chuang, J. (2015). The Challenges and Perils of Reframing Trafficking as "Modern-Day Slavery". *Anti-Trafficking Review, 5,* 146–149.

Cohen, L. E., Kluegel, J. R., & Land, K. C. (1981). Social Inequality and Predatory Criminal Victimization: An Exposition and Test of a Formal Theory. *American Sociological Review, 46,* 505–524.

Davidson, J. O. (2006). Will the Real Sex Slave Please Stand Up? *Feminist Review, 83,* 4–22.

Del Zotto, A., & Jones, A. (2002). *Male-On-Male Sexual Violence in Wartime: Human Rights' Last Taboo?* Paper Presented to the Congress of the International Studies Association (ISA), New Orleans, March [Online]. http://adamjones.freeservers.com/malerape.htm.

Gallagher, A. (2009). Human Rights and Human Trafficking: Quagmire or Firm Ground? A Response to James Hathaway. *Virginia Journal of International Law, 49*(4), 789–848.

Gilani, S. (2010). Transforming the 'Perpetrator' into 'Victim': The Effect of Gendering Violence on the Legal and Practical Responses to Women's Political Violence. *Australian Journal of Gender and Law, 1* [Online]. https://papers.ssrn.com/sol3/papers.cfm?abstract_id=2569106.

Hadijatou Mani Koraou V The Republic of Niger, Economic Community of West African States Community Court of Justice, Ecw/Ccj/Jud/06/08, Judgment of 27 October 2008.

Howard, N. (2014). Teenage Labor Migration and Antitrafficking Policy in West Africa. *The ANNALS of the American Academy of Political and Social Science, 653*(1), 124–140.

Hoyle, C., Bosworth, M., & Dempsey, M. (2011). Labelling the Victims of Sex Trafficking: Exploring the Borderland Between Rhetoric and Reality. *Social & Legal Studies, 20*(3), 313–329.

Jahic, G., & Finckenaeur, J. O. (2005). Representations and Misrepresentations of Human Trafficking. *Trends in Organised Crime, 8*(3), 24–40.

Kara, S. (2009). *Sex Trafficking: Inside of the Business of Modern-Day Slavery.* New York: Columbia University Press.

L.E. v. Greece, Appl. No. 71545/12, 21 January 2016.

Mawby, R. I., & Walklate, S. (1994). *Critica Victimology.* London: Sage.

McEvoy, K., & McConnachie, K. (2016). Victimhood and Transnatioal Justice. In D. Spencer, & S. Walklate, (Eds.), *Reconceptualizing Critical Victimology.* London: Lexington Books.

O'Brien, E. (2013). Ideal Victims in Human Trafficking Awareness Campaigns. In K. Carrington, M. Ball, E. O'Brien, & J. T. Marcellus (Eds.), *Crime, Justice and Social Democracy: International Perspectives* (pp. 315–326). Basingstoke: Palgrave Macmillan.

O'Connell Davidson, J. (2010). New Slavery, Old Binaries: Human Trafficking and the Borders of 'Freeom'. *Global Networks, 10*(2), 244–261.

R v. VSJ, ADC, VCL, NTN, DN, AA and Anti-Slavery International, [2017] EWCA Crim 36.

Rijken, C., & Römkens, R. (2011). Trafficking for Sexual Purposes as a Globalized Shadow Economy: Human Security as the Tool to Facilitate a Human Rights Based Approach. In J. Dijk & R. Letschert (Eds.), *The New Faces of Victimhood* (pp. 73–98). Dordrecht: Springer.

Scarpa, S. (2008). *Trafficking in Human Beings: Modern Slavery.* Oxford: Oxford University Press.

Schloenhardt, A., & Markey-Towler, R. (2016). Non-criminalisation of Victims of Trafficking in Persons—Principles, Promises and Perspectives. *Groningen Journal of International Law, 4*(1), 10–38.

Segrave, M., Milivojevvic, S., & Pickering, S. (2009). *Sex Trafficking: International Context and Response.* Portland: Willan Publishing.

Seibel, C. L. (2014). Human Trafficking and the History of Slavery in America. In M. J. Palmiotto (Ed.), *Combatting Human Trafficking: A Multidisciplinary Approach.* Boca Raton, FL: CRC Press.

Siller, N. (2016). Modern Slavery. Does International Law Distinguish Between Slavery, Enslavement and Trafficking? *Journal of International Criminal Justice, 14,* 405–427.

Sorensen, P. (2003). *New Perspectives and Policies on Protection of Victims.* Brussels: The European Parliament.

Srikantiah, J. (2007). Perfect Victims and Real Survivors: The Iconic Victim in Domestic Human Trafficking Law. *Boston University Law Review, 87,* 157–211.

Stoyanova, V. (2015). *Human Trafficking and Slavery Reconsidered: Conceptual Limits and States' Positive Obligations.* Lund: Lund University.

Stoyanova, V. (2016). *L.E. v. Greece: Human Trafficking and States' Positive Obligations* [Online]. https://strasbourgobservers.com/2016/02/02/l-e-v-greece-human-trafficking-and-states-positive-obligations/.

Stringer, R. (2013). Vulnerability After Wounding: Feminism, Rape Law, and the Differend. *SubStance, 42*(3), 148–168.

Turner, I. (2014). Positive Obligations and Article 4 of the European Convention on Human Rights: A defence of the UK's Human Rights Act 1998. *The International Journal of Human Rights, 18*(1), 94–114.

Tyler, K. A., & Beal, M. R. (2010). The High-Risk Environment of Homeless Young Adults: Consequences for Physical and Sexual Victimization. *Sociology Department, Faculty Publications, 96*, 101–115.

United Nations Office on Drugs and Crime (UNODC). (2009). *Anti-human Trafficking Manual for Criminal Justice Practitioners, Module 4—Control Methods in Trafficking in Persons* [Online]. https://www.unodc.org/documents/human-trafficking/TIP_module4_Ebook.pdf.

Van Dijk, J. (1999). Introducing Victimology. In J. van Dijk, R. R. H. van Kaam, & J. Wemrners (Eds.), *Caring for Crime Victims* (pp. 1–13). New York: Criminal Justice Press.

Von Hentig, H. (1948). *The Criminal and His Victim.* New Haven: Yale University Press.

Wilson, M., & O'Brien, E. (2016). Constructing the Ideal Victim in the United States of America's Annual Trafficking in Persons Reports. *Crime Law and Social Change, 65*(1–2), 29–45.

9

An Alternative Provision

Introduction

Holding trafficked persons liable can lead to institutional victimisation and is far from the victim-centred approach that is championed in anti-human trafficking discourse.

This book looked at the non-liability principle in Europe and showed that excusing victims of human trafficking who have been compelled to commit crimes is not only a legal problem, but it also involves moral arguments and social standpoints. The purpose of this book was to determine if European law—EU and Council—fulfils the aim of protecting trafficked persons from being held liable.

The issue involves an interplay of criminal law, human rights law and victimology. Within each of these fields, there is space and a reason to excuse a victim; the domains agree that under certain conditions the victim of human trafficking who committed a crime is not morally culpable and should not to be punished. The lack of desert to be punished is understood with reference to their trafficking situation, a situation where free will is distorted. Trafficked persons are not autonomous, they are acting under control and commit crimes because of

© The Author(s) 2019
J. M. Muraszkiewicz, *Protecting Victims of Human Trafficking From Liability*, Palgrave
Studies in Victims and Victimology, https://doi.org/10.1007/978-3-030-02659-2_9

unique circumstances they find themselves in. Their culpability is either significantly reduced or destroyed. That is to say, there is a lack of the foundation for responsibility. Of course, their actions can still be seen as wrong, but once they prove the relevant elements of their defence they should not be held morally responsible and be excused. As stated by Pham (2015: 3) "when an individual can be shown to have been 'compelled' to commit an unlawful act, the criminal law is reticent to impose the same criminal sanction as that imposed on an individual acting of his own free will."

Rationale for the non-liability principle is also explained through bearing in mind the purposes for why the law punishes people in the first place. Prosecuting or punishing trafficked persons serves none of the purposes of criminal law: retribution, incapacitation, rehabilitation and deterrence. Moreover, it is accepted that preventing compelled trafficked person from being held liable is part of the human rights doctrine. As articulately put by Piotrowicz (2009: 192): "[t]he essence of human rights law is that it makes the state accountable for failing to protect rights which it has the power and obligation to protect...." If a trafficked victim is held liable that act is attributable solely to the state and it is clear that such instances of acts or omissions contravene human rights responsibilities. The book showed why holding a person liable is a breach of human rights. Whilst human rights law does not contain a non-liability principle in the traditional human rights instruments, such a principle is in fact a fundamental right. The principle arises out of soft law, case law and is related to other key human rights. In brief: holding trafficked persons liable for crimes they were compelled to commit, is a human right violation because of the direct connection between the harm caused to the person (secondary victimisation, risk of trafficking, erosion of dignity, etc.) and the actions of the state, whereby the state omitted to carry out its responsibility to identify and protect the said individual. That duty is articulated in case law of the Strasbourg Court, in particular in the *Rantsev* case. The Court's premise is that human trafficking law needs to include protecting trafficked persons, including taking them out of a situation of risk. It is contended that a situation of risk extends to re-trafficking, which can be a product of holding trafficked persons liable. Such findings are in tune with the underlying premise of human rights, namely human dignity. This book also argued that by protecting victims from liability the state is safeguarding more traditional human rights laws such as the right to liberty or free movement. Acknowledging that a non-liability provision is rooted in human rights creates a strict responsibility whereby the "responsibility is neither an ideal nor a virtue nor a voluntary option for the wise policy maker, but legally imposed starting point for regulation" (De Hert 2012: 96).

The book also examined the definition of human trafficking to determine who exactly falls within the remit of the non-liability clause, and thus who is entitled to this human right. On a broad level, the chapter provided an answer: human trafficking is a crime that is made up of an action, a means and is committed for the purpose of exploiting another human being. Yet, much remains imprecise with regard to the characterisation and many practitioners involved in addressing trafficking in human beings will struggle to understand their tasks. Particularly problematic are the listed means, e.g. the abuse of position of vulnerability. And yet it is understanding the means element that is perhaps most crucial for the correct use of the non-liability provision. For as this book has shown, non-liability requires the defendant to show that he/ she acted under compulsion, this in turn is related to the means elements of the human trafficking definition. Accordingly, in order for a defendant victim to show that they were subjected to, for example, an abuse of position of vulnerability, they need the law and law enforcement officials to fully understand all the nuances that this can entail. For example, vulnerability can be related to gender, migration status, past experience. This will not be an easy task. The third element of the definition, namely the purpose, also leaves many questions unanswered. There is no clearly defined framework for the concept of exploitation.

This book then sought to have an impact on developing our understanding of the non-liability principle as found in Article 26 of the *2005 Council of Europe Convention on Action Against Trafficking in Human Beings* and Article 8 of Directive *2011/36 on preventing and combating trafficking in human beings and protecting its victims*. Both provisions seek to protect trafficked persons from liability. This is not a blanket immunity and there is general agreement that the principle of non-liability is applicable only where the offence was either integral or related to their trafficking situation.

Placing the existing European legislations at the foreground of analysis, this book hopes to have provided the reader with a critique of those laws. Notwithstanding the altruistic aim of both Articles, which are rooted in human rights, this book finds that the provisions have marginal scope to actually protect trafficked persons. This is for a number of reasons that were detailed. Primarily, the legal frameworks do not ask much of states. In the case of the Directive states are only obliged to ensure that competent national authorities are **entitled** not to prosecute or impose penalties on victims of trafficking. In the case of the Convention states only have to provide for the **possibility** of not imposing penalties on victims. Given that all criminal justice systems have some methods through which defendants of all crimes can be found non-liable, Article 8 and Article 26 are not actually asking much of states. States retain a wide margin of appreciation as to how they choose to implement the relevant provisions.

A telling sign of whether a provision is effective in protecting trafficked persons, is how it is realised in practice. Because Article 26 of the *2005 Council of Europe Convention on Action Against Trafficking in Human Beings* and Article 8 of Directive *2011/36 on preventing and combating trafficking in human beings and protecting its victims* do not outline the content of the right of non-liability we are left with an array of practices. Victims in the UK will have a different experience to victims in Poland. There is thus, worryingly, a lack of a uniform standard of protection. Moreover, some states will implement the obligations through inadequate ways. As shown in this book, states may refer to existing defences of duress or necessity as trajectories for competent authorities having an entitlement not to hold victims liable or showcasing that they provide for the possibility of not imposing penalties on victims. Although this is not wrong from the perspective of what the regional documents require of states, it may lead to trafficked persons not being protected from liability. Thus, the aim of the non-liability principle will not be achieved. For instance, with regard to duress, the book emphasised that duress is demarcated too narrowly and would not be applicable to a large number of circumstances in which trafficked persons commit crimes. The high threshold of existing defences and the fact that they were not designed in mind with the particular circumstances of the trafficked victim thwart their use. As to guidelines, which some states will use as a method of implementing the non-liability principle it was argued that they may lack statutory footing, they can be vague or grant too much discretion to the prosecution. Yet at the same time it is helpful to produce guidelines to different relevant persons, for guidelines can go more in depth than an Article in a legislation and can even use more accessible language. Essentially, this book argues that protection is more likely to be ensured if a non-liability defence is implemented in tandem with guidelines.

Noting the shortcomings of the existing regional provisions on non-liability a more enhanced provision is needed, one that would go beyond only entitling authorities not to prosecute or punish, and instead would ensure that they do not detain, prosecute or impose penalties on victims unless it is strictly necessary and in the public interest. In other words, it would confer an enforceable right on a victim of trafficking not to be held liable. Any new provision should not repeat the mistake of the Directive and refer to "direct consequences," for the principle of non-liability is significantly limited by this phrase. According to Article 8, a trafficked person will need to show that they have been compelled to commit a crime as a direct consequence of their trafficking situation. It is not immediately obvious what nexus "direct consequence" requires, there is a lack of *lex certa*. This book argued that the implication is that the proximity needs to be very close; there is a need for immediacy. Thus, historical victims—those who are no longer in a situation of exploitation (or in the danger of it)—do not fall within the ambit of direct consequence. This is regrettable, for there will be victims that despite the passage of time or distance from the trafficker can still feel compelled to commit a crime (see the case of T detailed previously). The current phraseology in many instances will frustrate the victim's interests because it will be hard at times to show that the crime was "directly" linked to human trafficking. Nevertheless, in many instances the crime committed will arise out of the context of the human trafficking experience. Consequently, this book suggests that non-liability should not be dependent on the direct consequence element and be afforded when a victim can show that they were compelled to commit a crime, and that compulsion was related to their trafficking experience. This is a causation approach whereby the offence committed by the trafficked person is related to the trafficking but not necessarily a direct consequence thereof. A trafficked person should only have to show evidence of compulsion, which arose out of the human trafficking experience and demonstrate that it severely reduced or extinguished their agency and free will.

Yet this is not without controversy; it undoubtedly opens up the defence to many more cases including those where the victim committed a crime many years after their trafficking situation. However, this author trusts that by requiring the victim to prove the relevant constituents (especially compulsion and the relation between the crime and their human trafficking experience), the criminal justice systems will not allow for fraudulent use of the defence.

What Happened to the Protection?

Why does the law have such a shortcoming? It is hard to pinpoint one reason. Much could have to do with the way the European Union and Council of Europe legislations were formed; a result of compromise that required drafters to tread lightly not to infringe state sovereignty too much. Persuading is also the argument on policy formation put forward by Broad and Turnbull: "[o]ver many decades, public policy scholars have criticised the assumption that policymaking is problem solving as a founding myth […]. Instead, policymaking practice is: characterized by partial solutions, incremental advances, and political compromise […]; pre-structured by the 'appreciative systems' or interpretive frames of policy actors […]; and concerns problem-setting and problem-structuring, more than goal-directed problem-solving" (Broad and Turnbull 2018). Equally interesting are the arguments offered by feminists well summarised by Mawby and Walklate (1994) that the states, and thus presumably the regional organisations that the state forms, are patriarchal. Various extensions of the state (or the regional body), such as the legislating body, work within a "system which operates from a deeply embedded patriarchal framework" (Mawby and Walklate 1994: 185).

Thus, because male power is systemic and seeps into the legislation, that legislation will undoubtedly be gendered and not neutral. This insight can help explain why women, who are seen as the ideal victims, may benefit from the non-liability principle whilst men are less likely to. The men are more likely to be judged by their crimes and by the masculinity, namely their conduct and behaviours. Moreover, it may explain why only certain women—passive—will be granted the relevant assistance. In other words, men and women who fail to reflect the gendered ideal victim image held in societies mind will struggle to successfully use the non-liability principle. Whether or not someone benefits from the non-liability principle may not necessarily depend on whether they have been compelled to commit a crime as a result of their trafficking situation, but instead depends of the factors of victimhood that are recognised by society and relevant stakeholders (e.g. police, lawyers, judges). These factors include gender, their personal circumstances, migration status, proximity to the criminal world etc.

Notwithstanding what ones' theories of why the regional bodies and the state have failed to implement adequate laws one thing can be agreed on: those that the state fails experience a strong miscarriage of justice. Consequently, further work is needed to ensure the efficacy of the non-liability principle, for male, female and transgender trafficked persons who are compelled to commit crimes. That work needs to be done at a legal level, reforming the existing principle, and at a social level. As to the latter, this includes reforming the status quo that victimisation is the privilege of those that fit an ideal victim image. It is recommended therefore that scholars, practitioners and policy makers think critically about how to impact the skewed understanding of victimhood so that all forms of suffering are recognised and consequently put right.

What Can Be Done to Improve the Law?

The central conclusion of this book is that regional legislators should have gone further in their attempt to protect trafficked persons, and perhaps in the next generation of legislations the European laws could be improved by way of the proposed alternative provision:

1. States shall, in accordance with the basic principles of their legal systems take the necessary measures to ensure that competent national authorities do not detain, prosecute, bring a civil case against or impose penalties on victims of trafficking in human beings, or victims of exploitation, for their involvement in unlawful activities (including violation of migration law) in relation to their status as victims of human trafficking, unless it is strictly necessary and in the public interest.
2. Special attention shall be paid to cases involving children, and Member States shall take into account the bespoke definition of child trafficking and the full range of rights and protections to which children are entitled.
3. Where possible relevant national authorities will work together with third parties such as civil society to ensure that all relevant elements have been considered.

It is suggested in this book that a more invasive provision, such as the one suggested above will not amount to a takeover of national powers to prosecute and would continue to allow states to maintain national sovereignty and legal diversity whilst at the same time embracing a human rights approach. It is not manifestly inappropriate and still deemed as proportionate. Proportionality is best imagined as a balancing exercise between the means used and the ends pursued, where the former needs to be proportionate to the latter. A more obligatory wording (such as the one proposed above) still maintains that balance. This is because the enhanced provision is suitable and necessary in order to successfully pursue the objective, which is the protection of the human rights of victims and the avoidance of further victimisation. A more obligatory provision is also a better and proper expression of our core values. Values that state, that a person should not be held liable for crimes they committed when their free will and agency were extinguished.

A more demanding provision is also proportionate for we do not have competing values. Not like in the case of e.g. increased surveillance as a method of combating terrorism. Here, the state is obliged to protect its people against terrorist threats but at the same time must safeguard their right to fundamental rights such as privacy. When it comes to more law to ensure non-liability, there is no balancing between conflicting values or principles. The use of more law and safeguarding human rights are related in this context, and thus perhaps easier to endorse. A claim that the trafficker may have their rights breached has been argued against in chapter 2. However, in brief, we can reiterate the reference to the most recent ECtHR case concerning human trafficking. Here the Court highlighted that there is independence between crime investigation against the trafficker and victim identification.[1]

The suggested provision is both legislatively feasible and also makes logical sense if protecting trafficked persons is really our priority. Importantly, this provision does not provide trafficked persons with blanket immunity; instead it strikes the balance between what is proportionate and within the regional bodies competence on one hand and on the other hand what human rights notions require. It also offers a "protection by design approach." Where protection is guaranteed at the outset, i.e. not after the victim is convicted and is serving a sentence. As examples in this book showed, there are victims who often get their retribution on appeal. The present law is used in such a manner that means that the rights owed to the victims come in after the conviction and often after the end of the sentence. Thus, "protection by design" regards being proactive rather than reactive in the endeavours to protect trafficked persons.

How should such a provision be transposed at a national level? This author encourages the use of an explicit, causation focused, non-liability provision that addresses the niche situation that trafficked persons find themselves in. Moldova as discussed in previous chapters provides us with a good example. Such a defence clause would ensure that trafficked persons accused of crimes have a tangible tool, recognised in national legislation, that they could evoke before the police, an administrative body, prosecution or a court. The defence clause should be accompanied by guidelines, which can elaborate on the provision, detail examples and ensure that there is evenness in the understanding of what the defence clause aims to achieve. The guidelines should also be widely disseminated to relevant persons including prosecution, police, defence lawyers, civil society, law clinics and academia.

We must here stress the role of civil society, which can provide insight into the victim's story. Civil society organisations are in a unique position, and better connected to victims than law enforcement officials, and are thus more likely better able to ascertain the exact circumstances that led the trafficked victim to commit a crime. That is why this author stresses that both the non-liability provision and guidelines that accompany it, should emphasise the importance of civil society.

Notwithstanding, in order to fully address the problem faced by victims, with regard to being held liable, it will be essential for the EU and the Council of Europe to firstly elaborate on the parameters of the human trafficking definition. Secondly, steps will need to be taken to combat the prevailing ideal victim image that society holds and also improve identification. In parallel, the law on non-liability ought to be reformed.

Note

1. The Court noted that an official identification "did not presuppose official confirmation that the offence had been established, and was *independent of the authorities' duty to investigate....* The question of whether the elements of the crime had been fulfilled would have to have been answered in subsequent criminal proceedings" J. and Others v. Austria, App; No. 58216/12, 17 January 2017, para. 115.

References

Broad, R., & Turnbull, N. (2018). From Human Trafficking to Modern Slavery: The Development of Anti-slavery Legislation in the UK. *European Journal on Criminal Policy and Research*, March, 1–15.

De Hert, P. (2012). From the Principle of Accountability to System Responsibility: Key Concepts in Data Protection Law and Human Rights Law Discussions. In D. Guagnin, L. Hempel, L. Ilten, I. Kroener, D. Neyland, & H. Postigo (Eds.), *Managing Privacy Through Accountability* (pp. 88–120). Basingstoke: Springer.

Mawby, R. I., & Walklate, S. (1994). *Critica Victimology*. London: Sage.

Pham, J. (2015). *Protecting Trafficking Victims from Prosecution: Analysis of the Modern Slavery Bill Defence* [Online]. http://files.magdalenecambridge.com/pdfs/Publications/peter_peckard_prize_jp_july_2015.pdf.

Piotrowicz, R. (2009). The Legal Nature of Trafficking in Human Beings. *Intercultural Human Rights Law Review, 4,* 175–203.

Index

© The Editor(s) (if applicable) and The Author(s) 2019
J. M. Muraszkiewicz, *Protecting Victims of Human Trafficking From Liability*, Palgrave Studies in Victims and Victimology, https://doi.org/10.1007/978-3-030-02659-2

Printed by Printforce, the Netherlands